Early praise for *Design It!*

Others have written about risk-driven architecture before, but only Michael Keeling uses his taste for guacamole to illustrate it. *Design It!* is full of pragmatism, personal experience, and useful tips. This book has something to offer anyone involved in software development, and it's fun to read.

➤ **Eltjo Poort**
   CGI, recipient of the Linda Northrop Software Architecture Award

Of the numerous books that talk about software architecture, there are a select few that are really, really good. This book runs the complexity of software architecture through the real world of software development and distills it into real, understandable concepts that can be applied to everyday software engineering practices. In *Design It!*, Michael gives you his recipes for applying these concepts, providing pragmatic guidance for success in a very tough discipline.

➤ **Will Chaparro**
   Software Development Manager, IBM Watson

What I like most about Michael's style is that it is inclusive: everyone on the team should become a better architect. His book gives us hands-on ways to achieve this by collecting many great ideas and tools that arose from the community. This book is for everyone who wants to build better software together.

➤ **Thijmen de Gooijer**
   IT Architect, Kommuninvest Sweden

This book covers the essentials of design and software architecture that all development teams need to know. It is definitely going on the recommended reading list for all my teams and anyone we bring on board!

➤ **Jørn Ølmheim**
Leading Advisor Software Architecture, Statoil ASA

What sets *Design It!* apart for me is its fresh perspective—that the technical undertaking of building software is an intensely social activity. Michael manages to uniquely fuse the mechanics of software architecture together with the chemistry of design thinking. You'll learn to move from architecture viewpoints into design mindsets and from managing architecture life cycles into telling architecture stories. This is a must-have reference book on modern software architecting.

➤ **Amine Chigani**
Chief Architect, GE Digital

This book is timely, valuable, accessible, and excellent. It is a clear, informed, and practical guide to the principles and practice of software architecture, for the aspiring architect as well as the established practitioner who wants to deepen and refresh his or her skills. Michael Keeling takes the reader on a clear and results-oriented journey, from the fundamentals of the field to the state of the art.

➤ **Eoin Woods**
CTO of Endava, editor of IEEE Software's Pragmatic Architect column, and author of *Software Systems Architecture*

Invaluable for growing your career and your team! The perfect balance between design theory and practical activities.

➤ **Joseph Kramer**
Software Engineering Manager, IBM

Design It!

From Programmer to Software Architect

Michael Keeling

The Pragmatic Bookshelf

Raleigh, North Carolina

Many of the designations used by manufacturers and sellers to distinguish their products are claimed as trademarks. Where those designations appear in this book, and The Pragmatic Programmers, LLC was aware of a trademark claim, the designations have been printed in initial capital letters or in all capitals. The Pragmatic Starter Kit, The Pragmatic Programmer, Pragmatic Programming, Pragmatic Bookshelf, PragProg and the linking *g* device are trademarks of The Pragmatic Programmers, LLC.

Every precaution was taken in the preparation of this book. However, the publisher assumes no responsibility for errors or omissions, or for damages that may result from the use of information (including program listings) contained herein.

Our Pragmatic books, screencasts, and audio books can help you and your team create better software and have more fun. Visit us at *https://pragprog.com*.

The team that produced this book includes:

Publisher: Andy Hunt
VP of Operations: Janet Furlow
Development Editor: Susannah Davidson Pfalzer
Indexing: Potomac Indexing, LLC
Copy Editor: Liz Welch
Layout: Gilson Graphics

For sales, volume licensing, and support, please contact *support@pragprog.com*.

For international rights, please contact *rights@pragprog.com*.

Printed in the United States of America.
ISBN-13: 978-1-68050-209-1
Printed on acid-free paper.
Book version: P1.0—October 2017

Contents

Part III — The Architect's Toolbox

Acknowledgments

The most memorable moment for me writing this book was when my wife and five-year-old son helped me figure out how to organize Chapters 1 and 2. One Saturday morning, Marie asked probing questions and listened to me talk things out while Owen, sharpie in hand, helped me write ideas on sticky notes and move them around our kitchen window for over an hour. You are both amazing. Thank you for your love and patience.

Deadlines do indeed make a strange *whooshing* sound as they pass. The best deadline, and the only one I didn't let slip while writing this book, was Finn. Welcome to the world!

Mom, Dad, Ryan—this book was only possible thanks to your support and encouragement throughout my life. Chris and Russ, thank you for helping me find the time to write (and for the lasagna). Leia, thanks for listening.

I've been fortunate to learn from, collaborate with, and hang out with many smart software architects and designers who greatly influenced my thinking, including David Garlan, Mary Shaw, George Fairbanks, Len Bass, Rebecca Wirfs-Brock, Simon Brown, Ariadna Font, Matt Bass, Tony Lattanze, Dave Root, and Ipek Ozkaya.

I had an army of technical reviewers who, through their pointed feedback, made this book significantly better. Those reviewers are David Bock, Will Chaparro, Javier Collado, Fabrizio Cucci, George Fairbanks, Kevin Gisi, Thijmen de Gooijer, Rod Hilton, Michael Hunter, Maurice Kelly, Joe Kramer, Nick McGinness, Ryan Moore, Daivid Morgan, Emanuele Origgi, Ipek Ozkaya, Will Price, Antonio Gomes Rodrigues, Jesse Rosalia, Tibor Simic, Stephen Wolff, Eoin Woods, Peter W A Wood, and Colin Yates. Thank you to everyone at IBM Pittsburgh for being willing guinea pigs for many of the design methods.

Susannah Pfalzer, the most amazing editor a first-time author could ask for, thank you for shepherding me through the writing and publishing process. Andy and Dave, thanks for giving me a chance to try to improve the way we build software.

Foreword

When I picked up the final draft of this book, at first I was surprised to see that it was missing any mention of Agile software development. Michael and I have been chatting about this book for years now, and I thought I knew what the book was about and why it must be written: software architecture ideas, as traditionally described, have been hard to use in Agile processes, but Michael has figured out how to do just that. So how could "Agile" not be on every page of the book?

Michael is a modern Prometheus, fascinated by technology and determined to tame it for all of humanity. He is a true believer in the benefits of Agile and an expert in software architecture. I know of no one else who was walking the walk as an Agile team leader during the day while mentoring Carnegie Mellon software architecture students at night. I know him best through our involvement in the SATURN software architecture conference, where he has brought ideas and thought leaders from the Agile community to rub elbows with the architecture community. He has been looking for the best of both worlds, a mixture of Agile and architecture that is not oil and water.

There have been other attempts to reconcile the differences, but they have all been limited. Early attempts tried to shoehorn Agile into the implementation phase of a waterfall process. Others implicitly assumed there was still a "corner office architect" making the important decisions. Almost all of them were based in theory rather than reporting on what they had successfully applied and were written by an author in one camp trying to pull in ideas from the other.

This book is a different, better synthesis of Agile and architecture, which is why the word "Agile" is not on every page. It starts with a deep understanding and appreciation for Agile values and describes design techniques that are compatible. Michael has invented or adapted many of the techniques himself, but it thrills me to see that he's also plucked the best ideas from conferences over the past few years, techniques that are not yet in any other book. If you glance at Part III, "The Architect's Toolbox," you will not see "Architect chisels stone tablets for the team." You will see activities that fit within even week-long iterations, encourage team ownership of the design, and promote the design as a first-class concern of the team. It also has pictures of teams actually applying these techniques.

The same thought leaders who overthrew bureaucratic software processes also cautioned us that Agile was not a disguise for undisciplined cowboy coding. Those bureaucratic pre-Agile processes were, for the most part, disciplined, and you knew which design activities you should do and when. Despite teams self-reporting that they are following Agile processes, my experience is that there is a lot of undisciplined cowboy coding happening today.

Now that this book exists, the question is: what happens next? It is hard to make predictions, especially about the future, but here is what I foresee. We are on the cusp of a transition to a stable state of software development where we have learned to blend agility and discipline. Our processes will use the quick feedback loops popularized by Agile and will guide us to design techniques that drive quality. Unmistakably, they will be software processes, with activities and techniques uniquely appropriate for software development.

We are not there yet, but this book moves us in that direction. Let's go build the future we want to live in.

George Fairbanks
Author of *Just Enough Software Architecture*

Welcome!

Software architecture is the foundation on which awesome software is built. A great architecture alone isn't enough to guarantee your software will be a smashing success, but the wrong architecture almost guarantees failure. Software architecture is so important that every software developer should know how to design it.

In this book, you'll learn how to design great software architectures. Just to be clear, this isn't a lesson in Ivory Tower, high-abstraction software design. You also won't find any *magic bean* solutions—frameworks and technologies that magically solve any problem. You will learn how to apply essential design principles and practices, which will make you a stronger programmer, architect, and technical leader.

Designing great software requires more than mastery of principles and practices. How you go about designing a software system is just as important as the final result. In this book, you'll learn how to use design thinking and human-centered methods to design software architectures collaboratively with your team. This approach to architecture design helps you forge a stronger connection between the design decisions you make and the humans affected by those decisions. Putting people first allows you to make better design decisions and, as a result, better software.

Who Should Read This Book?

This book is for anyone who has ever stood at a whiteboard and sketched boxes and lines while trying to answer tough questions.

If you're completely new to software architecture design, then this book is the perfect introduction. We'll start with the basics and work our way through the core fundamentals you need to know to be an amazing software architect.

If you're a programmer who already knows a thing or two about architecture, then this book will help you organize your thoughts. As you read, you may find concepts you intuited on your own but didn't know the name, or perhaps you'll find gaps you didn't know you were missing. After reading this book, you'll be able to explain why you do what you do, which puts you in a better position to lead others.

If you're already a software architect and this isn't your first rodeo, then this book will give you a fresh perspective on how to lead your team. The junior programmers of today expect to have a greater say in the software they build. The focus on fundamentals in this book will prepare you to teach and mentor today's programmers—the architects of tomorrow—so they can fully participate in the design process. The collaborative design approaches described throughout this book will give you new techniques for safely and productively collaborating with less experienced teammates as you design a software system together.

How to Read This Book

This book is divided into three parts. Parts I and II are designed to be read start to finish. Part III is designed for easy reference.

In Part I you'll learn the basics of software architecture and design thinking needed to become an architect.

In Part II you'll learn the essential skills and knowledge all software architects possess.

Part III includes a set of practical architecture design methods. There are no silver bullets, but every software engineer has a silver toolbox filled with practices, methods, and techniques that together allow them to ship amazing software. The methods in Part III come from my silver toolbox and it is my privilege to share them with you.

Each chapter in Parts II and III focuses on a different design mindset, which you'll learn more about in Chapter 2, *Design Thinking Fundamentals*, on page 15. Design mindsets are a way of thinking about the world to help us focus our attention on the right details at the right time. There are four design mindsets: understand, explore, make, and evaluate. Look for the icon at the start of each chapter to tell you which mindset you'll be learning about next.

Community Tips and Advice

When you opened this book, you joined a community of software architects who help one another by sharing advice, tips, and good practices. To officially welcome you to the community, I've asked some fellow software architects to share tips and advice they think you should know. You'll find their stories and advice in sidebars throughout the book.

Our extraordinary community contributors are Len Bass, Bett Bollhoefer, Simon Brown, George Fairbanks, Thijmen de Gooijer, Patrick Kua, and Ipek Ozkaya. You can learn more about them in Appendix 1, *Community Contributor Bios*, on page 315.

Case Study

When talking about abstract things, it's all too easy to stay abstract. To prevent that from happening I've included a case study—Project Lionheart—based on real systems I've worked on in the past. The case study is introduced in Chapter 1. You'll see examples from the case study as the book progresses.

Get Your Hands Dirty Exercises

Great software architects have dirty hands. To become a great software architect, you have to practice design, not just talk about it. Anytime you see this icon it's time to think critically and put the theory into practice. Like architecture design in the real world, *Get Your Hands Dirty* exercises have many right answers. How you arrive at an answer—the journey—is as important as the solution itself.

Online Resources

This book has its own web page[1] where you can find details about this book, post to the discussion forums, and report errata such as typos and content suggestions. The discussion forums are the perfect place to talk shop with other readers and share your answers to the exercises.

Welcome, thank you for joining me, and let's get started!

---

1. https://pragprog.com/book/mkdsa/design-it

Part I

Introducing Software Architecture

Before we can dive in, we need to cover some basic concepts. These include both core architecture principles as well as design fundamentals.

CHAPTER 1

Become a Software Architect

I'm not exactly sure when I became a software architect. I do remember the first time someone else called me one. We were at an important client meeting and someone asked a tough technical question. The project manager chimed in: "Michael is the architect on this project. He'll dig in and send you an update by the end of the week."

Just like that, I was a software architect. The rush of power. The anticipation of career advancement. I am an architect! Soon a slight feeling of dread set in. I am an architect. Now what do I do? How is being a software architect different from being a software engineer?

Software architects have a number of responsibilities in addition to programming. They define the problem from an engineering perspective. They divide the software system into implementable chunks, but also keep an eye on the big picture to ensure the system still works as a consistent whole. Architects decide trade-offs among quality attributes and manage the inevitable growth of technical debt. Perhaps above all, architects develop their team's architecture skills, because they know the best teams are filled with architects.

In this chapter, you'll learn what architects do. You'll also learn why knowing about software architecture will make you a better programmer and technical leader. You'll also learn how to get started on the path to becoming a software architect in your professional career.

What Software Architects Do

Software architects are in a unique position on the team. They aren't project managers, but architects decide when and how software is delivered. They aren't product managers, but architects make sure the software meets its business goals. They write code, but architects design more than only algorithms and code. Software architects have a distinct set of responsibilities and are seemingly at the center of everything.

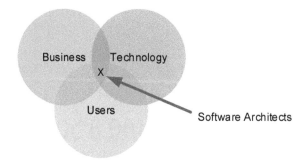

Most of us start our software careers focusing purely on technology. Knowing how to program, design efficient algorithms, test that everything works, and deploy software are all essential skills for software architects too. Growing from programmer to software architect requires you to accept some new responsibilities.

Define the Problem from an Engineering Perspective

Software architecture design is a human-centered design discipline. Everyone with a stake in the software can help you understand what is expected of it. Software architects work with product managers, project managers, and other stakeholders to define business goals and requirements for the software to be built.

On many teams, product managers define the features. Features are great, but there is another kind of requirement called a *quality attribute* that architects care the most about (see *Reason about Quality Attributes (and Other System Properties)*, on page 10). In addition to defining quality attributes for the system, architects keep an eye out for design constraints and features that might force the architecture down a specific path.

Defining the problem with the architecture in mind ensures you can build a system everyone wants. You'll learn how architects approach requirements in Chapter 5, *Dig for Architecturally*, on page 49.

Partition the System and Assign Responsibilities

Have you ever watched little kids play soccer? The only tyke to stay in position is the goalie, who remains glued to their team's goal while the other children form a glob of kicking feet and chase the ball from one end of the field to the other. It's adorable. Once the kids grow up a bit, they learn to play set positions. Playing positions is important since it lets the coach create a game strategy, which increases the team's likelihood of scoring.

Some software systems are designed like a children's soccer team: one great big clump of software chasing after a release. Software development, similar to soccer games, goes smoother when the software is divided into pieces and each piece is assigned a responsibility, a position to play.

Architects partition (a fancy word for *divide into pieces*) the software system so they can develop a strategy for achieving quality attributes and other system requirements. For example, you might assign functional responsibilities by designing one component to register users and another to identify pictures of cats. Or you could assign different teams to develop different modules. Or you might split things that read data from things that write data so the software system will be more reliable, available, and scalable.

Partitioning a system is important not just because it lets you develop a strategy for achieving quality attributes. Smaller things are easier to reason about, easier to test, and easier to design. Of course, since you broke the system into pieces, you'll also have to make sure everything can come back together again.

Keep an Eye on the Bigger Picture

Every software system lives in the context of a bigger world. The world in which software lives includes the users who interact with it, the team who builds it, the hardware it runs on, and even the purpose for developing the software in the first place. Ideally, the architecture lives harmoniously within this broader context.

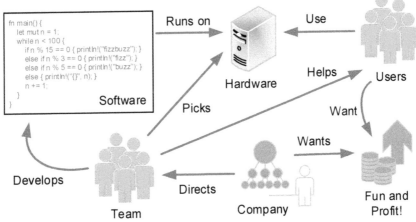

Software always lives in the **context** of a **system**.

Thinking about the system as a whole means architects deal with more than just technology. People, processes, business needs, and many other technical and nontechnical factors play a part in the final software system. Even simple design decisions can have far-reaching consequences. Architects must look beyond a small neighborhood of design decisions and think about the system as a whole.

Software design is a constant struggle to find the right balance between the things you want and the reality you must accept. This means you must think about and make trade-offs.

Decide Trade-offs among Quality Attributes

Say high availability is an important quality attribute for your stakeholders and you need your software to respond to 99.9 percent of requests. One way to promote availability is to introduce redundant elements. Designing for this is simple, but there's a catch. You now must purchase twice the hardware, which doubles your costs. In this case, you traded costs to get higher availability.

It is common in software development to give up something you want to get something you need. Architects identify the trade-offs and work with stakeholders to decide which compromises make the most sense.

Software systems are never partitioned perfectly. You'll make compromises. You'll make mistakes. As you build the system, you'll introduce technical debt into the architecture.

Manage Technical Debt

Software architects know the details about how the system is partitioned. They keep an eye on the big picture and guide how everything comes together. They also connect technology decisions with business needs. Knowing all this puts architects in the perfect position to manage technical debt.

Technical debt is the gap between your software system's current design and the design you need it to have so you can continue to deliver value. You can measure the amount of technical debt by estimating the effort required to close that gap. All software has technical debt. Technical debt is an inevitable byproduct of success. The best software development teams use technical debt strategically to ship faster and regularly pay debt down so they can continue shipping value over time.

Architects make technical debt visible and help stakeholders decide which actions to take to manage it.

Grow the Team's Architecture Skills

Software architects are teachers and mentors for their teams. There is no use in designing an awesome architecture that nobody can understand. As the architecture expert on your team, it is your responsibility to share your knowledge with your team so they can successfully develop an amazing software system.

Architects teach design skills and architecture concepts just-in-time. To pass on your knowledge, you'll pair design with teammates, create documents that educate and inform, and share constructive criticism. Perhaps the most important thing you can do to grow the team's architecture skills is to include them in the design process. Architecture design is a social activity. Skills development is crucial to your team's success.

Now you know what architects do, but we haven't defined what we mean by software architecture yet. Let's do something about that now.

What Is Software Architecture?

A system's *software architecture* is the set of significant design decisions about how the software is organized to promote desired quality attributes and other properties.

A design decision might be significant for any number of reasons. It might represent a point of no return or influence quality attributes, schedule, or costs. A significant decision might be one that affects many people or forces other software systems to change. In any case, significant design decisions are costly to change later if you get them wrong.

To *promote* a quality attribute means to encourage it to appear in the software system. When the architecture is well organized, it will boost the quality attributes stakeholders want and downplay or eliminate the quality attributes stakeholders don't want. Architecture can promote other properties too. For example, the right architecture for the job will let you ship on time, on budget, and without requiring too much overtime.

Define the Essential Structures

A skyscraper has a foundation and frames. A body has bones. Software has *structures*. A structure defines how a software system is arranged. Structures are in the code you write, the software you run, and even your collaborations with other people.

To create a structure, take any *element* and connect it to another element using a *relation*. Think of elements and relations like the bricks and mortar of software. The bread and peanut butter. The duct tape and...well, you get the idea. Elements are the fundamental building blocks of software. Relations describe how elements work together to accomplish some task.

It's easy to design an architecture on paper with no bearing on reality. To avoid this trap, you'll build architectures using three types of elements and relations. *Software Architecture in Practice [BCK12]* defines these three types as *module, component and connector* (C&C for short), and *allocation*. To create a structure, combine elements and relations of the same type.

Here are some example elements and relations of each type.

	Example Elements	Example Relations
Module	class, package, layer, stored procedure, module, configuration file, database table	uses, allowed to use, depends on
Component and Connector	object, connection, thread, process, tier, filter	call, subscribe, pipe, publish, return
Allocation	server, sensor, laptop, load balancer, team, Owen (a person), Docker container	runs in or on, responsible for, develops, stores, pays for

Module structures exist at design time. You interact with module structures when you write code. Module structures live on the file system and stick around even when the software is not running.

Component and connector structures come into existence at runtime. At runtime, components can create connections to other components, spawn new processes, and instantiate new objects. Unlike module structures, C&C structures cease to exist when the system is not running. You might only know a C&C structure existed from the artifacts it left behind, such as a log file or database entry.

Allocation structures are created by showing how module and C&C elements correspond with each other and the physical elements that exist in real life. Allocation structures are sometimes called *mapping structures* since they show how different elements map to one another. Does an element run on the client machine or the server? Which teams are building which parts of the system? Allocation structures help us answer questions like these.

Joe asks:
Are Components and Modules Different Things?

In your software development career you may have heard the words module and component used interchangeably and in different contexts. Technically a component is a different concept from a module. A *module* refers to a design time element whereas a *component* is a runtime idea.

Sometimes this precision in language is important. Using a term with specific meaning to describe something general can create confusion. Anytime you want to describe a generic building block of an architecture instead of using component or module, use the word *element*.

All that said, arguing about semantics is not the best way to get your ideas across. While I encourage you to use proper and precise terminology, your ideas will sometimes get better mileage by adapting your language so others understand you.

Different kinds of structures are useful for thinking about different properties you want in your system. For example, you can think about testability and maintainability using a module structure. A C&C structure helps us think about runtime concerns such as availability or performance. You also might know there's a gap in our understanding if you see mixed structures such as a static element using a dynamic relation.

Structures determine the shape of our system. The shape is important since it decides the quality attributes and other properties your users will experience. In the next section you'll see how to use structures to reason about quality attributes, but first, it's time get your hands dirty with a quick exercise.

Get Your Hands Dirty: Elements, Relations, and Structures

Find a few teammates from a recent project. Working alone, list or sketch module, component and connector, and allocation structures from that project. Share your lists with one another. How do they compare? Are there structures your teammates identified that you didn't? Discuss the similarities and differences in the structures different teammates identified.

Here are some things to think about:

- Be specific when naming the elements. Don't forget about the relations!

- Think about the module structures: What methods or classes are used? Do the classes live in different packages or namespaces? What dependencies are included in package managers or build scripts?

- Think about the C&C structures: Does the software interact with other processes or systems at runtime? Who calls the system and how does it change in response?

- Think about the allocation structures: Who is responsible for building different parts of the software? How is the software deployed?

Reason about Quality Attributes (and Other System Properties)

Say you're building a calculator app and you want to add two numbers together. Sounds easy, right?

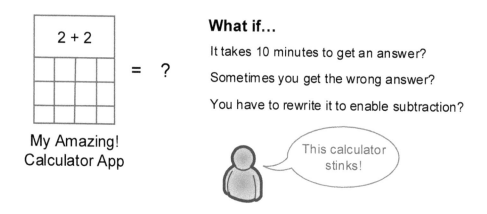

2 + 2

= ?

My Amazing!
Calculator App

What if...

It takes 10 minutes to get an answer?

Sometimes you get the wrong answer?

You have to rewrite it to enable subtraction?

This calculator stinks!

Wait. Did you want a calculator that adds two numbers and is fast, reliable, scalable, and maintainable? Why didn't you say so! If we hadn't asked about these quality attributes, we might have designed the wrong system altogether.

A *quality attribute* is any externally visible characteristic by which stakeholders judge a software system's goodness. Some examples include scalability, availability, maintainability, and testability. You experience quality attributes when you interact with the software.

When you choose an architectural structure, you are choosing the quality attributes you want to be promoted in the software system. Thinking about software architecture makes sure you design a software system that supports the quality attributes you want within the context of all the other concerns vying for attention.

Quality attributes make software unique. The circumstances of every system are different—different team, different budget, different market conditions, even different technology trends. As a result, no two architectures will ever be the same even if the feature sets are identical.

Up for the challenge? In the next section, you'll learn some strategies for becoming your team's architect.

Become an Architect for Your Team

On some teams, *architect* is an official team role. On other teams, there is no explicit role and teammates share the architect's responsibilities. Some teams say they don't have an architect, but if you look closely, someone is fulfilling the architect's duties without realizing it.

Architects are leaders, but being a *software architect* also implies a person who thinks about software design in a certain way. No matter what the title on your business card reads (mine still reads *software engineer*, my choice), you can be a software architect. Every team has at least one architect. The best teams have several.

If your team doesn't have an architect, congratulations, you've got the job! You don't need permission to inject architectural thinking into your team's design discussions. Start asking questions about quality attributes. Point out when the team makes trade-offs. Volunteer to write up design decisions and begin accepting more architecture design responsibilities.

If your team already has an architect, then ask that person how you can help. When possible, work closely with your architect and take advantage of every learning opportunity you can. Developing a software system is a big job. The more people who pay attention to the details, the greater your chance of success. Every team should be so lucky as to have many knowledgeable software architects!

Make the Move from Programmer to Software Architect

An average software architect has developed three to five software systems with increased technical responsibility on each software system. Depending on the software you build, as your architecture responsibilities grow you may find you have less time for programming. This is normal, though software architects should never stop programming altogether.

To measure your growth from programmer to software architect, create a project portfolio. For every software system you build, no matter your role, briefly describe the software system and what you learned during your time developing it. This kind of reflective practice is essential for all technical leaders but especially software architects.

Here are some questions you should answer about each project in your portfolio:

- Who were the stakeholders and what were the primary business goals?
- What did the high-level solution look like?
- What technologies were involved?
- What were the biggest risks and how did you overcome them?
- If you could do it all over again, how would you do it differently?

Whether your goal is promotion or simply professional growth, be patient. You might have the chance to design a software system of meaningful complexity only every three to five years. If you are lucky, you will see between 8 and 15 software systems throughout your entire career. Be prepared to take advantage of architecting opportunities as they arise. Work with your teammates to give everyone a chance to grow their skills. I promise there is more than enough interesting architecture work for everyone!

Always remember, *software architect* is a way of thinking, not just a role on the team. When you're wearing your programmer hat, you'll make dozens of design decisions daily. Some of these decisions have architectural significance. Anyone who makes a decision that influences the structures of the software system becomes the *architect pro tempore*. It's up to you to make good decisions and uphold architectural integrity no matter what the title on your business card reads.

Build Amazing Software

There are lots of things that have to go right when building a software system. Architecture connects them all together and provides a foundation for success. Here are six ways software architecture helps you in your quest to build spectacular software that your stakeholders will love:

1. Software architecture turns a big problem into smaller, more manageable problems.

   Modern software systems are large and complex, and they have many moving pieces. The architecture precisely explains how to partition the system into smaller, bite-sized chunks while also ensuring the system as a whole is greater than the sum of its parts.

2. Software architecture shows people how to work together.

   Software development is as much about human communication as it is technology. Software architecture describes how the whole system comes together, including the people who build it. When you know the architecture, then you can see how people can collaborate to develop software. The larger the software system, the more important this becomes.

3. Software architecture provides a vocabulary for talking about complex ideas.

If I don't understand what you're talking about, then we won't be able to collaborate. Instead of spending all our time inventing vocabulary and concepts, we can use the essential concepts and core vocabulary of architecture as the starting basis for collaboration. Now we can spend our time solving our users' real problems.

4. Software architecture looks beyond features and functionality.

Features and functionality are important, but they are not the only thing that determines whether or not software is awesome. When designing architecture, you'll consider not only the features but also costs, constraints, schedules, risk, the ability of the team to deliver, and most importantly quality attributes—things like scalability, availability, performance, and maintainability.

5. Software architecture helps you avoid costly mistakes.

In *Who Needs an Architect? [Fow03]*, Martin Fowler defines software architecture as "...the important stuff. Whatever that is." The important stuff is nearly always what we think will be difficult to change without significantly increasing complexity. Grady Booch echoes Fowler's sentiment by defining architecture as the "...significant design decisions (where significant is measured by the cost of change)."[1] Software architects are not omniscient, but designing an architecture will help you discover the challenging (and interesting) parts of the problem that might cause big trouble later.

6. Software architecture enables agility.

Your software should respond to change like water, by bending around obstacles with ease. If software is like water, able to take any shape, then software architecture is the container that holds it. That container can be rigid like a box or flexible like a plastic bag. It can be thick and heavy or lightweight. Without an architecture, software, like water, follows the path of least resistance and sprawls uncontrollably. A software system's architecture provides the structure within which change is possible.

We'll expand on these ideas throughout the remainder of the book.

---

1. Grady Booch. *Abstracting the Unknown*. SATURN 2016. http://resources.sei.cmu.edu/library/asset-view.cfm?assetID=454315

Case Study: Project Lionheart

As we cover new ideas in each chapter, we'll apply them to a case study, Project Lionheart. The case study is based on a real system, but the names and situations have been changed for teaching and legal purposes.

Design an Architecture to Solve This Problem

The City of Springfield is facing budget shortfalls and needs to cut costs. Mayor Jean Claude van Damme (no relation to the action hero) has hired our team to streamline the city's Office of Management and Budget (OMB).

When a city employee needs to purchase something for more than a few thousand dollars, the OMB issues a Request for Proposals (RFP) in the local newspaper. Businesses bid on the RFPs and the OMB awards a contract based on the competitiveness of the bid and other factors. The OMB monitors more than 500 active contracts and RFPs for everything from toilet paper to medical supplies to basketballs. The OMB manages all this data in spreadsheets.

Mayor van Damme hopes modernizing the OMB will improve a few strategic areas.

- Over half of all RFPs have a single bid. The city is potentially overpaying for lower-quality services.

- Finalizing a contract takes months. Many businesses get lost in the multistep process.

- Publishing a new RFP takes up to 6 weeks. This process must be faster.

Throughout Part II, we'll flesh out this case study and work together to design a plausible architecture to solve some of these problems.

Next Up

Software architects are responsible for quite a lot. Designing interesting, complex software systems and working with different people feels good and is well worth the effort. Becoming a software architect is not an overnight journey. If you focus on the architect's core responsibilities and do your best to apply the architectural fundamentals, mainly selecting structures to promote desired quality attributes, then you'll do great.

In this chapter, you learned what architecture is and what architects do. In the next chapter, you'll learn how to use design thinking to figure out what should go into the architecture.

CHAPTER 2

Design Thinking Fundamentals

On your first day working with any software system the architecture is always TBD—to be discovered. Whether we start from a blank page or must uncover structures in an existing software system, the architecture we need is out there, somewhere, waiting for us to discover it. To design a software system's architecture we explore solutions at the same time we're working to uncover the problem to be solved.

To help you perform this challenging task, you'll learn a creative and analytical approach to problem solving that puts humans at the center of attention called *design thinking*. Focusing on the people affected by your design decisions helps you concentrate on the exact problems that must be solved. It also grounds your solution exploration by reminding you that your purpose is to build software that helps people.

In this chapter, you'll learn how to apply design thinking to software architecture. You'll start by learning the core principles of design thinking. Next, you'll learn how to use different design mindsets to keep your architecture moving forward in (mostly) the right direction. Finally, you'll see an approach for picking design mindsets.

The Four Principles of Design Thinking

Design thinking is less a process and more a way of thinking about problems and solutions from the perspective of the people affected by them. While design thinking is not a process, there are still rules to guide our design activities. In *Design Thinking: Understand - Improve - Apply (Understanding Innovation) [PML10]* Christoph Meinel and Larry Leifer propose four universal principles of design. These principles apply to software architecture as well as to detailed program design, user interaction design, or any other design-focused discipline.

Here are the four principles of design:

1. Human rule. All design is social in nature.

2. Ambiguity rule. Preserve ambiguity.

3. Redesign rule. All design is redesign.

4. Tangibility rule. Make ideas tangible to facilitate communication.

We'll use the acronym HART to help remember these principles. Let's examine the HART principles as they relate to software architecture design so we can see how to apply design thinking in the context of software architecture.

Design for Humans

Design is an inherently human-focused endeavor. We design software *for* people. We design software *with* people. Every design decision in the architecture helps individuals in some way. Every design decision must be understood by and shared with other humans.

Architects must empathize with all stakeholders. We care about end users as much as the people the end users help, the programmers who write the code, the testers who verify it, and even the managers who keep tabs on the development schedule. As we design a software system, we'll collaborate with the other humans on our team and show them respect by listening, assuming positive intent, and using human-centered design methods.

The Human rule also reminds us that architects are not separated from our teams. We work directly with them to design the architecture together. Building software is an intensely social activity. The idea of an *ivory tower architect* who designs the architecture isolated from the team is a myth. Software architects are an integral part of every team. Separating the architect from the team severs the human connection the architect shares with everyone touched by the architecture.

Empathizing with the humans who directly and indirectly interact with the architecture makes us a better designer, communicator, and leader.

Preserve Ambiguity

Ambiguity in engineering is dangerous. Once we've made a design decision, we must share it with precision and clarity. Allowing requirements, design decisions, and commitments to remain ambiguous is the best way to destroy a project. Before we solidify a design decision, we can use ambiguity to keep options open.

Since the goal of software architecture is to arrange structures that promote desired quality attributes, we'll focus our attention there. In *Less is more with minimalist architecture [MB02]*, Ruth Malan and Dana Bredemeyer suggest architects design a *minimalist architecture*. A minimalist architecture only shows how high-priority quality attributes are achieved and reduces risks for promoting those quality attributes. All other design decisions are left open for downstream designers to determine.

Architecture minimalism implies that we want to defer binding design decisions for as long as responsible. Design decisions that do not directly influence a quality attribute or reduce risks threatening our ability to deliver software are more about detailed design than architecture. Such decisions can safely be left open for downstream designers to settle outside the architecture. You'll learn more about preserving ambiguity in *Design for Change*, on page 75.

Preserving ambiguity allows us to deliver software even as the world around us changes.

Design Is Redesign

In *A Pattern Language: Towns, Buildings, Construction [AISJ77]*, Christopher Alexander and others cataloged over 253 civil engineering problems with known good solutions. Topics ranged from construction materials to community organization techniques to building architectures. If you've ever enjoyed a perfect spring morning while sipping coffee at a sidewalk cafe, then you can thank Christopher Alexander for documenting the *sidewalk cafe* pattern as a *community building* solution.

The redesign rule encourages us to look to think about what we already know by exploring patterns and past designs. As time goes on and as we build more software, our institutional knowledge about how to design great software improves. Other teams have probably seen a problem similar to the one you face currently. Hopefully, someone documented a pattern you can use as a starting point for your architecture. Maybe someone built a framework designed to solve your exact problem?

When designing software architectures, we'll spend more time refining existing designs than we'll be creating new ones. One of the least effective ways to design software architecture is to ignore the software systems that came before us.

Make the Architecture Tangible

While the structures in the architecture can exist in code, this does not make the architecture any more tangible. Code is difficult to read and does not make discussions about quality attributes, coarse-grained components, design rationale, or the consequences of our decisions any easier. If we want to share an architecture with others, then we need to make it real in a way code by itself will not allow.

There are many ways to make architecture tangible. Draw it. Make it come alive in the code you write. Build prototypes that let people experience structures and quality attributes. Create simple models that show how some part of the architecture works. Create relatable metaphors. Act out parts of the control flow of the system.

The tangibility rule is closely related to the Human rule. Humans must be able to relate to ideas to internalize them. The only way to share an architecture is to make it tangible.

The HART principles form the philosophical basis of our architecture design approach. These principles guide our decision making and permeate our thinking. These four principles describe why we do things the way we do them. Now that you understand the underlying principles behind design thinking, let's explore how to apply these principles by learning how to select architecture-focused design practices.

Adopt a Design Mindset

Designing a software system requires us to think about the architecture from the perspective of different *design mindsets*. A design mindset is a way of thinking about the world so that we focus our attention on the right details at the right time.

There are four design mindsets: understand, explore, make, and evaluate. Each design mindset comes with a set of practices. To design the architecture, we'll choose a mindset, pick a practice in that mindset, apply the practice to learn something new about the architecture, and repeat.

The chapters in Part II will show you how to put each mindset into practice. Look for the icon, shown in the image on page 19, at the start of each chapter to tell you what the focus will be. For now, let's learn what it means to embrace each of the four design mindsets.

Understand the Problem

In the *understand mindset* we actively seek information from stakeholders and work to describe the problem. The understand mindset is as much about requirements as it is empathy. To understand the problem, we must learn about the people who will be touched by our system and what they need.

Four Design Mindsets; Use in Any Order

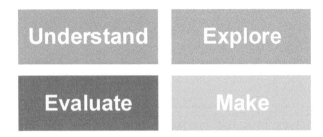

To understand the problem, we'll need to investigate business goals and quality attributes that are important to our stakeholders. We'll also have to learn how our team operates and get a deeper sense of the priorities and trade-offs among design decisions.

Explore Ideas

In the popular ethos, design thinking is all about brainstorming and sticky notes. Brainstorming is powerful, but it is only one practice in the *explore mindset*. When we explore, we create multiple design concepts and identify engineering approaches for solving some aspect of a problem.

Exploring software architecture means we try combinations of structures until we find a combination that best promotes desired quality attributes. To find the best mix of structures, we'll need to survey a broad range of patterns, technologies, and development practices. When we're planning the architecture, we'll spend a lot of time in the exploration mindset, but this mindset is also useful when working with stakeholders.

Make It Real

As you learned in *Make the Architecture Tangible*, on page 17, ideas are great but if you can't transfer them from your brain into someone else's brain, then your ideas are useless. Making ideas real gives us a way to share them but also provides an opportunity for testing an idea. In the *make mindset* we turn our design concepts into real-world artifacts.

The most common ways we make architecture real is by creating models. Making goes way beyond box and line diagrams. You can make the architecture real by building prototypes, writing documents, crunching numbers, and a variety of other approaches.

The make mindset is useful for communicating our plans. We'll also make the architecture real as we build the system—for example, by organizing our code so that it's possible to *see* module structures in the architecture. Making is also an excellent way to push your team out of analysis paralysis.

Evaluate Fit

How do you know if a design decision will solve the problem? When we embrace the *evaluate mindset*, we determine the fitness of our design decisions relative to our current understanding.

Evaluation is not an all or none proposition. We can evaluate all or part of the architecture, even only a single model, concept, or idea. The most common approach is to walk through a piece of the architecture with different scenarios, but we can also test design decisions directly by running experiments or examining the risks surrounding a decision.

The evaluate mindset comes in handy when we want to verify the planned or built architecture, but this is only the beginning. This mindset will help us inspect anything we make and decide whether that artifact is serving our need.

Using design mindsets requires a process with a tight feedback loop so we can quickly move from one mindset to the next. In the next section, we'll learn how to use a simple, iterative approach to help us choose and use design mindsets.

Get Your Hands Dirty: Understand, Explore, Make, Evaluate

The four design thinking mindsets reflect how people solve problems. Even without training in design thinking, you have probably used these mindsets before. What are some examples of how you embraced each of these mindsets so far in your software development career? Try to name at least two examples of how you worked in each design mindset.

Here are some things to think about:

- When have you worked with people to *understand* a problem? Did you follow a particular method?

- How have you collaborated with others to *explore* ideas and generated alternatives?

- Looking beyond code, how do the things you *make* change how you interact with stakeholders and teammates?

- How do you *evaluate* your designs? What techniques have you used to test solution hypotheses?

Think, Do, Check

Every day, for as long as we work on a software system, we learn interesting things about the software. Every new thing we learn might force the architecture to evolve to reconcile the new information. For us to keep tabs on this ever changing landscape, we need a design approach with a tight feedback loop that gives us the opportunity to change our mindsets often.

There are three steps in our approach: think, do, and check. Each iteration of the think-do-check cycle focuses on a particular design mindset.

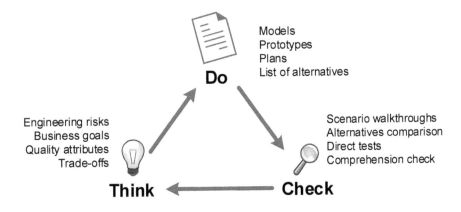

Iterate to Learn

An iteration can be as brief as a few minutes or as long as a few days. We prefer shorter cycles over longer ones, but sometimes more time is required for in-depth research. Every iteration follows the same steps, though the execution will vary depending on the design mindset we adopt.

Think What do we hope to learn? What questions do we need answered? What are our top risks? Thinking involves creating a plan to learn what we need to answer specific questions or reduce risks.

Do Execute the plan. Create something tangible that quickly and cheaply uncovers information needed to check our thinking and share our ideas.

Check Critically examine what we accomplished during the *do* step so we can decide our next move. The insights coming out of the *check* step tell us what to do next. Repeat at the *think* step.

A software system is never finished; it is only released. Since software is never done, our design approach has no end. Anytime you need to revisit some aspect of the architecture, whether it's to evolve an existing design or create something new, the same approach applies.

Adopt Mindsets in Any Order

Think of the four design mindsets like four tool boxes, each containing tools tuned for a particular type of design work. When the need arises, embrace the mindset required to learn more about the world or reduce a risk.

In the understand mindset, we'll focus on stakeholders needs and how to specify those needs as requirements. In the explore mindset, we'll brainstorm ways to solve the problem as we understand it by looking at patterns, technology, and other solutions. In the make mindset, we'll model the system so we have something concrete to reason about and share. In the evaluate mindset, we'll put our models and requirements to the test.

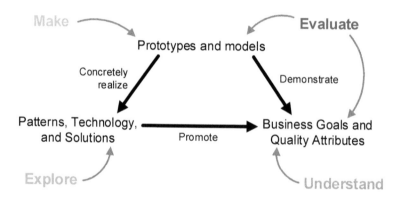

Mindsets shift frequently and quickly. During a single conversation, we might change mindsets several times. During a workshop, we will create situations that force participants to adopt new mindsets so that we can arrive at a desirable outcome. You'll see an example of this in Chapter 9, *Host an Architecture Design Studio*, on page 113.

Experienced architects are often unaware that they attack architecture from varying perspectives. They fly by instinct and adopt different mindsets intuitively (thanks to years of practice). Awareness of the four design mindsets gives us new techniques for getting out of a rut. If you get stuck, choose a new mindset to get yourself unstuck.

Plot Your Course: Think-Do-Check and Mindsets in Action

Let's see a concrete example of how the think-do-check cycle and design mindsets might play out in practice. Say a stakeholder just gave us a new constraint and this increases the risk that the architecture will be unable to satisfy performance requirements.

- *Think.* We know system performance is important, but we don't know what it means to have *good* performance. Since we need information about the problem, let's adopt the *understand* mindset. Looking through some practices in Chapter 14, *Activities to Understand the Problem*, on page 191, we decide to capture quality attribute scenarios.

- *Do.* We brainstorm some performance scenarios and record them in a document.

- *Check.* The team and stakeholders review the scenarios and provide feedback.

Based on what we learned, new risks arise. Can we achieve the performance quality attribute scenarios given the new constraint?

- *Think.* Since we need to verify that our decisions promote a specific quality attribute let's adopt the *evaluate* mindset. We plan an experiment so we can directly test the constraint's impact on performance.

- *Do.* We write some simple scripts to drive existing parts of the software system and collect data. We run the experiment.

- *Check.* With data in hand, we examine the results and conclude that the new constraint negatively impacts performance but only by a few 100 milliseconds.

We think we've done a thorough job, but performance is funny. Hurting performance might not be a big deal until it degrades too much. We need to share these results with our stakeholders and discuss the implications of the new constraint.

- *Think.* Since making ideas tangible facilitates communication, we'll adopt the *make* mindset and create a simple prototype. We want stakeholders to experience the impact of the new constraint. Graphs aren't enough.

- *Do.* We develop a throwaway prototype that demonstrates the application workflow and simulates different assumptions about performance.

- *Check.* We give the prototype to our stakeholders and explain why the performance of the system was impacted. On paper, a few 100 milliseconds is tiny, but experiencing the slowdown firsthand shows that this dip in performance isn't acceptable.

The prototype helped our stakeholders learn something about the problem nobody knew was important until now. Next, we'll adopt the *understand* mindset and refine our new requirements. We check our understanding a few minutes in the same meeting by selecting the *explore* mindset. And the cycle continues.

The think-do-check cycle is extremely flexible. How you use it depends on the complexity and size of the system, your team's size and skills, and your experience with having simultaneous design initiatives in flight.

Next Up

Design thinking gives us a way to connect the highly technical world of software development with the humans affected by the software we build. The four HART principles are the means by which we'll give our software heart (pun 100 percent intended). Design mindsets are the way we'll decide what needs to be done to help our stakeholders.

Now that we've covered the theory, it's time to get down to business.

Since the invention of software, we have debated how much architecture design should happen up front and how much can emerge as we implement a solution. Like any discussion about extremes, the real answer lies somewhere in the middle. In the next chapter, you'll see how to define a design strategy appropriate to your situation and choose design mindsets by considering the risks in the software system.

Part II

Architecture Design Fundamentals

In Part I you learned about design thinking principles and mindsets. In Part II you'll see how to put those principles and mindsets into practice to design software architectures.

CHAPTER 3

Devise a Design Strategy

Designing software architecture always feels a bit chaotic. Despite the swirl of uncertainty surrounding every software system, it's important to have a plan. With a solid design strategy, we can feel our way through the mists of uncertainty.

Design thinking is perfect for finding solutions to complex problems. Instead of trying to solve the problem perfectly on the first try, design thinking emphasizes learning and experimentation. Testing an architecture might be impossible without implementing it, but it may be possible to verify pieces of the architecture incrementally as we design them. We can use design mindsets and the think-do-check cycle to decide where to focus our attention next.

In Chapter 2, *Design Thinking Fundamentals*, on page 15 you learned the basic rules of design thinking and how to use design mindsets. In this chapter, you'll learn how to choose design mindsets as part of a broader design strategy by thinking about the risks in the software system.

Find a Design That Satisfices

In a rational world, we'd fully define the problem before designing a perfect architecture to solve it. Too bad we don't live in a perfect, rational world. In *The Sciences of the Artificial [Sim96]*, Herbert Simon coined the term *bounded rationality* to describe the theoretical barrier created by limits in time, money, skills, and knowledge that make rational design challenging for complex problems such as software architecture.

Instead of rationally seeking an optimal design, our goal is to find an architecture that *satisfices*. A satisficing design is both satisfactory and sufficient—good enough—for our needs.

Instead of thinking of software architecture as a design optimization problem, we'll look for a satisficing design by emphasizing the following activities.

Treat solutions as experiments. Architects are not omniscient sages of technology who know all things. Think of every potential solution as an experiment to be validated. The sooner, faster, and cheaper we can validate (or invalidate) our hypotheses, the sooner we'll find the right combination of structures that will help our stakeholders and the sooner our stakeholders will gain value from our designs.

Focus on reducing risks. Value is only one variable that must be considered. Architecture is the foundation of the software system. If it fails, then everything fails. Architects must constantly worry about what could go wrong and design for these scenarios. We can use risk to help us decide what to design next.

Work to simplify problems. Simple problems often have simple solutions. There are many ways to simplify the problem. Reducing the number of stakeholders will decrease the variety of competing perspectives influencing the system. Adding or removing constraints, or focusing on a subset of the problem can reduce complexity. Identifying the *routine problems* makes it easier to focus on redesign. Routine problems have a known solution so we can start with pattern catalogs and apply our collective experience when exploring solutions.

Iterate quickly to learn quickly. The faster we learn, the more we can explore, and the greater confidence we'll have in our solutions. If we're wrong, let's find out as quickly as possible. Failing fast means learning fast. Favor short, tight design iterations with concrete outcomes over longer design iterations that only focus on abstract goals.

Think about the problem and solution at the same time. In *Notes on the Synthesis of Form [Ale64]*, Christopher Alexander shows how problems are always defined with a solution in mind. The boundary around a problem is created by the solutions that could potentially solve it. To understand the problem, we must explore solutions. To do a better job of exploring solutions, we must improve our understanding of the problem. Designing software architecture requires us to think about problems and solutions simultaneously. Writing some code early in the design process is one strategy for dealing with the reciprocal relationship between problems and solutions.

Avoiding rational design does not mean we suddenly become irrational architects. Architecture is the foundation of every software system, so we still need do some design work up front. We'll need to decide how much of the architecture we'll design up front and how much we'll allow to emerge over time. Selecting a design strategy early in a software system's life tells our team how we want to grow the architecture and instills confidence in our stakeholders.

Decide How Much to Design Up Front

Architecture is a necessary investment. Every software system has an architecture. One way or another, you will spend time designing it. If we spend time designing architecture up front, then we'll reduce the cost of future rework. Of course, time spent planning architecture also delays implementation thus potentially delaying value for stakeholders. If we spend no time up front on architecture, then we are more likely to make changes to the architecture after developing parts of the software system.

Depending on the software system's size and requirements variability, every software systems has a *design sweet spot*, an optimal amount of time to spend designing architecture before diving into implementation.

Find the Design Sweet Spot

In *Architecting: How Much and When? [BWO10]*, Barry Boehm shows us that the combination of development time, architecture planning, and rework are major contributing factors to the overall project schedule. Rework includes activities such as fixing design defects, rewriting code, and undoing mistakes. To find the sweet spot, we must account for both design costs and the inevitable rework required to complete the software system.

> Development Time
> Architecture and Risk Reduction Time
> **+** Rework Time (fixing defects, rewrites, mistakes)
> _____
> **Total Project Time**

Note: Time spent on architecture can speed up development and reduce rework!

The architecture sweet spot is highly dependent on the size, requirements volatility, and complexity of the software you're developing. The graph on page 30 from *Boehm's data [BWO10]* shows how the amount of rework decreases as more time is invested in architecture planning. The solid green

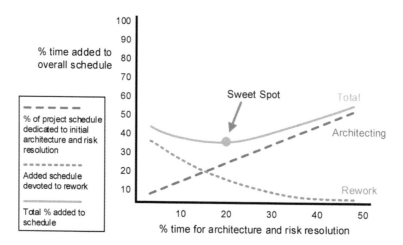

line represents the sum of architecture design effort (dashed blue line) and the cost of rework (dotted orange line).

In this case, spending less than about 20 percent of the original project schedule on architecture has a diminishing return. While the amount of rework decreases with a greater investment in architecture, the total project schedule increases. Similarly, spending less time on architecture raises the amount of rework, creating a longer overall project timeline.

In the same research, Boehm also shows how the sweet spot moves depending on the estimated size of the software system. Use this data to decide if the amount of time you plan to dedicate to up-front architecture design is in the right range.

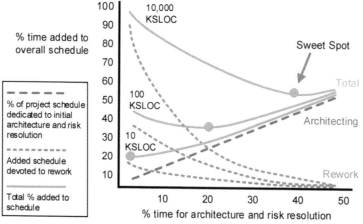

This graph is packed with important implications, so let's break down the essential points.

The bigger the software system, the greater the benefits you'll reap from up-front architecture design. From Boehm's research, spending upward of 37 percent of the total estimated development schedule on architecture design for large (10,000 KSLOC, where a KSLOC is 1,000 equivalent source lines of code) software systems would be a wise decision.

Smaller (10 KSLOC) software systems gain little from up-front architecture planning. From Boehm's research, as little as 5 percent of the total estimated development schedule might be spent on up-front architecture design. In some cases, it can be faster to rewrite a small software system than to spend significant time designing architecture up front.

Expect violent thrashing if you invest little into architecture design. Avoiding up-front architecture design in smaller software systems might be more cost effective and result in a shorter overall schedule, but rework will still be necessary. Be prepared for this and account for design churn in your plans. Bigger systems will experience even more thrashing with less architecture design up front.

The more you invest in architecture, the less rework will be required. Planning architecture helps avoid mistakes. If you favor predictable project schedules over schedule efficiency, you will benefit from more planning up front, even on smaller software systems. Up-front planning is a must in larger software systems.

Size is a nice predictor since it's easy to measure and estimate, but *many teams also use complexity [WNA13]* to decide how much architecture design work might be required. Large systems can be complex, but not all complex systems are large. If a solution is routine, then your team might get away with less up-front planning even when the system is large.

Another factor to consider is requirements volatility. Changes to architecturally significant requirements can invalidate the best-laid plans. If you anticipate a high degree of change, delay making binding decisions and focus on using lighter-weight design and documentation methods.

Example: Impact of Architecture on Total Schedule

Say we are developing a software system with an estimated size of 100 KSLOC and an initial development schedule of 100 days. Per Boehm's data, if we spent 5 percent of our time on architecture, then the total project schedule would increase by about 43 percent. Had we spent a little more time on architecture, say 17 percent of the estimated development schedule, then the total project schedule would have increased by only 38 percent.

Of course, more architecture does not always mean we'll have a shorter schedule. If we spent a third of the estimated development time on architecture, we'd increase the total development schedule. While we'd spend significantly less time on rework, the extra time dedicated to architecture doesn't pay off since the overall project schedule increases by about 40 percent.

Here are the numbers assuming our estimated 100-day initial development schedule:

Days Spent on Architecture	Days Spent on Rework	Days in Total Schedule
5	38	143
17	21	138
33	7	140

The Constructive Systems Engineering Model (COSYSMO) includes Boehm's findings. I suggest you try the COSYSMO and COCOMO II tools with your project data.[1]

Thanks to Boehm's work, we have a general idea for how much time to spend on architecture design, but we still don't know when to do the design work or when to adopt the different design mindsets introduced in Chapter 2, *Design Thinking Fundamentals*, on page 15. It turns out Boehm also has an answer for this (yes, he is that awesome). In *Using Risk to Balance Agile and Plan-Driven Methods [BT03]*, Barry Boehm and Richard Turner propose using risk to decide when to focus on architecture. If we think about risk in the right ways, we can also use it to determine what to design and how to involve stakeholders in the design process.

Let Risk Be Your Guide

Shortly after the first stakeholder meeting on a new software project, I always feel a giant pit grow in my stomach. If I didn't have that feeling, then I would be worried. Software worth building always has risks. You *should* feel a bit uncomfortable at the start of a new project. After all, if you knew everything at the outset and had no questions about what you were going to build, then why would an architect be needed?

We can use that slight sinking feeling in our guts to our advantage. Risk is an excellent indicator of what might prevent us from succeeding. To harness the power of our guts, write down all the things that worry you about the software

---

1. http://sunset.usc.edu/csse/research/cocomoii/cocomo_main.html

system. Next, prioritize the items on your list so that the things likely to cause the most trouble are highest on the list. Finally, pick one of the top things you're worried about and choose a design mindset to reduce the risk.

Gut feelings are a good start, but guts alone don't give us much to go on. I don't know about you, but I hate going to my boss with gut feelings. *Hi, Will, so I'm not sure if it was the burrito I had for lunch or what, but I've got a bad feeling about how the system is going to scale as we add data.* Gut feelings tell us there is something wrong, but we can do a much better job than just listening to our lower intestines.

Identify Conditions and Consequences

A *risk* is something bad that might happen in the future. If it already happened, then it's called a problem. If it starts with *what if...*, then it's pure speculation. We could play *what if...* all day and never get any closer to designing a useful architecture. Instead of speculating, we'll use what we know about the architecture today to help us decide what to design next.

There are two parts to every risk. The *condition* is a fact about the world that is currently true. The *consequence* is something bad that might happen in the future as a direct result of the condition. We record risk statements using the simple template from *A Construct for Describing Software Development Risks [Glu94]*, *<Condition>; might <Consequence>*.

Here's a risk statement in the condition-consequence format.

There are many ways we could reduce or remove this risk:

- Reduce the probability. Hire catering to bring in food a few days a week, and hold an info session on responsible meal portions.

- Reduce the impact. Keep a supply of antacids in the office.

- Push out the time frame of the risk. Schedule meetings at lunch so people can eat burritos only for dinner.

- Remove the condition. Move the office to a new location. Change the shift schedule so that everyone works at night when the new restaurant is closed.

- Accept it and do nothing. Sometimes people eat too many burritos (*mmmm… guacamole*). We'll deal with the repercussions if the risk converts into a problem.

Knowing the condition and the consequence creates hooks for deciding what to do about the risk. Compare our *<Condition>; might <Consequence>* risk with these other, less effective risk statements:

Bad Risk Statement	Why It's Bad
New burrito restaurant opened.	So what? The negative impact is unclear. In fact, this sounds great. We love burritos!
The team might overindulge in burritos.	This sounds bad, but why should we be worried about this now?
Eating too many burritos can make you sick.	True, but what does this have to do with my team?
If a teammate eats too many burritos, he or she will get sick.	And if a radioactive meteorite falls on the office, we'll get sick too. What led you to be worried about burritos?

OK, enough about burritos. Let's get back to software design.

Use Risk to Choose a Design Mindset

Software architecture design is an exercise in risk reduction. Every time you think, *I've got a bad feeling about this,* it's a sign there's a risk looming nearby. If you can pick a condition and consequence that captures the essence of your bad feeling, then we can use that information to guide our design activities.

Here are some example risks from a past project I worked on and the design activities the team used to reduce the risk:

The Model Training service was originally built for a different purpose; might overload it with new requests.

Design Mindsets: Understand, Evaluate

What we did: Talked to the team who built the Model Training service to understand scalability, ran experiments to measure throughput.

Data processing is time consuming and resource intensive; might not be able to finish processing jobs without failures.

Design Mindset: Explore

What we did: Brainstormed approaches for promoting reliability, researched job scheduling patterns, and sketched alternative designs that might reduce processing time.

A lot of data is needed to train a statistically significant model; might not be profitable due to data storage costs at scale.

Design Mindset: Make

What we did: Created a cost estimation model. The model demonstrated pros and cons of different design options to stakeholders. Pushed out the risk's time frame by changing backlog priorities.

Stored data may contain sensitive customer information; might require stricter data isolation than we can provide.

Design Mindset: Evaluate

What we did: Rated available compute platforms based on how well each met our needs.

Engineering risks help us decide what to design. Design mindsets help us devise a strategy to decrease the risk. When facing a risk that must be reduced, first decide which parts of the risk you can address—condition, impact, probability, or time frame. Next, choose a design mindset. Here are some questions to help decide which design mindset might be appropriate:

Try...	If...
Understand Mindset	The risk is about the problem. Do you need a deeper understanding of stakeholders or other system actors?
Explore Mindset	The risk about the solution. Have you seen enough solution alternatives?
Make Mindset	The risk is about communication. Do stakeholders fully understand design concepts at play and can they see the architecture?
Evaluate Mindset	The risk involves a design decision or the design's overall fit. Do we need to make a design decision?

Risks are the GPS for our design process. They tell us where we are, where we're going, and how much we have left to design. With each loop through the think-do-check cycle discussed on page 21, think about the risks and use them to decide what to do next.

Shift to Passive Design Once Risks Are Reduced

In *Just Enough Software Architecture: A Risk-Driven Approach [Fai10]*, George Fairbanks tells us that architects should work to reduce technical risks to the point where architecture is no longer the biggest source of risk in the system. Once we have reduced enough of the architectural risks, whatever that means for the software system, then our time is better spent elsewhere.

Once architecture is no longer the greatest source of risk in the system, shift from *active design* to *passive design*, as shown in the graph. With active design, we drive the design process in the pursuit of reducing risk. With passive design, we observe the architecture as it manifests in the working system and take corrective actions as necessary.

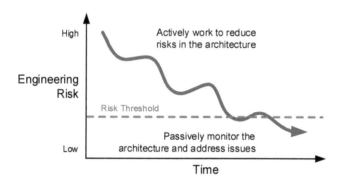

Don't be tricked by the name. There is still a lot for an architect to do in passive design mode. We might correct errant documentation or improve missing documents. We'll make minor adjustments to the architecture as new information emerges. We'll teach our teammates about the architecture by pairing and reviewing code. Most importantly, we're on the front line in the fight against architectural erosion and other issues, discussed on page 172.

Even with careful vigilance, architecture could reemerge as a significant risk. New risks might emerge. The implemented system could drift too far from our plans. We could learn that our assumptions about the world are wrong or that the world around us changed. When these things happen, switch back to active design and adjust the architecture based on the new realities.

Now that you know how to use risk to help you decide what to design, let's pull together everything you've learned in this chapter by ceating an architecture design plan.

Create a Design Plan

Design plans outline a general strategy for how the team will spend their time on architecture. Will we do more analysis up front? Are we expecting change later? When do we start writing code? A good design plan sets expectations and explains these details.

A design plan doesn't have to be a formal schedule, but you do need to put some thought into it. Here are a few things every design plan should include: Capture your plan in a lightweight document such as an inception deck described on page 269.

Stopping conditions for design Will you time-box up-front design work, or will you reduce risks no matter how long it takes? Will you do minimal up-front design before starting to write code, or do you want more of the architecture laid out? Can implementation start piecemeal, or do some areas need to start together? There is no single right answer. Stopping conditions depend heavily on the team, stakeholders, and project context.

Required design artifacts Tell everyone how you plan to document the architecture before starting. Are you OK with pictures of whiteboards, or do you need a more traditional document? Does your team use specific templates? Where should design artifacts be stored?

Time line Describe the key design milestones within the project schedule. Many large projects have a dedicated elaboration phase for gathering requirements and exploring architecture. Smaller projects or continuously maintained software systems might regularly schedule design spikes.

At a minimum, the time line should include milestones for reviewing architecturally significant requirements, reviewing draft designs, and conducting evaluations. Also, include any major workshops with stakeholders. Call out when you think implementation will start and what is in scope for early implementation.

Top risks Since we are using a risk-driven design approach, include the top risks in the design plan as context. Revisit your risk list throughout the software system's life, especially during any up-front architecture design.

Notional architecture design Start with a potential solution. Recall that we need to think about the solution to help us define the problem. A notional architecture can be a lightweight sketch, just enough to communicate the essence of your initial design thoughts.

The amount of time spent on design could be hours, days, or even months depending on the software system. No matter your time horizon, if we use the four principles of design thinking covered on page 15 and focus on finding a satisficing solution discussed on page 27, then we should arrive at a working solution by the time we need it.

Project Lionheart: The Story So Far...

Next week you'll go on site to gather requirements from the mayor and other stakeholders. We have a fixed final due date in about six months. We need to focus on value up front and deliver as fast as possible. It also sounds like the core functional requirements will be based on an existing process, so there is a low probability of requirements churn.

The solution seems like a classic data-driven web application with some search features. Based on the mayor's description, security and privacy could be a key concern. We also know that the city's IT department will take over the software system after us. That group may impose some unique constraints.

You send Mayor van Damme an agenda for the on-site visit. Our biggest risks right now can be addressed by digging for information, so for now you'll focus on getting to know our stakeholders. We think we can get away with very little up-front design and want to concentrate on delivering value faster, even if that means rewriting parts of the application later. The team wants to start writing code immediately after a two-week design spike.

Next Up

One way or another, you'll pay for your architecture either through up-front design or downstream rework. In this chapter, you learned how to use risk to plan our design activities. Risks can help us decide how much work to do up-front. We can also use risk to decide which design mindsets to adopt.

One of the first risks many teams face on a new software system, even if it's only new to you, is understanding who the software is meant to help. In the next chapter, you'll learn how to embrace the understand mindset by developing empathy for the humans who benefit from the software you develop. When you can walk in your stakeholders' shoes, you'll get a deeper understanding of their actual needs. Understand stakeholders' real needs, and you improve your chance of solving the right problem.

CHAPTER 4

Empathize with Stakeholders

Knowing what problem to solve is sometimes easier said than done. Since we create software to help people, we must understand the people whose lives will be affected by the software we make to understand the problem thoroughly. The better we empathize with their needs, the better we'll see and understand the real problems that need to be solved.

We call people with an interest or concern in our software *stakeholders*. It's the architect's job to identify stakeholders and understand their needs. Our stakeholders' expectations for the system will directly or indirectly influence how we design it.

Empathy is the engine that drives design. When you empathize with the people affected by your software, then you'll make better software. In this chapter, you'll learn how to decide who to talk to about the problem you're solving and what you need to learn from them to start designing the architecture.

Talk to the Right People

Stakeholders usually, but not always, have a business interest in the software. They might pay for the software or directly profit from it. Users are important stakeholders but so too are the people who build and maintain the system. Other people might not even realize how our software might affect them, but it's sometimes necessary to consider their concerns as well.

In the wild, stakeholders rarely travel alone. We use the term *stakeholder group* to highlight this fact. Working with groups is different than working with individuals. Two people from the same stakeholder group can provide inconsistent or conflicting information. We must work to understand the whole group's concerns and sometimes even help them reach consensus.

Here are some stakeholders for the Project Lionheart Case Study, introduced on page 14. In this picture, the icons represent specific people or roles while speech bubbles show stakeholders' thoughts and feelings.

Some Project Lionheart Stakeholders

We want to make awesome software!

Dev Team

I love security. I hate downtime.

System Administrator

We need to cut the city's operating costs.

Mayor ($$$)

We manage the city's contracts and find the best prices.

Office of Management and Budget (User)

We make a living selling goods and services to the city.

Local Businesses (User)

Stakeholders are interested in what we're building and will influence the architecture we design. Since we'll want to invite these people to future design workshops, we should find out who they are. Enter the stakeholder map.

Bett says:
It's About the Customer

By Bett Bollhoefer, software architect at General Electric

Architecture is about the customer. If I create an architecture that doesn't give value to the customer, I am wasting my time. When I talk to customers, I often hear horror stories about how their current systems were developed by someone in an ivory tower who didn't understand them or their work. How do I make sure I am bringing value to customers through my architecture?

My answer is to use a customer-centric design process. I start with who the customer is and what they want to do. I divide the system into tasks the customer performs. For each task, I find out how they start it and where they run into issues.

You might be thinking, "This doesn't sound like architecture—it sounds like user experience!" Yes, it is, but many UX designers don't understand the technical aspects of the system well enough to determine the architecture. My process goes beyond the surface to ensure the deep structures support the customer's values. I call it *Customer Experience Architecture.*

Step 1: Determine what matters to the customer, including their functional require-ments and quality attributes, by watching how they do the task in their natural environment and asking lots of *why's*.

Step 2: Design the system around the customer's needs and document it in a proto-type. The prototype should be as interactive as possible, not just a flowchart.

Step 3: Review the prototype as early as possible with the customer. Make sure they really understand what is changing in the new system and how it will impact them.

Step 4: Revise the architecture based on feedback from the customer's review.

Using these four steps, you can create value for your customer through your archi-tecture and become their hero, or at least not the person in the ivory tower who is ruining their life.

Create a Stakeholder Map

A *stakeholder map* is a network diagram showing all the people involved with or affected by the proposed software system. Stakeholder maps are ideal for visualizing relationships and interactions among people. They also give you a snapshot of what motivates different stakeholders. Use stakeholder maps to decide who the most important people are to talk to about their concerns.

Every time I create a stakeholder map, I'm surprised to see how many people I might touch with the software I build. There's a partial stakeholder map for Project Lionheart on page 42.

There are several stakeholders not shown on this diagram for the sake of sim-plicity. Additional stakeholders include IT vendors we might have to collaborate with, the Chamber of Commerce (or other lobbying organizations), the deputy mayor, and various community groups who receive services from the city. The *city departments* stakeholder can be made more precise by dividing it into the board of education, parks and recreation, public works, sanitation, and so on. If these groups have a similar stake in the system, then they could be lumped together as shown. As a rule of thumb, it's best to be as specific as possible.

Step back and look at the stakeholder map after you've created it. Who is paying for the software? Who is using it? Are there network hubs with many incoming or outgoing arrows? Are there stakeholders with potential conflicts of interest? These people are all excellent candidates for interviews and further research.

Project Lionheart Stakeholder Map

Icons represent roles

Arrows show relationships

When I look at the Project Lionheart stakeholder map, I see a few interesting areas that we should investigate further.

1. Mayor van Damme hired us and we report to him, but the Office of Management and Budget receives policy direction from both the mayor and city council.

2. Our software will affect many city departments, but we won't be able to talk to all of them. We should identify a few representative stakeholders and carefully validate our findings with the larger group.

3. Some local businesses rely on lawyers to navigate the Request for Proposal process. Different interaction patterns for the potential software might exist, which could influence the architecture.

4. The Office of Management and Budget (OMB) sits at the center of several key user interactions, but they aren't paying the bills. We should talk to the OMB directly. It's possible that the mayor and city council have budgeted for a system that does not solve the OMB's real problems.

You can build a stakeholder map by yourself, but it's more fun to create them in groups. The steps for this activity are outlined in Activity 10, *Stakeholder Map*, on page 221.

👥 Get Your Hands Dirty: Create a Stakeholder Map

Pick an open source project you use or contribute to and create a stakeholder map for it. Take a picture of it and share it on this book's forum.[1] Here are some things to think about:

- Is there an organization that oversees or funds the project? Are there subgroups within the organization who might have different vested interests?

- Who are the biggest contributors to the project?

- How is the project licensed? Who benefits from the choice of license?

- Who uses the project? What problems are they trying to solve?

Discover the Business Goals

Every software system is built to serve some fundamental purpose. *Business goals* describe what stakeholders hope to accomplish with the software. Business goals also seed conversations about quality attributes, trade-offs, and technical debt.

Business goals are a primary architectural driver and help prioritize competing concerns. The better everyone understands stakeholders' needs, the better you'll be able to help them. Here's a summary of common business goal categories:

Who wants it	What they want
Individuals	Increase wealth, power, reputation, personal enjoyment, or knowledge
Organizations	Increase revenue, maximize profits, grow the business, become a market leader, improve stability, enter a new market, beat a competitor
Employees	Interesting and meaningful work, increase knowledge, help users, become recognized as an expert
Development Team	Improve specific quality attributes, reduce costs, add new features, implement a standard, improve time-to-market
Nations, governments	Security, civic welfare, social responsibility, legal compliance

---

1. http://pragprog.com/book/mkdsa/design-it

Capture business goals as simple need-based statements that explain what stakeholders will get from the software system.

Record Business Goal Statements

Great business goal statements are measurable and have clear success criteria. Human-centered business goals allow your team to understand the people you are ultimately serving through the software you build.

Good business goal statements include three things:

Subject A specific person or role. If the stakeholder or group has a name, use it. *United Hamster Trainers Union* is better than *union groups*.

Outcome Express the stakeholder's need as a measurable outcome. How does the world change if the system is successful? You will design an architecture to achieve this outcome. For example, maybe the United Hamster Trainers Union needs a way to help members stay in touch with one another.

Context Context shares an insight about a stakeholder's need and helps build empathy. Ideally context is insightful and not completely obvious. For example, knowing that the United Hamster Trainers Union's most important annual meeting has over 5 million members attending virtually creates deeper understanding about the previously discussed outcome.

There are some business goals for Project Lionheart in the table on page 45. Putting business goal statements in a slick-looking table sometimes makes them easier to read.

Most systems only have only three to five business goals. More than this and the goals become confusing and difficult to remember. When working with many stakeholders, it's useful to record goals' relative importance. A simple *must have* or *nice to have* designation is good enough for this purpose.

Help Stakeholders Share Their Business Goals

Stakeholders usually know what they want, but many stakeholders find it difficult to articulate their needs as measurable statements. Every architect should have a few simple templates in their toolbox to help stakeholders find their voice. The point of view (POV) mad lib on page 45 is a fun alternative that is similar to a user story but describes the value expected from the whole system instead of functionality. Other business goal formats are described in Activity 8, *Point-of-View Mad Lib*, on page 215.

Stakeholder	Goal	Context
Mayor van Damme	Reduce procurement costs by 30%	Avoid making budget cuts to education or other essential services in an election year.
Mayor van Damme	Improve city engagement with local businesses, measured by the number of applications from first-time local businesses, percentage of overall RFPs won by local businesses.	Improve the local economy by ensuring local businesses win city contracts.
Office of Management and Business	Cut the time required to publish a new RFP in half.	Improves services across the city and reduces costs at the same time. Citizens suffer when city services go unfunded. Think: *No toilet paper at the girls' basketball game* or *not enough hypodermic needles for emergency medical crews.*
Office of Management and Business	Review historical procurement data for the past 10 years.	Businesses behave similarly over time and historic data gives the city a leg up when reviewing contract bids.

Mayor van Damme **needs to** reduce procurement costs by 30%
(stakeholder)   *(stakeholder's need)*

because he wants to avoid cutting essential department funding.
(context)

Collaborate closely with your product manager or other business-focused stakeholders to identify the system's business goals. They can usually describe a system's business goals without breaking a sweat. Be prepared to help stakeholders or product managers if they struggle to articulate business goals, but remember they own the business goals.

🏃 Get Your Hands Dirty: Create Business Goals for This System

What are the business goals for this proposed system? Create a few point of view mad libs for this scenario.

> *Bouncing Bean Grocery* is a regional grocery store chain. A few months ago an *Organic Plus!* store opened and *Bouncing Bean* has seen a decline in sales. Hoping to entice customers to their stores, *Bouncing Bean* has hired your team to develop a mobile application in which potential shoppers can create shopping lists, search recipes, and clip e-coupons. *Bouncing Bean* hopes the app will attract customers and provide customer data to drive targeted advertising.

Here are some things to think about.

- Who are the stakeholders? What do they hope to gain?

- Who are the users? What are they trying to accomplish? (Hint: It has nothing to do with software.)

- What's the worst that can happen? Sometimes thinking about failure can help uncover a business goal. People usually want to avoid failures.

Project Lionheart: The Story So Far...

Mayor van Damme gave our product manager a good starting point with his key strategic directives. The first thing she did was verify the mayor's business goals with other stakeholders. After looking at our stakeholder map (described on page 42), our product manager scheduled meetings with the head of the Office of Management and Budget and two members of city council.

Our product manager led the stakeholder interviews. You observed the interviews to develop a bit more empathy for our stakeholders' needs. Our product manager summarized the business goals using the standard goals template shown on page 45. The whole team reviewed the business goals with Mayor van Damme and the Office of Management and Budget to verify that we understood the business goals correctly. Our product manager added our business goals to the project wiki so that everyone could read them.

While talking to stakeholders about business goals, you heard many requests for features and a few pain points around quality attributes. Since we have a good handle on the business goals, it will be easier for us to focus our design efforts as we dig for additional architecturally significant requirements.

Next Up

Empathy is the engine that drives design. When we know who our stakeholders are and how they hope the software will help them, we will make better design decisions on their behalf. Business goals are a straightforward way to help the team internalize stakeholders' hopes and dreams for the software.

Knowing who the stakeholders are and understanding the business goals is important but doesn't tell us what the software should do or how it is expected to behave. We capture this information as requirements. Architects need different information than what traditional requirements specifications typically offer. In the next chapter, you'll learn how to look at requirements from the perspective of software architecture.

CHAPTER 5

Dig for Architecturally Significant Requirements

Every design discussion starts with *who*, *what*, and *why*. In Chapter 4, *Empathize with Stakeholders*, on page 39 you learned how to identify *who* is affected by the software system and *why* they care. In this chapter, you'll learn how to define the *what*, the requirements, from the perspective of software architecture.

An *architecturally significant requirement*, or ASR, is any requirement that strongly influences our choice of structures for the architecture. It is the software architect's responsibility to identify requirements with architectural significance. You'll do this by thinking about four categories of requirements:

Constraints Unchangeable design decisions, usually given, sometimes chosen.

Quality Attributes Externally visible properties that characterize how the system operates in a specific context.

Influential Functional Requirements Features and functions that require special attention in the architecture.

Other Influencers Time, knowledge, experience, skills, office politics, your own geeky biases, and all the other stuff that sways your decision making.

Let's take a closer look at these categories of ASRs and learn how to work with stakeholders to define them.

Limit Design Options with Constraints

A *constraint* is an unchangeable design decision you are given or choose to give yourself. Most software systems have only a handful of constraints. All constraints limit choice, but well-chosen constraints simplify the problem and can make it easier to design a satisficing architecture. Sometimes constraints create a living hell for architects by limiting options so severely we are unable to satisfy other requirements.

Constraints can influence technical or business concerns. Business constraints limit decisions about people, process, costs, and schedule. Technical constraints limit decisions about the technology we may use in the software system. Here are some examples of each:

Technical Constraints	Business Constraints
Programming Language Choice	Team Composition and Makeup
Anything that runs on the JVM.	*Team X will build the XYZ component.*
Operating System or Platform	Schedule or Budget
It must run on Windows, Linux, and BeOS.	*It must be ready in time for the Big Trade Show and cost less than $800,000.*
Use of Components or Technology	Legal Restrictions
We own DB2 so that's your database.	*There is a 5 GB daily limit in our license.*

Capture Constraints as Simple Statements

To capture a constraint, describe the decision and its origin in a brief statement. There are some constraints for the Project Lionheart system in the table on page 51, introduced on page 14.

Constraints, once decided, are 100 percent non-negotiable. Be conservative in accepting constraints. There is a huge difference between *this must be done or you will fail* and *this should be done unless you have a good reason not to do it.*

As the software system emerges, design decisions can become constraint-like. Distinguishing between the constraints we created and the ones we were given becomes more difficult as the system grows. Like barnacles on a ship, software slowly gains cruft and becomes less nimble, less clean, less malleable. Eventually, it may become so difficult to amend the architecture that those early design choices become constraints for future designers.

As constraints emerge, be careful to distinguish the constraints chosen for you from the constraints you give yourself. Though it may be difficult, you always have the option of changing a constraining design decision.

Constraint	Origin	Type	Context
Must be developed as open source software.	Mayor van Damme	Business	The City has an Open Data policy and citizens must have access to source code.
Must build a browser-based web application.	Mayor van Damme	Technical	Decreases concerns about software delivery and maintenance.
Must ship by the end of Q3.	Mayor van Damme	Business	Avoids end of fiscal year budget issues.
Must support latest Firefox web browser.	City IT	Technical	Officially supported browser.
Must be served from a Linux server.	City IT	Technical	City uses Linux and open source where possible.

Define the Quality Attributes

Quality attributes describe externally visible properties of a software system and the expectations for that system's operation. Quality attributes define how well a system should perform some action. These *-ilities* of the system are sometimes called *quality requirements*. Here is a list of some common quality attributes from *Software Architecture in Practice [BCK12]*.

Design Time Properties	Runtime Properties	Conceptual Properties
Modifiability	Availability	Manageability
Maintainability	Reliability	Supportability
Reusability	Performance	Simplicity
Testability	Scalability	Teachability
Buildability or Time-to-Market	Security	

Every architecture decision promotes or inhibits at least one quality attribute. Many design decisions promote one set of quality attributes while inhibiting others that are also important! When this happens, we'll trade one quality attribute for another by choosing a structure for the architecture that favors one quality attribute but harms others.

When digging for ASRs, we'll spend most of our time working with quality attributes. Quality attributes are used throughout the design process to guide technology selection, choose structures, pick patterns, and evaluate the fitness of our design decisions.

> ### Joe asks:
> ## Are Quality Attributes Non-functional Requirements?
>
> Traditional software engineering textbooks usually discuss two classes of requirements. *Functional requirements* describe the behavior of the software system. *Non-functional requirements* describe all system requirements that aren't functional requirements, including what we're calling quality attributes and constraints.
>
> When you are designing a software architecture, it's useful to distinguish between functionality, constraints, and quality attributes because each type of requirement implies a different set of forces are influencing the design. For example, constraints are non-negotiable whereas quality attributes can be nuanced and involve significant trade-offs.
>
> Yes, quality attributes are non-functional requirements, but it is strange to use this term to describe them since quality attribute scenarios (sometimes called quality requirements) have a functional piece to them. Quality attributes make sense only in the context of system operation. In a quality attribute scenario, an artifact's response is the direct result of some function.

Capture Quality Attributes as Scenarios

A quality attribute is just a word. Scalability, availability, and performance are meaningless by themselves. We need to give these words meaning so we understand what to design. We use a *quality attribute scenario* to provide an unambiguous description of a quality attribute.

Quality attribute scenarios describe how the software system is expected to operate within a certain environmental context. There is a functional component to each scenario—stimulus and response—just like any feature. Quality attributes scenarios differ from functional requirements since they qualify the response using a response measure. It is not enough just to correctly respond. How the system responds is also important. The diagram on page 53 visually depicts the six parts of a quality attribute scenario.

Stimulus The stimulus is an event that requires the system to respond in some way. The stimulus kicks off the scenario and will vary depending on the type quality attribute. For example, the stimulus for an availability might be a node becoming unreachable whereas the stimulus for a modifiability scenario might be a request for a change.

Source The source is the person or system that initiations the stimulus. Examples include users, system components, and external systems.

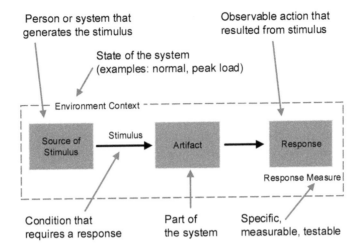

Artifact The artifact is the part of the system whose behavior is characterized in the scenario. The artifact can be the whole system or a specific component.

Response The response is an externally visible action that takes place in the artifact as a result of the stimulus. Stimulus leads to response.

Response Measure The response measure defines the success criteria for the scenario by defining what a successful response looks like. Response measures should be specific and measurable.

Environment Context The environment context describes the operational circumstances surrounding the system during the scenario. The environment context should always be defined even if the context is *normal*. Abnormal contexts, such as peak load or a specific failure condition, are also interesting to consider.

Here is an example portability scenario for an interplanetary robotic explorer based on examples from *the NASA Jet Propulsion Laboratory [WFD16]*.

Portability Scenario for a Mars Rover (via NASA JPL)

Raw scenario: Processors and platforms are typical variation points project to project. Enabling projects to select processors and platforms with minimal effects to applications allows for system optimization.

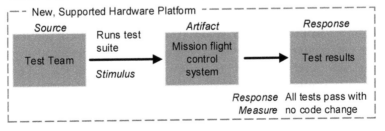

Notice that the *raw scenario* in our example doesn't mention specific response measures. Raw scenarios are simple descriptions that form the basis for more precise quality attribute scenarios. We call them raw because they need further cooking to become a good scenario. Think of a raw scenario as the start of a conversation.

Specifying all six parts of a formal quality attribute scenario is not always necessary. You can often get by with a simple statement that includes the stimulus, source, response, and response measure. Add the environment whenever the scenario does not describe a *normal* environmental context.

Here are some quality attribute scenarios for the Project Lionheart case study:

Quality Attribute	Scenario	Priority
Availability	When the RFP database does not respond, Lionheart should log the fault and respond with stale data within 3 seconds.	High
Availability	A user's searches for open RFPs and receives a list of RFPs 99% of the time on average over the course of the year.	High
Scalability	New servers can be added during a planned maintenance window (less than 7 hours).	Low
Performance	A user sees search results within 5 seconds when the system is at an average load of 2 searches per second.	High
Reliability	Updates to RFPs should be reflected in the application within 24 hours of the change.	Low
Availability	A user-initiated update (for example, starring an RFP) is reflected in the system within 5 seconds.	Low
Availability	The system can handle a peak load of 100 searches per second with no more than a 10% dip in average response times.	Low
Scalability	Data growth is expected to expand at a rate of 5% annually. The system should be able to grow to handle this with *minimal* effort.	Low

A good-quality attribute scenario communicates the intent of the requirement so anyone can understand it. Great scenarios are precise and measurable. Two people who read the same quality attribute scenario should come away with the same understanding of the system's *scalability* or *performance* or *maintainability*.

Strive for Specific and Measurable Response Measures

To create a response measure, start by estimating potential values based on your own experience. Use a straw man to kick off a conversation with stakeholders (see Activity 9, *Response Measure Straw Man*, on page 219). What if it took nine months to migrate the system to a new microcontroller platform, would that work? How about six months? Eventually, you'll find a response measure that resonates with stakeholders.

Good response measures are testable. Early in the system's life, the architecture might exist only on paper, but it's just a matter of time before you have a running system. If you can't write a test using your scenario, then the scenario does not have a specific, measurable response measure.

Choose Appropriate Response Measures

I was once on a team responsible for building a simulation testbed for a military combat system. The purpose of the testbed was to connect a dozen military bases across the world so we could play simulated war games. To run a test, we would play a scenario that generated fake aircraft. The hardware and software at each site would detect the simulated aircraft, and the combat systems would process the sensor data as if it were from the real world.

The simulation testbed had extremely aggressive latency requirements. If all sites did not receive the same simulation data within a narrow window of time, it would seem as if aircraft were appearing and disappearing from the sky. Even worse, aircraft might be visible only to some sites in the network. Too much latency would invalidate the system tests.

After crunching some numbers, we determined our testbed would need to transfer data faster than the speed of light for everything to work. The performance and availability response measures were nowhere near reality. Once quantum entangled networks become viable, it will be interesting to revisit this problem.

⚒ Get Your Hands Dirty: Refine These Notes into Quality Attribute Scenarios

During a meeting, Project Lionheart stakeholders shared the following statements. For each statement, identify the quality attribute and create a formal, six-part quality attribute scenario.

- There's a small number of users, but when a user submits a question or problem we need to be able to respond quickly, within a business day.

- Releases happen at least once a month. Ideally, we'll ship code as it is ready.

- We need to verify that the RFP index is built correctly. The verification should be automated.

- We need a new, permanent dev team to come up to speed quickly after the current team of contractors we've hired leaves.

Here are some things to think about:

- What quality attribute is suggested by each statement? It's OK to make up an *ility* if it helps describe the concern effectively.

- Are there implied responses or response measures?

- What missing information can you fill in based on your own experiences?

Look for Classes of Functional Requirements

Functional requirements, often captured as use cases or user stories, define the software system's behavior but are only sometimes interesting when designing the architecture. All functional requirements are essential to the success of the software system, but not all system features have architectural significance. When a functional requirement drives architectural decision making, we call it an *influential functional requirement*.

Influential functional requirements can be referred to as *architecture killers*. If your architecture doesn't allow you to implement one of these high-value, high-priority features, you'll be forced to raze your architecture and start over.

Identifying influential functional requirements is equal parts art and science. It becomes easier with experience. Here's how I do it:

1. Start with a notional architecture sketch that summarizes your current thinking about the architecture.

2. Identify general classes of requirements that represent the same type of architectural problem.

3. For each problem class identified, walk through the notional architecture and show how to achieve each requirement group. If it is not immediately obvious how you would implement the feature based on the known coarse-grained requirements, it might have architectural significance.

The goal of step two is to reduce a giant list of functional requirements down to a small number of representative categories. Here are a few strategies:

- Look for functional requirements that might be implemented within the same architectural elements. For example, features that require persistence go in one group whereas features that require user interaction go in another.

- Look for functional requirements that seem difficult to implement. These could be significant to the architecture.

- Look for high-value, high-priority functional requirements.

Here's an example. Recall the simple calculator example on page 10. Adding two numbers together is an important functional requirement but has little influence on the architecture, so let's spice it up a bit. Here's a new feature: *as an Adder User I can review my addition history even if I've lost my phone.* "People love looking at past stuff they've done," the marketing team assures us. "It's going to be A-Mazing!"

Historical information? OK, no problem. We can save the user's actions to a local database. Wait... even if they've lost their phone?!?! Now we need a remote database server, which opens up a ton of new questions. What happens when the user's phone is offline? What about availability? Scalability? Hosting costs? Syncing the app when the schema changes? The list goes on.

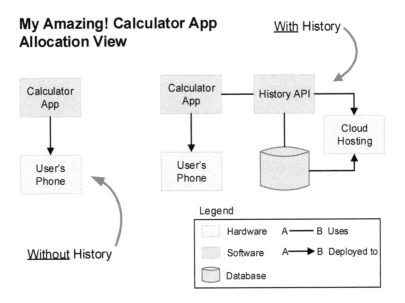

That one seemingly innocent feature request introduces a swirl of complexity. In our simple calculator example, we can reduce any mathematical operation to the same general problem. To solve the newly requested history feature, we need remote storage. This one feature takes the architecture in a new direction that other functional requirements did not.

Reference any influential functional requirements in your architecture documentation but avoid duplicating the requirements engineering effort. Our goal is to call attention to critical features that influence our decision making.

Find Out What Else Influences the Architecture

In addition to ASRs, there is a slew of other factors that will affect the architecture both directly and indirectly. Here is a list of some of the factors that might influence the architecture:

What Influences the architecture?

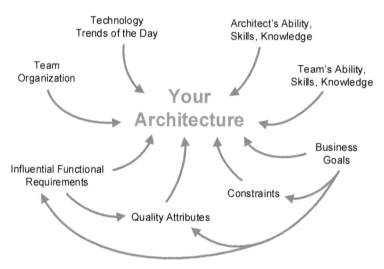

Your skills and experience as an architect determine how you approach design and the architecture options available to you. Your knowledge and your team's knowledge of technology defines your design vocabulary. If all you know is Ruby on Rails, then the chances are good you'll find some way to wedge it into the architecture. When all you have is a hammer, you will find plenty of nails to hit.

Architecture always seems to follow hot technology trends. As new hardware, software, and design paradigms emerge, some will permanently alter the software engineering landscape. Others might just be marketing veneer on old ideas. There's a good chance your architecture is already proudly sporting the design equivalent of a mullet hairstyle.

Learn to Live with Conway's Law

How your team is organized and prefers to collaborate influences the architecture design. Conway's Law, coined by Melvin Conway in 1967 and popularized by

Fred Brooks in the *Mythical Man Month [Bro95]*, describes the relationship between team organization and architecture.

> …organizations which design systems…are constrained to produce designs which are copies of the communication structures of these organizations.

If you have three teams, you'll end up with three components. Communication boundaries among people manifest as element boundaries in the architecture. Conway's Law works both ways. Communication paths designed into the architecture will also influence how you organize your teams. If you want to design the best software possible, then you must be prepared to reorganize your team.

Other influencers are usually only recorded as part of the rationale for design decisions. So many things can influence the architecture that it is practically impossible to document all the potential influencers prior to making design decisions.

Dig for the Information You Need

Architecturally significant requirements are hidden all around us. You'll find ASRs in user stories, implied by a manager's request, and hinted by stakeholders who know what they want but don't quite know how to explain it.

The product backlog contains a treasure trove of ASRs. Quality attributes are implied or assumed in nearly every functional requirement. Sometimes a user story will plainly describe response times, scalability needs, or how to handle failures. Highlight these details as quality attribute scenarios lest they get lost in the feature backlog.

Talk to stakeholders. Find out what worries them. Ask stakeholders what excites them. Share the risks and open questions you see. Here are some additional methods you can use to dig out interesting ASRs:

- Use Activity 3, *Goal-Question-Metric (GQM) Workshop*, on page 199 to connect business goals and quality attribute response measures with concrete data requirements.

- Use Activity 4, *Interview Stakeholders*, on page 202 to uncover quality attribute scenarios and constraints. Interviews work especially well with technical stakeholders.

- Use Activity 5, *List Assumptions*, on page 205 to flush hidden requirements into the open.

- Use Activity 7, *Mini-Quality Attribute Workshop*, on page 210 to quickly and effectively define high-priority quality attribute scenarios. This workshop works for nearly any kind of project and with stakeholders of different skills and backgrounds.

- Use Activity 24, *Inception Deck*, on page 269 as a checklist for kicking off a new project. Architecture is the main topic for several slides in the inception deck.

Build an ASR Workbook

Once you've identified requirements with architectural significance, record them in an *ASR Workbook*. At the beginning of a new software system, the ASR Workbook is a living document and changes rapidly. As the architecture coalesces, you'll edit the workbook less frequently but reference it more often. Executable tests and source could eventually supplant portions of the ASR Workbook as a source of truth, though the document will remain an important historical record.

The ASR Workbook provides context and information for programmers, testers, and of course, architects. The more people who understand the ASRs, the less architectural oversight will be required.

Here is a sample ASR Workbook outline. Use the outline as a checklist for planning requirements elicitation.

Sample ASR Workbook Outline
Purpose and Scope
Intended Audience
Business Context
Stakeholders
Business Goals
Architecturally Significant Requirements
Technical Constraints
Business Constraints
Quality Attribute Requirements
Top Scenarios
Influential Functional Requirements
Top Users or User Personas
Use Cases or User Stories
Appendix A: Glossary
Appendix B: Quality Attributes Taxonomy

Thijmen says:

Learn to Be an Active Listener

by Thijmen de Gooijer, IT Architect

Understanding your stakeholders and their goals is the first step to successfully delivering value with software. Taking someone else's perspective and showing empathy will help you understand their expectations of your software. Technical training and experience then turn requirements into implementable ideas. However, you will need excellent communication skills to get developers and management to share your vision and turn ideas into code.

One of the most useful communication skills I had to learn is active listening. Hearing what someone says is only the first step. You also have to understand it. Here is a surprisingly challenging exercise that I learned during a course on communication. You can try this exercise with a partner.

Person A tells a story to person B, for example about an achievement or describing a problem they solved. The trick is that person B is not allowed to say a word until person A indicates they are finished. Only then is person B allowed to ask questions to increase understanding of what person A said. The questions cannot be covert feedback or critique. Person B's goal is to reach an understanding. Now reverse roles to experience the other side of the relationship.

Imagine how hard this exercise can be! You probably know a colleague who talks a little bit too much or a shy and quiet intern. How would you ensure that you understand their requirements?

Writing down directly what a stakeholder tells you probably won't lead to an implementable requirement. Human language is messy, complicated, and full of culturally loaded messages—nothing like COBOL, Java, PHP, or Python. Culture does not only differ between countries or religions. Cities, companies, schools, and sports clubs have cultures, which influence how people communicate.

As an active listener, you need empathy to put words into their cultural context and understand them. Remain quiet, don't judge, and ask questions to help you understand.

Communication skills are hard to learn from books, yet I recommend two to assist you on your way to becoming an amazing software architect. *How to Win Friends and Influence People [Car09]* by Dale Carnegie is a classic book that gives actionable guidance on how to build better relationships with people. In *Culture Clash 2: Managing the Global High Performance Team [Zwe13]* Thomas D. Zweifel provides an easy-to-understand framework for identifying and overcoming cultural differences.

Use the ASR Workbook to introduce architectural concepts to your team and stakeholders. Briefly teach readers what business goals, constraints, quality attributes, and influential functional requirements are, and they'll have a finer appreciation for the information in the document.

Project Lionheart: The Story So Far…

During a user experience workshop facilitated by our product manager, you discover dozens of new features. You add these features to the product backlog and make a note in the few functional requirements that seem to have architectural significance. You also jot down several potential constraints to verify with stakeholders.

A few days after the requirements workshop, you facilitate a mini-quality attribute workshop with several stakeholders. During the workshop, you elicit and prioritize nearly two dozen quality attribute scenarios. You don't formally record all the concerns raised during the workshop, but you collaborate with participants to refine the top seven highest-priority scenarios.

Up to this point, our primary focus was to understand the problem. We made several artifacts so we could share what we know about the problem with our stakeholders. You uncover a lot in a few short days on site. Looking at the team's list of open questions, you think we have enough information to embrace the explore mindset and start choosing structures for the architecture.

Next Up

Many different architectures could implement the same set of features. Features alone are not enough information for us to design a software system. It's the architecturally significant requirements, especially quality attributes, that drive architectural decision making.

Solutions flow from our understanding of the problem. We do not need to wait until we understand everything about the problem before thinking about potential solutions. We'd never build anything if we waited to define the whole problem! As you explore solutions, you'll uncover new insights about the problem. Discovering there is more to the problem than you knew is natural and expected. In the next chapter, you'll learn how to use what we currently know about the problem to explore design options and make decisions.

CHAPTER 6

Choose an Architecture (Before It Chooses You)

Every software system has an architecture. That doesn't mean you'll end up with one you want. When you leave design decisions to fate, there is no telling what fate will deliver. Actively making decisions about how to organize the software system significantly increases our chances of getting an architecture that meets our needs.

Designing software architecture is all about making decisions under uncertainty. Design decisions are loaded with *trade-offs*, decisions that force us to compromise—give up something good to avoid something bad, or accept something bad to get something better. If we make acceptable trade-offs, then we'll achieve our architecturally significant requirements and help our stakeholders reach their business goals. Yay!

In this chapter, you'll learn how to choose structures for the architecture by using architecturally significant requirements to drive your decision making.

Diverge to See Options, Converge to Decide

Making a decision implies we've seen multiple options from which to choose. If there is only one option, then we didn't decide anything; the decision was made for us. To ensure we see many options, we need to explore the design space.

Design exploration is an iterative journey of divergence and convergence. Once we've identified a problem, we *diverge* our thinking and generate design alternatives that can solve that problem. Once we have a few options on the table, we'll *converge* our thinking by building consensus and eliminating options that are a poor fit for the current problem.

Human brains crave options. Our confidence in a decision increases after seeing multiple alternatives. Unfortunately, there isn't time to explore every possible option and all aspects of a software system's design. Architects need to focus on and champion quality attributes, structural organization, and design decisions that will influence these things.

Explore the Architecturally Significant Things

Grady Booch has said, "All architecture is design, but not all design is architecture."[1] As you learned in *What Is Software Architecture?*, on page 7, a system's software architecture is the set of significant design decisions about how the software is organized to promote desired quality attributes and other properties. Architects must explore these significant design decisions and actively choose how to organize the software to achieve desired quality attributes.

Here are areas of a software system's design architects will typically explore:

Explore elements and their responsibilities to determine the general composition of structures in the architecture.   Recall from *Define the Essential Structures*, on page 7 that structures in the architecture are made up of elements. In a well-designed architecture, every element has clear responsibilities. Any element without a well-defined responsibility should be eliminated. Exploring design options requires that we explore combinations of elements with varying responsibilities.

Explore relations and their interfaces to determine how elements interact with one another.   Relations describe how two elements in the architecture work together to accomplish a task. A component's interface is one example of a relation. Both the communication mechanism (for example, HTTP, TCP, or shared memory) and the rules for communication (such as APIs, response objects, or required data) define the interface. The rules

---

1.   Grady Booch. *Abstracting the Unknown.* SATURN 2016. http://resources.sei.cmu.edu/library/asset-view.cfm?assetID=454315

governing interfaces and element communication are inherently architectural, at least up to a point. We can defer some details—such as method names and sometimes the fields returned in a response—to downstream designers.

Explore the domain to understand the world the architecture models. Every problem has its own terminology and concepts, which describe the world in which it exists. The concepts from the domain, be they objects or events, must be accounted for somewhere in the architecture. The better we understand the problem domain, the better we'll partition elements and assign responsibilities to them in the architecture.

Explore technology and frameworks to bootstrap promoting quality attributes. Modern software development technologies are loaded with architecture assumptions. Frameworks, middlewares, libraries—any off-the-shelf technology—comes with attitude. The technology will tell you how and when to use it. Opinionated technologies force decisions on to the architecture.

When the technology aligns with our needs, then life is rainbows and unicorns. When our needs fall outside the bounds of what the tech thinks we need, then prepare for a battle royal between you and the framework.

Explore construction and deployment methods to ensure the architecture can be shipped. How we design the architecture influences how the software is constructed and deployed. If we desire continuous delivery, if we want to have multiple developers working in parallel, if we require the use of specific testing strategies, then we must design the architecture to support these requirements.

Explore past designs to gain perspective and guide decision making. All design is redesign. Most architecture explorations start by looking at what we already know about how to design software. We can codify design knowledge as a rule of thumb or a documented pattern. Knowledge can come from your own experience or as legends passed from architect to architect over the ages.

Since we want to create a clear connection between our design decisions and stakeholders' needs, we'll use the categories of architecturally significant requirements from Chapter 5, *Dig for Architecturally*, on page 49 to organize our approach to exploration and decision making.

Len says:
Don't Forget Deployment

By Len Bass, independent consultant and co-author of Software Architecture in Practice [BCK12], Documenting Software Architectures: Views and Beyond [BBCG10], and DevOps: A Software Architect's Perspective [BWZ15]

One of the most easily overlooked items when designing a system or service with multiple instances during execution is deployment. There are two basic methods for deploying a new version of a service with multiple instances: red/black or rolling upgrade.

A red/black deployment (some names use different colors like blue/green) allocates sufficient virtual machines for all instances of the new version, deploys the new version into those instances, and then switches to use the new instances. A rolling upgrade will upgrade one instance at a time.

In either case, there are possibilities of inconsistencies. For example, suppose you have a chain of services—Service A depends on Service B, which in turn depends on Service C. Now one of your developers deploys a new version of Service B. This new version may change the syntax or semantics of the interface. What happens when Service A invokes Service B and gets an incorrect error because the semantics of an interface has changed? What happens when the new version of Service B assumes a new version of Service C, and the new version of Service C has yet to be deployed?

If you are deploying new versions using a rolling upgrade strategy, then it is possible that two different versions of Service B with different interfaces will simultaneously be executing.

There are a collection of techniques used to overcome these inconsistencies—enforcing backward compatibility, using feature toggles, gracefully handling unknown responses from a dependent service—but the first step is recognizing that deployment and deployment strategies can cause inconsistencies when multiple instances of a service are being run.

Accept Constraints

In *Limit Design Options with Constraints*, on page 49 you learned that constraints are predetermined design decisions that cannot be changed. Recall there are two types of constraints: technical and business. Technical constraints limit your technical options whereas business constraints focus on people, process, cost, and schedule.

We have no choice but to embrace technical constraints and incorporate them into the architecture. If we agree that *the system must be written in .NET*, then there is no point lamenting over the loss of your favorite Java framework.

Business constraints are a bit more nuanced. You also have to accept these, but their impact on the architecture is not always evident. For example, say you've agreed to a business constraint that the system must be ready in time for a trade show at the end of July. You might consider several architectural decisions to satisfy this constraint:

- Choose a pattern that promotes concurrent development effort.
- Choose a pattern that promotes incremental delivery.
- Choose technologies the team is familiar with to reduce risks.
- Choose technologies that support automation and development speed.
- Choose to skip planning, accept technical debt, and build a ball of mud.
- Choose combinations of all these ideas.

Business constraints can also be satisfied outside the architecture—for example, by emphasizing craftsmanship and early testing, or by using a subcontractor with lower hourly rates.

Remember that early design decisions can become constraining, but they are not constraints. Like the load-bearing walls of a house, these early design decisions hold everything else in place. Moving a load-bearing wall in a house might be costly and challenging, but it is technically possible. Always distinguish between the constraints you are given and the constraints you give yourself.

While constraints strongly influence the architecture, most of our design decisions (and trade-offs) in the architecture will focus on promoting desired quality attributes.

Constraints Can Have Far-Reaching Consequences

Years ago a start-up I worked for was acquired by a much larger and more risk-averse corporation. Shortly after the acquisition, our new corporate legal team informed us about some new policies. One of the big policy changes required that we no longer use open source software released under certain licenses.

This new constraint, handed down by the legal team, created nearly a year of new development work. The lesson: Stakeholders don't always understand how a constraint might impact the architecture. When a constraint causes significant pain, talk with your stakeholders about the ramifications of their requirements. In our case, we couldn't sway the lawyers, but sometimes hard constraints become soft when the impact is understood.

Promote Desired Quality Attributes

Selecting structures for the architecture is like making a smoothie. Smoothies (like software) are tasty but difficult to make well. While many things must go right to create great software, there is only one thing you need to get right for a great smoothie: use the proper blender. OK, there are lots of things that can wrong with smoothie making too (berry seeds, ugh!), but the blender is a crucial smoothie-making tool.

You'd think picking a blender would be easy. It's not. Do you want one that's easy to clean? Something that stores easily and fits on your countertop? Something quiet? Or powerful? Or portable so you can blend on the beach? We can express these needs as blender quality attributes.

Here are three types of blenders capable of making smoothies. Each blender is designed to promote different quality attributes and, as you can see, no two blenders are the same.

Chainsaw Blender photo credit: Mike Warren

The standard blender is dishwasher safe and has a sturdy base for sitting on a kitchen counter top. But it requires electricity, so you're limited to the kitchen. The battery-powered hand blender is small, portable, and easy to clean, but trades power for portability. Finally, the gas-powered chainsaw blender has the best power and portability.[2] Too bad the 37cc two-stroke, motorcycle-throttle-controlled chainsaw engine is a tad loud and emits an exhaust unsafe for indoor use.

---

2. Yes, this is a real, working blender. Instructions for making your own can be found at http://www.instructables.com/id/Chainsaw-Blender/.

Here is a summary of how well our top-quality attributes are promoted by each blender:

	Standard Blender	Hand Blender	Chainsaw Blender
Cleanability	Neutral	Positive	Neutral
Counter top-ability	Positive	Negative	Strongly Negative
Quietness	Neutral	Positive	Strongly Negative
Power	Neutral	Negative	Strongly Positive
Portability	Strongly Negative	Positive	Strongly Positive
Safety	Neutral	Neutral	Negative

Each blender performs the same basic function (blending). They have interchangeable parts. For example, the same glass pitcher works with the standard and gas-powered chainsaw blenders. In addition to the blender quality attributes, the designers considered costs, manufacturing techniques, interfaces with external systems (human and machine), and other properties. The structures we see in the final designs were chosen to promote properties the designers highly valued.

Just like the blenders, architects choose structures to promote quality attributes in the software system. The most common way to select structures is by exploring patterns. Remember, all design is redesign! Find patterns that promote desired quality attributes and use those patterns as a starting point for the architecture.

Explore Patterns with Quality Attributes in Mind

We'll explore architecture patterns in greater detail in Chapter 7, *Create a Foundation with Patterns*, on page 79. For now, let's see a simple example of how we can use quality attributes to choose an appropriate pattern.

Say we want to build a web-based, data-driven application. What patterns would you choose for this application? There are three decent options: 3-tier, publish-subscribe, and service-oriented as shown in the figure on page 70.

Option A: 3-Tier Pattern. Introduced on page 92, each tier is responsible for different application concerns. For a web application, the display tier renders the UI, the business tier operates server side to verify business rules, and the database stores data.

Option B: Publish-Subscribe Pattern. Introduced on page 88, each element publishes messages to an event bus. Interested components may subscribe

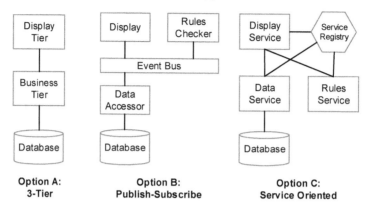

Which architecture pattern would you choose for a data-driven web application?

to message types. Depending on the rules of the message system, events might not be delivered in order and delivery might not be guaranteed.

Option C: Service-Oriented Architecture Pattern. Introduced on page 86, services register with a central registry so that callers can find them. Components look up and call those services directly and the service responds with the requested information—or doesn't if something goes wrong.

Each of these patterns promotes and inhibits different quality attributes. Which one would you choose?

The 3-tier pattern is ideal in many situations. It's easy to test, easy to deploy, and easy to describe. This simplicity comes at a cost. The multi-tier pattern does not promote quality attributes such as scalability and availability. Depending on other quality attribute scenarios, this pattern may not address all our needs without augmenting the architecture with other patterns.

The publish-subscribe pattern is highly modifiable and extremely flexible. This flexibility makes it easy to build loosely coupled systems. While this flexibility and modifiability are attractive, there is a downside. Message order matters to the events in our data-driven application, but the publish-subscribe pattern alone can't guarantee message order. With the right message bus technology, we might make this pattern work, but it feels awkward.

Like the other patterns, service-oriented architecture is modifiable, flexible, and testable. Service-oriented systems are also scalable and promote availability easier than our other options. It's also the most complex of the three patterns under discussion and has the steepest infrastructure curve. Depending on our specific quality attribute scenarios, this pattern could be overkill.

We could successfully implement the functional requirements with any of these patterns. The quality attributes are what really drives our decision making. With quality attributes, there is rarely a single *right* or *wrong* design, only designs that are *better* or *worse* relative to desired system properties. To make a decision we need to do some analysis.

Create a Decision Matrix

The *decision matrix* is a simple tool for summarizing the trade-off analysis among architecture design options. Use it to make decisions about any architectural choice from patterns to functional responsibilities to technology choice. Here is an example:

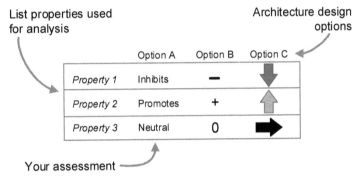

To use a decision matrix, list properties you plan to use for the analysis in the first column of a table. Each row represents a particular property. Each column represents your analysis of a design option.

Summarize the results of your analysis with an easy-to-read notation such as words, arrows, symbols, or colors. The idea is to create a visual representation that shows how each option influences properties you think are valuable. Here is an example:

Strongly Promotes	The design option actively helps you to achieve the system property.
Promotes	The design option allows you to achieve the system property.
Neutral	The design option neither helps nor hurts the system property.
Inhibits	The design option makes achieving the system property slightly more difficult.
Strongly Inhibits	The design option makes it costly or significantly difficult to achieve the system property.

The best decision is often obvious once it's in the matrix. Use a scale like the following to summarize the analysis of each architecture design option. Immediately eliminate any design option that prevents you from achieving a required system property.

We already saw a decision matrix for smoothie blenders on page 69. Let's create another decision matrix, this time for the Project Lionheart patterns discussed on page 69. Here is a decision matrix, which shows some of the analysis for the quality attribute scenarios we defined in *Capture Quality Attributes as Scenarios*, on page 52:

Project Lionheart Decision Matrix

	3-Tier	Publish - Subscribe	Service Oriented
Availability (Database unavailable)	+	O	+
Availability (Uptime requirements)	O	O	O
Performance (5-second response time)	O	–	+
Security	O	–	O
Scalability (5% annual growth)	O	O	+
Maintainability (Team knowledge)	+	–	O
Buildability (Implementation risks)	++	–	– –

Legend

Strongly Promotes ++	Strongly Inhibits – –	Neutral O
Promotes +	Inhibits –	

Looking at the decision matrix, which pattern would you choose? Are there other factors not captured in the matrix that might influence your final decision?

The work that goes into creating the matrix is more important than the matrix itself. The decision matrix is a convenient way to summarize findings and facilitate discussions with stakeholders. We want stakeholders to have a robust discussion about trade-offs among design decisions. Be prepared to explain the scores in the matrix.

Using numbers in the matrix is tempting. Don't. Numbers give a false sense of confidence and precision in the analysis. Eventually, someone will try to adjust scores with weighted stakeholder preferences, sum the columns, consider aggregate averages, or some other dreadful idea. It's just bad news.

See Activity 32, *Decision Matrix*, on page 292 for further details on this method. An alternative method for helping discuss trade-off priorities is the trade-off sliders activity described on page 192.

Assign Functional Responsibilities to Elements

Every element in the architecture has a job to do. As we choose structures, we'll assign specific functional responsibilities to each element so we can achieve all the essential functional requirements.

Let's look at an example from our case study system, Project Lionheart. Here are some functional requirements gleaned from interviews with people from the Office of Management and Budget.

An Office of Management and Budget user can:

- Search existing and past city contracts

- Paginate through all results

- View basic information about a company including the name, phone number, address, and list of past and active contracts

- View basic information about a contract including the type, status, expiration date, PID, bidding companies, and who won the contract

- Subscribe to receive alerts about contract updates

Several responsibilities are implied by these functional requirements, in addition to the things directly mentioned:

- Since users can search, this suggests it must be indexed.
- To show contract and company information it must be stored.
- Subscriptions require that the system stores email addresses.
- To alert users about changes implies something can recognize when a change has happened.

Here is one view of a set of elements that will allow us to achieve these functional requirements shown in the figure on page 74.

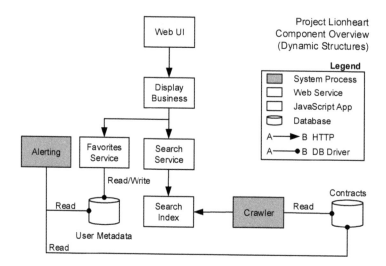

Here is an *element responsibility catalog* for this diagram:

Element	Responsibility
Web UI	Renders a user interface for the user in their web browser, handles user interactions.
Display Business	Authentication and authorization, proxy for other backing services, verifies business logic for application use.
Search Service	Core processing for query parsing, search, pagination, filtering.
Favorites Service	Normalizes tags, writes favorites to persistent storage.
Alerting Service	Scheduled to look for recent changes, sends email based on subscriptions stored in user metadata database.
Crawler	Reads data from the Contracts DB, transforms it for search, uploads to index.
User Metadata DB	Persistent storage for user subscriptions and other user-added content.
Search Index	Optimized representation of contract data designed for search. All contract data to be displayed in the UI is searchable, sortable, and stored.
Contracts DB	Persistent storage. System of record for city RFP data.
HTTP Relation	Communication among services over standard HTTP protocols. APIs are assumed to be RESTful.
DB Driver Relation	Native driver/client for the to-be-selected database.

The element responsibility catalog describes the essential duties each element in the architecture has the authority to perform. We created this element responsibility catalog by running down the list of the known influential functional requirements and ensuring each function was owned by one and only one element. Also, each element in the architecture should have at least one function for which it is responsible; otherwise, that element is without purpose.

Influential functional requirements make for a great checklist when assigning responsibilities to elements. One approach for identifying responsibilities is to model the system with component responsibility collaborator cards as described on page 232.

Design for Change

So far in this chapter, you've learned how to explore options and make decisions using your understanding of the ASRs. Making significant design decisions is supremely important for having a robust architecture, but if there is one constant in software, it's change.

All great architectures account for the inevitability of change. We design for change by choosing when to make a decision and by moving design decisions out of the architecture.

Defer Binding Decisions until the Most Responsible Moment

Making a decision that cannot be easily reversed—an architectural decision—is a big deal. One strategy for avoiding dead ends and wrong turns is to defer making binding decisions for as long as responsible. Delaying design decisions until they must be decided creates time for research and exploration.

In *Lean Software Development: An Agile Toolkit for Software Development Managers [PP03]*, Mary and Tom Poppendieck introduced the idea of the *last responsible moment*, the time when a decision must be made to avoid losing important design alternatives. Instead of thinking about the last responsible moment, we want to try to make design decisions at the *most responsible moment*, the time at which a design decision has the greatest positive impact on the software system.[3]

---

3. http://wirfs-brock.com/blog/2011/01/18/agile-architecture-myths-2-architecture-decisions-should-be-made-at-the-last-responsible-moment/

Ideally, the last responsible moment is also the most responsible moment to decide. In practice, the most responsible moment to make a decision leaves extra time for external dependencies beyond our control, consensus building, education, and design validation. The most responsible moment is often earlier than we think it is.

Here are some questions I use to help me decide whether now is the right time to make a design decision:

- Does a lack of a decision prevent forward progress?
- Does the decision resolve a problem that cannot wait?
- Does the decision create more options or new opportunities?
- Does delaying the decision introduce significantly more risk?
- Do I understand and accept the implications of the decision?
- Do I have a clear rationale for why I am making this decision now?
- Do I have the time to undo this decision if it is wrong? Can I afford to make a mistake?

Even if we can identify the most responsible moment to decide, that doesn't mean we'll always have enough information to make a good decision. Luckily we have a cheat to help us avoid catastrophes when this situation arises. We can move things likely to change out of the architecture.

Move Design Decisions out of the Architecture

If a design decision is easy to change later, then it is no longer an architectural concern. When possible, design the architecture so that decisions likely to change are left open for downstream designers to decide.

Many of the design principles we know from programming are just plain good design principles. For example, applying SOLID principles to architecture yields many of the same benefits to architecture as they do to object-oriented design. SOLID is a mnemonic to help remember the single responsibility, open/closed, Liskov substitution, interface segregation, and dependency inversion design principles. When elements in the architecture have a single responsibility it's easier to isolate changes. Depending on abstractions and creating elements with clean interfaces creates flexibility.

There are many ways to move design decisions out of the architecture, including pluggable architectures, external configuration, self-describing data, and dynamic discovery. In each of these examples, we chose to alter the system's behavior at design time or runtime without modifying the architecture and, ideally, without adversely affecting essential quality attributes.

Project Lionheart: The Story So Far...

The day after the mini-quality attribute workshop (see Activity 7, *Mini-Quality Attribute Workshop*, on page 210), our team gathers to discuss architecture options. We knew we were building a data-driven web application, but beyond that we didn't have much else to go on. What overall patterns would we use to organize the system? What technologies will we use for the web application? How will the code be deployed and hosted? How will the code be organized?

You review the constraints with the team as well as some of the more interesting functional requirements. Looking at the influential functional requirements you point out that we'll need a database and a search engine. Most of the team has prior experience with MySQL, so you guide the team into choosing that for the database. After the review meeting you create a task in the backlog to explore search engine technologies and select one.

Before we start coding, we still needed to make some basic decisions about organizing the code and how the coarse-grained components in the system will come together. Using the think-do-check cycle as a guide, you take a moment to *think* and plan our next steps.

You start writing open questions on the whiteboard and ask the team to share their concerns too. Soon there is a long list of questions and risks on the whiteboard. You shift to the *do* part of our design process. "We'll cover more ground if we divide and conquer (see Activity 15, *Divide and Conquer*, on page 239) to find answers," you say. "Half the team will explore patterns that let us achieve our quality attributes. The other half will explore our technology questions." To *check*, you decide that everyone will reconvene in one week to share findings and make decisions.

Next Up

Choosing structures is easy. Choosing appropriate structures is difficult. In this chapter, we solved some of the mysteries behind the thought process that goes into architectural decision making. Accept the constraints. Find the interesting functional requirements and ensure the architecture can achieve them. Explore patterns to help promote desired quality attributes. Make decisions at the right time and always promote changeability when practical.

Making design decisions is never easy, but it becomes easier with experience. In the next chapter, you'll bootstrap your design experience by learning some common architecture patterns.

CHAPTER 7

Create a Foundation with Patterns

For hundreds of years, engineers have captured solutions to common problems as reusable patterns. Software engineers follow this tradition as well. Seasoned software architects know many patterns. When facing a new problem, experienced architects explore their catalog of design patterns to find likely solutions before attempting to design something new. Once they've identified a suitable pattern, they'll fill in details for the particular problem at hand and adapt it to meet their current needs.

Every software system employs a small number of thematic patterns as a foundation on which we make all other design decisions. Using patterns is like having the greatest minds in software architecture on your team. When you use a pattern, you gain the benefits of others' wisdom without investing much work on your own.

Hundreds of architecture design patterns are available that span a variety of domains and contexts. In this chapter, you'll explore some of the most common architecture patterns and briefly discuss how to adapt those general patterns to meet specific needs.

What Is an Architecture Pattern?

Many of the technical problems software architects face are not new. As a broader software architecture community, we've been building scalable, maintainable, reliable, highly available, testable software systems across a variety of technical domains for decades. Apart from a small handful of emerging problem areas, many of today's software design problems have known solutions. Patterns describe these known solutions.

An *architecture pattern* is a reusable solution to a specific problem. Software architecture patterns show how to promote specific quality attributes by using a specific combination of structures. Choose the right patterns for our problem, and we can avoid nasty traps that may otherwise cause trouble had we attempted to design the architecture from scratch.

Patterns have many other benefits. Since many patterns are widely known, we get communication bonuses by using them. If a picture is worth a thousand words, a pattern is worth a thousand pictures. Popular patterns are baked into frameworks and platforms, making it easier to adopt them.

Let's explore some of the more common architecture patterns in use today. The mini-catalog here is far from a complete list. More information about each pattern can be found easily on the web and in existing architecture literature.

 Joe asks:

What Is the Difference between a Design Pattern and an Architecture Pattern?

Design patterns are an essential design tool for all designers regardless of design discipline or granularity of abstraction. You'll find design patterns for user experience, testing, database design, and even engineering processes, in addition to programming, software architecture, and enterprise architecture. All design patterns have a place in modern software development.

Architecture patterns differ from programming design patterns, such as those cataloged by the Gang of Four in *Design Patterns: Elements of Reusable Object-Oriented Software [GHJV95]*, by the types of problems they aim to solve. The Gang of Four's design patterns shows how to organize object-oriented programs to promote reusability and maintainability. Architecture patterns define solutions for a variety of quality attributes scenarios—design time, runtime, and conceptual—and often deal with multiple components of a software system. The scope is broader in an architecture pattern regarding both the quality attributes and the granularity of abstractions in play.

In practice, distinguishing programming design patterns from architecture design patterns isn't so important. After all, one person's architecture might be another person's detailed design.

Layers Pattern

The *layers pattern* is one of the most used (and abused) architecture patterns. Most software systems have multiple contributors. Partitioning code into distinct and independent layers organized around a specific set of related concerns enables developers to work together better. Layers promote decreased coupling between the layers and higher cohesion within, which promotes maintainability. Use layers any time you need to change code modules independently of one another.

Category	Module
Elements	*Layer*—group of functionally cohesive modules.
Relations	*Allowed to use*—indicates which layers may use modules within another layer.
Rules for Use	Every module must be allocated to one and only one layer.
	Layers above are allowed to use layers below, but this relation only goes one way. The *allowed to use* relation can be limited so the current layer may only use the layer immediately below it. Cyclical dependencies are not permitted.
Strengths	Promotes maintainability, portability, reusability, testability, design time modifiability. Conceptually simple to implement. Layers can be made visible in the code.
Weaknesses	Each layer introduces additional abstractions between the highest layers and the lowest. These additional abstractions increase complexity and may harm performance. Too many layers or leaky abstractions can make development painful for programmers.

Here are examples of layered diagrams. The diagram on the left explicitly shows the *allowed to use* relation, whereas the diagram on the right implies relations among elements.

Layers Pattern Examples

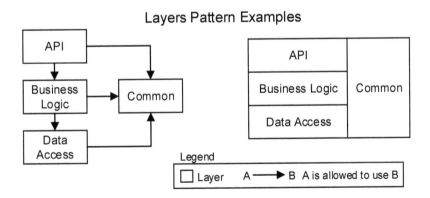

There many variants of the layered pattern. No matter how it's drawn or how many layers are involved, the elements, relations, and rules for their use are the same.

Ports and Adapters Pattern

The *ports and adapters pattern* isolates core business logic so it can be used in a variety of contexts and tested in isolation from components that provide data and events. At runtime, pluggable adapters for specific input sources can be injected into the core business logic to provide access to events and data. Adapters can be swapped at build-time or runtime to create different configurations of the software system. Use this pattern when the system must support multiple input devices or when there is a risk that input devices could change.

This pattern was initially described by Alistair Cockburn under the name *Hexagonal Architecture.*[1] See the table on page 83.

Here is an example of a ports-and-adapters diagram. In this example, radar simulators can be swapped for adapters to real radar systems without changing the core business logic. The logging and communication bus can also be exchanged depending on the situation.

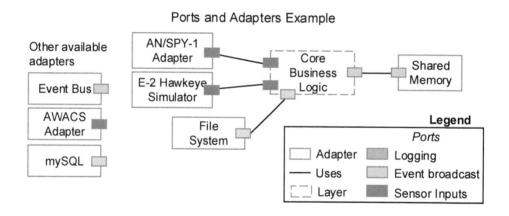

Ports and Adapters Example

---

1.   http://alistair.cockburn.us/Hexagonal+architecture

Category	Module or Component & Connector
Elements	*Layer*—Contains domain or business logic that has no knowledge of where data or events it uses originates.
	Port—Describes the interface between a layer and an adapter. Ports allow layers to be decoupled from concrete adapters.
	Adapter—Code that interacts with external data sources, devices, or other components that layers can use to gain access to data or events.
Relations	*Exposes*—Indicates the ports available from a specific layer.
	Implements—Describes the ports which constrain an adapter.
	Injects—Indicates which adapters will be available to a given layer.
Rules for Use	Layers usually but are not required to expose ports. Layers without ports are sometimes referred to as *inner layers*.
	Adapters may satisfy the constraints of one or more ports.
	An adapter may only be injected into a port when that adapter implements the interface required by that port.
	Depending on the mechanisms used to realize elements and relations, the pattern may refer to design-time or run-time interactions. Be clear and consistent in your models whether you are showing module or C&C structures.
Strengths	Promotes testability, maintainability, and modifiability. Different teams can work on different layers or adapters.
Weaknesses	Mechanisms must be developed to select adapters used at runtime. Runtime qualities such as security and reliability are decided by the adapters. Third-party adapters should be selected with care.

Pipe-and-Filter Pattern

With the *pipe-and-filter pattern*, each component called a filter is responsible for a single transformation or data operation. Data is streamed from one filter to the next as quickly as possible, and data operations occur in parallel. Loosely coupled filters can be reused and combined in different ways to create new pipelines.

The pipe-and-filter pattern is prevalent in data analysis and data transformation use cases. If you've ever piped Unix commands together in a terminal window, then you have firsthand experience with the pipe-and-filter pattern. See the table on page 85.

Here is an example diagram of the pipe-and-filter pattern:

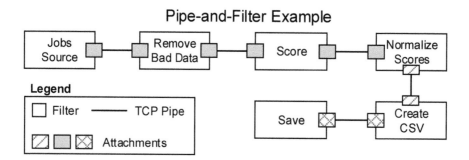

The *batch sequential pattern* is similar to pipe-and-filter but has one major difference. The stages of a batch-sequential system operate in turn, one at a time instead of in parallel like in a pipe-and-filter system. Instead of streaming data from one stage to the next, batch sequential systems usually write all data to disk for the next stage in the sequence to read.

Category	Component & Connector
Elements	*Filter*—A component that reads data, transforms it, then writes out the transformed data. Filters may begin processing data as soon as it is read. Filters must define expected inputs and produced outputs.
	Pipe—A connector, which transports data from one filter to the next, preserving data order. Pipes have a single input and output, and do not alter the data in transit.
	Some variants of this pattern also include *source* and *sink* elements. The former only produces data whereas the latter only receives it.
Relations	*Attachment*—Connects the output of one filter with the input of another by way of a pipe.
Rules for Use	Pipes can only connect filters with compatible inputs and outputs. Filters should be completely independent of one another and have no knowledge of upstream or downstream filters.
Strengths	Promotes performance, reusability, and modifiability.
Weaknesses	Pipe-and-filter systems are not interactive and cannot include a user interface without modifying the pattern. Reliability is not specifically promoted by the pattern but can be designed in by introducing filters to handle error cases. A naive implementation can harm performance because having many filters running in parallel can be computationally expensive.

Service-Oriented Architecture Pattern

In a *service-oriented architecture*, independent components are implemented as services, which provide specific functionality. Services are combined at runtime to define the software system's behavior. For this to work, service consumers must be able to locate and use services without knowing about implementation details behind the services they use.

Service-oriented architectures (SOA) can be implemented in many ways. Traditional SOA relies heavily on message buses and communication via SOAP. Modern SOA encourages the use of fine-grained microservices connected by lightweight message protocols such as HTTP.

Complex organizations will often turn to SOA to design large software systems in which different departments own different pieces of the system. SOA allows each department to work independently within their area of expertise and hide information systems but also provides broad access to those subsystems without compromising design integrity. See the table on page 87.

Here is an oversimplified example diagram showing a single view of a service-oriented system. Service-oriented architectures are complicated and involve many architectural components. This diagram shows two services attached to the service registry. Services must check the registry to look up connection information for other services they want to call.

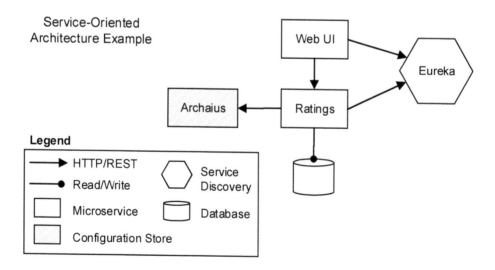

Category	Component & Connector
Elements	*Service*—An independently deployable unit, which provides functionality behind a well-defined interface.
	Service registry—List of all available services, used by a service to discover other services to use.
	Message system—The specific element type depends on the flavor of SOA and other design decisions around service communication. Some examples include SOAP, REST (representational state transfer, usually over HTTP), gRPC,[2] and asynchronous messaging.
Relations	Varies depending on the constraints in the SOA system. With the smart endpoints, dumb pipes approach popularized by Netflix, *calls* might be the only relation. If your SOA system uses asynchronous messaging, *publish* and *subscribe* might be the relations in play.
Rules for Use	Services have no knowledge about the implementation details of the services they use. Services must discover other services via an external component, either a service registry or message bus in the case of asynchronous message passing.
Strengths	Promotes interoperability, reusability, and scalability. This is a well-studied pattern with many, many subpatterns defined.
Weaknesses	SOA systems are distributed systems and include all the complexity that comes with distributed computation. SOA systems have many parts and can be complicated to assemble. Properties that can be handled easily at design time in other patterns are a runtime concern with SOA. For example, it's impossible to know the version of an SOA system without knowing what services were running at a snapshot in time. Availability, reliability, and performance are inhibited by this pattern.

---

2.   http://www.grpc.io/

Avoid Architectural Mismatch

Architectural mismatch, described in *Architectural Mismatch: Why Reuse Is So Hard [GAO95]*, is a phenomenon that occurs when the assumptions made about how a component will be used conflicts with that component's current use. In the best case, a system experiencing architectural mismatch will be difficult to develop and maintain. In the worst case, key quality attributes will be unattainable.

Architectural mismatch can occur at the conceptual level when a selected pattern is in direct tension with high-priority quality attributes. For example, if performance is the number one quality attribute, then selecting service-oriented architecture might be a mismatch. Picking the wrong pattern can significantly harm the architecture's ability to promote required properties.

Architectural mismatch can also occur when the technology selected to implement the system does not align with assumptions laid out in the architecture. For example, if the architecture describes a publish-subscribe pattern, using a relational database as the primary mechanism for message passing would undermine the properties promoted by the publish-subscribe pattern. When a mismatch occurs on my team, we will talk about how we are *fighting the framework*. To avoid creating a mismatch, choose technologies that match the assumptions made in the architecture.

Publish-Subscribe Pattern

In the *publish-subscribe pattern*, producers and consumers exist independently and unaware of one another. Numerous consumers subscribe to events published by various producers. Producers and consumers communicate indirectly via an event bus, which is responsible for connecting published events with interested subscribers. The choice of event bus technology greatly influences the systems properties. Choose the publish-subscribe pattern when multiple, independent components need access to the same information. See the table on page 89.

Here is an example diagram of a publish-subscribe system:

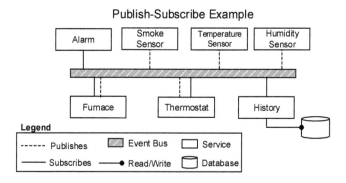

Category	Component & Connector
Elements	*Publisher*—any component that publishes an event. Specific events published should be described in design documentation.
	Subscriber—any component that subscribes to an event.
	Event Bus—responsible for registering component subscriptions and delivering published events. The properties promoted by the event bus vary on the specific technology and its configuration.
Relations	*Publish*—Indicates that a component publishes events to the event bus.
	Subscribe—Indicates that a component registers an event subscription.
Rules for Use	All communications in this pattern take place via the event bus. As such all components, must be connected to the bus. Components may be both a publisher and subscriber.
Strengths	Promotes extensibility, reusability, and testability. Depending on the selection of event bus and how it is configured, availability, reliability, and scalability might also be promoted.
Weaknesses	It is difficult to reason about performance in publish-subscribe systems given the independent, asynchronous nature of component communication. The choice of event bus is ultimately responsible for making or breaking a publish-subscribe system. Choose your event bus with care and learn everything you can about how to use it.

Most publish-subscribe systems define an *event specification*, which describes events to which components may subscribe. This document also describes event formats as well as the components responsible for publishing events.

Shared-Data Pattern

In the *shared-data pattern*, multiple components access data through a common data store. No single component is entirely responsible for the data or data store. This pattern is particularly useful when multiple components require a large amount of data. With shared-data systems, data and the data source is the primary medium of interaction. Compare this to event-based systems in which components communicate via procedure calls or message passing. See the table on page 91.

The following diagram shows an example of a shared-data pattern.

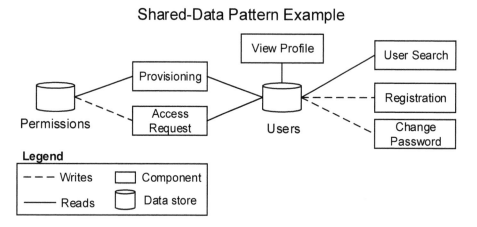

The shared-data pattern blends well with other patterns. Many large information systems will use this pattern somewhere within the architecture.

Category	Component & Connector
Elements	*Data store*—holds the data shared among accessors. Choice of the data store and the constraints placed on it determine the quality attributes achieved with the pattern. *Data accessor component*—components that use the data in some way.
Relations	*Reads*—indicates that a data accessor component may read data from the shared-data store. Some read relations might require specific protocols or place limits on the amount or types of data that can be read. *Writes*—indicates that a data accessor component writes data to the shared-data store. Write relations can be transactional, throttled, protected, or otherwise constrained in a variety of ways.
Rules for Use	Only data accessors may interact with the shared-data store.
Strengths	Promotes reliability via data consistency, security, and privacy. Scalability and availability are also promoted when the data store is tuned well and data accessors are thoughtfully partitioned.
Weaknesses	The shared-data store creates a single point of failure, which can harm availability and performance. Maintainability can be harmed if the data store changes, since all data accessors may be required to change as well. This pattern is simple to implement and prone to abuse. Sharing data can solve many problems, but depending on the context other architecture patterns could be a better fit.

Multi-Tier Pattern

In the *multi-tier pattern*, runtime structures are organized into logical groups. These logical groups may be allocated to specific physical components, such as a server or cloud platform. The multi-tier pattern is conceptually similar to the layers pattern. Layers are a module structure and deal with design-time elements, whereas tiers are either a component and connector or allocation structure and deal with runtime elements.

Any system in which components will live on different platforms or hardware will benefit by thinking about the tiers at play and which components reside on different tiers. See the table on page 93.

Here is a diagram depicting the multi-tier pattern. In this example, components in the application tier are allocated to the customer's servers. Components in the middle tiers are allocated to a common platform but have different functional responsibilities. Components in the data tier are hosted on a different cloud platform and may only include databases.

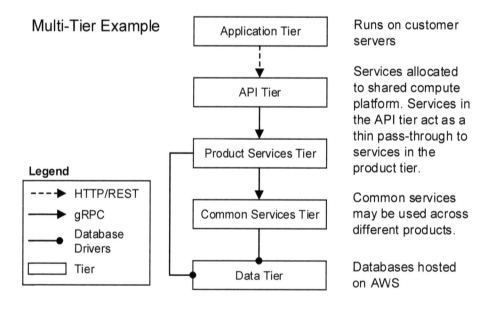

Category	Component & Connector or Allocation
Elements	*Tier*—a logical grouping of runtime components. There are many ways to partition tiers. Some examples include functional responsibilities, compute platforms, team responsibilities, communication mechanisms, security requirements, and data access.
Relations	*Belongs to*—used to group components into a tier.
	Communicates with—shows how tiers or the components within interact with one another. This relation may be specialized to include information about protocols and communication constraints.
	Allowed to communicate with—indicates which tiers may communicate with components in other tiers.
	Allocated to—maps tiers to physical compute platforms.
Rules for Use	A component may belong to only one tier. Components within a tier are only allowed to communicate with other components within the same. Additional constraints describing tier communication can enhance reasoning and improve maintainability. A common approach is to allow communication only among adjacent tiers.
Strengths	Promotes security, performance, availability, maintainability, modifiability. Can be used to reason about costs and deployment.
Weaknesses	As a runtime construct, tiers can be difficult to enforce in large systems. Systems with many tiers can inhibit performance and maintainability.

Center of Competence Pattern

In the *center of competence pattern*, a team of experts is charged with defining patterns, establishing best practices, developing support tools, and providing education for a subset of the architecture. The center of competence (CoC) is not expected to build and deliver this part of the system but rather help other teams excel in their day-to-day development work. CoC teams can be organized around technologies, use cases, patterns, and high-risk areas.

Creating a CoC will make it easier for development teams to implement patterns and technologies we want in the architecture. Since the CoC is a support group, its primary goal is to increase development speed and improve the overall quality of the software system.

Category	Allocation
Elements	*CoC Team*—group of developers and architects.
	Responsibility Area—subset of the architecture. Can be a pattern, technology, or use case.
Relations	*Responsible for*—connects a CoC team with their responsibility areas.
Rules for Use	Typically a CoC is responsible for only one type of technology or use case.
Strengths	Promotes reusability and scalability of experts. Greater access to experts and reusable assets can positively influence many quality attributes, including security, scalability, performance, reliability, and maintainability.
Weaknesses	Centers of competence create pockets of expert knowledge, which can be easily disrupted by turnover. Weak CoCs can create confusion and slow down development.

Here is an example of how one company, consisting of a few hundred developers, organized center of competence teams.

CoC Team	Responsibility Area
Job Scheduling Use Case	Develop a framework for the job scheduling use case and create tools so teams can instantiate the framework on clusters themselves.
Performance	Consult with teams about load and performance testing, provide tools for testing and data collection, collect and organize data sets and other testing assets.
Database Technologies	Consult with teams to select supported database technologies appropriate to use case, maintain tools for provisioning databases, create or distribute training materials.
Core Platform	Maintain common container management system, provide supported Docker base images, create tools for day-to-day tasks such as log aggregation and health checks.

Open Source Contribution Pattern

In the *open source contribution pattern*, teams are given responsibility for developing specific architectural components but are not expected to be the only contributing developers. When this pattern works well, a team will act as a *benevolent dictator* over their components, reviewing submitted changes to a component for quality and conceptual integrity. This pattern allows for limited centralized control across the architecture. Use this pattern when there are experts available from multiple development teams or when there is a common dependency on specific components.

For this pattern to be successful, teams must know they are responsible for specific components and have a firm understanding of where their components fit within the larger context. Provide only the owning team with write access to enforce architectural responsibility for the component. All other teams should have the ability to submit changes for review. Create style guides, design for testability, and impose constraints on technologies and build platforms, to make it easier for developers to contribute.

Category	Allocation
Elements	*Team*—a group who may submit or review component changes.
	Repository—version control repository containing software components.
Relations	*Owns*—indicates a team responsible for reviewing changes and maintaining conceptual integrity over a repository. The owner is sometimes called the repository's benevolent dictator.
	May contribute to—indicates a team who may submit changes to a repository.
Rules for Use	Repositories typically have only one owner but this is not a strict rule. Teams to contribute to many repositories.
Strengths	Promotes reusability, maintainability, and development speed
Weaknesses	This pattern is strongly tied with the component partitioning strategy. In many cases the learning curve for contributions is so steep this pattern becomes impractical. May require the owning teams to adopt other open management practices to be successful.

The open source contribution pattern pairs well with any architecture patterns that also promotes reusability. Giving teams the ability to contribute changes can create opportunities for reuse that might not exist otherwise.

Big Ball of Mud Pattern

The *big ball of mud* pattern is less a pattern you choose as it is a pattern you find in the real world. The big ball of mud is described by Brian Foote and Joseph Yoder in *Pattern Languages of Program Design 4 [FHR99]*.

The big ball of mud pattern has no defined elements or relations. Big balls of mud don't promote any qualities in particular. As you can imagine, or have yourself experienced, big balls of mud inhibit maintainability and extensibility. Both module and module and component and connector structures can be big balls of mud. Simon Brown has observed that many microservices systems can evolve into distributed big balls of mud just as easily as monolithic systems.[3]

Since big balls of mud are found only in the real world, not on paper, the one positive thing we can say about them is that they promote short-term development speed at the cost of long-term design integrity. Big balls of mud often emerge due to undisciplined development practices and a general lack of understanding of the architectural principles at play in the software system.

Some big balls of mud are created on purpose to ship value sooner such as when a team strategically decides to accept technical debt in exchange for faster initial development. The dangers of this approach lay in not retiring or paying down the debt in a timely fashion.

Discover New Patterns

Patterns are born from experience. New patterns emerge every day. Some patterns might apply to a variety of systems and teams. Others might be hyper local, perhaps only applicable to a single organization. New patterns spontaneously emerge all the time, though one does not simply invent a new architecture pattern.

Architects discover patterns in much the same way an entomologist discovers a new species of insect. Spend time in the field. Observe the world around you. When you've identified a possible pattern, describe it and classify it relative to existing patterns. If your discovery is similar to something that exists,

---

3. http://www.codingthearchitecture.com/2014/07/06/distributed_big_balls_of_mud.html

add your knowledge to our collective wisdom of the existing pattern by publishing a blog post or paper. If your discovery is new, then add it to your team's pattern catalog.

There are two primary approaches to discovering patterns: problem focused and solution focused. With the problem-focused approach, you start by looking for a common problem. Once you've seen the same problem a few times, your goal is to develop a generalized solution. Survey the existing solutions. Look for similarities and differences among the current solutions. Based on your analysis, attempt to describe the solution pattern.

With the solution-focused approach, you start by looking for solutions that are used again and again, perhaps without developers realizing it. Describe the solution pattern as you've observed it. Do some analysis to uncover the common problem being solved and attempt to define it.

Once you have a pattern, send it out for feedback. Look for people who are familiar with the problem or have implemented the solution before. The final test of your pattern will be in its first implementation. Use the feedback from your reviewers and the early implementation attempts to improve the pattern.

Project Lionheart: The Story So Far…

The team gathered in a conference room to share findings from their recent design exploration. Choosing a search technology was easy. The group gave a short presentation of the available technologies, shared a brief demo, and recommended a technology that seemed reasonable enough. Finalizing the basic patterns in the architecture, it seems, is a different matter.

"What if we go with a simple 3-tier system?" Leia suggests. She steps up to the whiteboard and sketches some boxes and lines. An impromptu whiteboard jam (described on page 255) breaks out. Owen counters, "I've been reading about microservices. It seems like a slick solution." Owen explains the microservices pattern to the team. Finn pipes up, "Microservices sound exciting but also seem like a lot of work for a simple web application."

The whiteboard jam continues for several minutes as teammates propose new patterns and discuss the merits of each pattern in turn. "Lots of good discussions," you chime in, "but we're losing focus and need to make a decision. How do the proposed solutions influence our top-quality attributes?"

Next Up

In this chapter, we've only just scratched the surface on a topic that goes very deep. There are many, many published patterns catalogs in the software design literature. The more patterns you know, the better a software designer you will become.

As we choose patterns and make design decisions, we must share our decisions with others. In the next chapter, you'll see how to make the design tangible by identifying the essential design concepts in the architecture and creating models.

CHAPTER 8

Manage Complexity
with Meaningful Models

Complexity is an inevitable by-product of every successful software system. More users will push the limits of availability, scalability, and performance. New features will be bolted on and wedged in wherever they fit. As software grows, the sheer size of the system can overwhelm the teams who develop it. Without constant vigilance, software systems eventually become victims of their own success.

All hope is not lost. When complexity rears its ugly head, we have options for keeping it in check. We can make the software smaller again by altering the requirements and snipping out code. We can divide big, complex things into smaller things that are easier to reason about and manage. We can also hide details and think about the software from the perspective of coarser-grained abstractions.

In *Define the Essential Structures*, on page 7 you learned that architecture is made up of structures, which in turn are composed of elements and relations. In this chapter you'll learn how to use these basic building blocks to create meaningful models that help us reason about our designs.

Reason About the Architecture

There is a finite amount of information we can keep in our heads at any given time. Over the years, software developers have created cheats to work around the limitations in our brains. One cheat is to turn problem solving into a massively parallel operation by collaborating with other humans. Another involves creating new, abstract concepts to represent chunks of knowledge.

These tools—collaboration and abstraction—give us what we need to think through, analyze, and understand our architectures.

Abstractions help us focus on specific details at the expense of others. For example, an interface of a class in object-oriented programming describes the public methods but says nothing about how we should implement those methods. The concrete implementation of the interface provides those details. Removing these distracting details tightens focus on what you want to think about: the interface.

Of course, the perfect abstraction is not useful if we can't share it. Anyone can draw boxes and lines. Creating a genuinely useful *model* of the architecture takes serious thought. A model, unlike any old sketch, is a precise and accurate description of some piece of the architecture that enhances communication and can be used to reason about the system.

Good architecture models have many benefits:

Models establish the vocabulary of design. Words matter. A good element name will convey meaning and intent. Each model we create extends the software system's vocabulary. We use this vocabulary in our day-to-day discussions, but it also permeates the code we write and shapes the way we see the world.

Models direct our attention to interesting details. In software development, details are everything. Just because all details are important it does not mean we want to (or have the cognitive capacity to) think about all the details at the same time. Models let us hide some details so we can focus only on what is needed at this moment to answer a specific question.

Models allow us to reason about quality attributes and other system properties. Models make it easier to think about and describe how the system would behave. If we build the right models of our architecture, we can use them to test our designs before implementing the system too. We'll still need to run experiments and build prototypes so that we can learn how to create accurate models. Even then, running an experiment is significantly cheaper and faster than learning that the design stinks after we built the whole system!

Models capture the architect's intent. All developers should understand why we designed the system the way we did. Great models express the intent behind the structures. The more people who understand this intent, the greater the chance we'll have of maintaining the system's conceptual design integrity as we evolve the system over time.

Models are born from our perception of the world and our struggle to communicate the deeper meaning behind our design intent. Every model has concepts and rules, which describe how to use those concepts. Correctly applying the rules keeps the model consistent with our perception of the world.

> **Joe asks:**
> ## What if I Want to Skip All This Modeling Stuff and Start Writing Code Now?
>
> Gregor Hohpe, author of *Enterprise Integration Patterns: Designing and Deploying Messaging Solutions* [HW04] and *37 Things and Architect Knows: A Chief Architect's Journey* [Hoh16], has a saying: *A month of coding can save an hour of architecting.* We know that architecture flaws are cheaper and faster to fix while we're still designing architecture than when we're writing code, running acceptance tests, or (*gasp!*) reviewing customer complaints after release. Gregor knows that an architecture problem is much faster to fix while it's on a whiteboard than captured in thousands of lines of code.
>
> Writing code is a fantastic way to learn about the system and how to design it. We should write code early. We should run experiments and build prototypes while we're discovering the architecture. Thinking about models is not a substitute for firsthand experience. It is impossible to predict everything about a software system only with diagrams.
>
> As you learned in *Decide How Much to Design Up Front*, on page 29, we'll end up with an architecture whether we design it up front, let it emerge as we write code, or do a little of both. Before you skip modeling the architecture and jump straight into writing code, think for a moment. When do you want to pay for your design and how much rework can you afford? A month of coding can save an hour of architecting.

Design the Meta-Model

A software system's *architectural meta-model* defines the concepts used in a model and the rules for how those concepts are applied. The meta-model is like a cognitive grammar for design. It constrains our thinking and creates the vocabulary we use to talk about the architecture.[1] The diagram on page 102 summarizes these ideas.

Defining a meta-model makes it easier to describe the architecture, set expectations for our audience, and reason about the models we create. To create a meta-model, start by defining the concepts at play. These will be the elements and

---

1. George Fairbanks. *Teaching the Architecture Metamodel-First.* SATURN 2014. http://resources.sei.cmu.edu/library/asset-view.cfm?assetID=89518

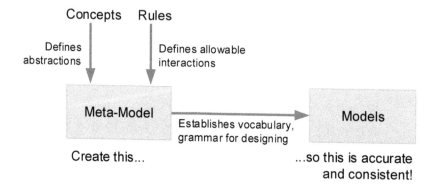

relations in the architecture. Once we've described the concepts, establish the rules for using those concepts.

Individuate New Concepts

Concept individuation is the cognitive process by which we recognize ideas as being distinct from one another. As we individuate new ideas in the architecture, we update our understanding of the world and the models that represent it.

You have individuated concepts naturally since birth. Imagine the first time you encountered a door as a toddler. By watching adults use doors, you surmised that you could open doors by turning knobs. You individuated the concept of a door as distinct from a wall because you figured out that doors have knobs. One day you turned a knob to open a door, and it didn't budge. Through this discovery, you individuated the concept of a locked door as distinct from an unlocked door and updated your internal mental model of the world.

To individuate concepts, we follow a simple process called the *curiosity cycle* *[Mug14]*. This process applies when defining any model, whether it is a model of our world or a software system's architecture.

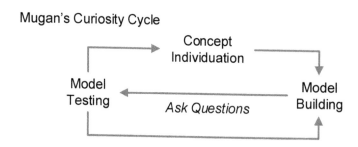

Start the process by asking a question. This question forms the basis for a test. Through the test, we'll either find the answer in our model or find a gap in our current understanding. If we find an answer, then we reinforce our existing model. When we find a gap, we must figure out how to change our model to fill it.

Here's an example of the curiosity cycle in action. Say stakeholders have prioritized availability, but we also need to keep costs down. Under these circumstances, we might ask the following questions:

- *Question*: Which components cost us the most if they are unavailable?

- *Test*: I can't answer this question with our current model. I see components, but I can't discern their costs.

- *Individuate a new concept*: Let's introduce cost.

- *Build new model*: We can use color in our meta-model to represent costs. White means no loss whereas a dark red box means we're losing a lot of money. The darker the color, the greater the loss.

- *Test*: Ah-ha! Now I can see that component Foo is going to cause the most if it is unavailable.

After updating the meta-model to include the concept of *cost*, we can now create a new model that lets us reason about the relationship between costs and other quality attributes.

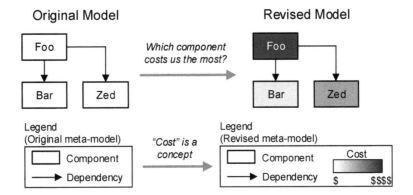

It takes time to arrive at the *ah-ha!* moment. There is also a risk that we may not have the knowledge or experience necessary to individuate concepts required to design the right system. Starting with an existing meta-model, such as an architecture pattern, can reduce this risk.

Pick a Pattern to Seed the Architecture

As discussed in *The Four Principles of Design Thinking*, on page 15, all design is redesign. Patterns are the ultimate example of the redesign rule in action. Architecture patterns describe a prepackaged meta-model relevant to a specific problem. Pick an appropriate pattern, and the meta-model is free.

We explore several popular patterns in Chapter 7, *Create a Foundation with Patterns*, on page 79. Notice how each pattern describes the elements, relations, and rules. Each pattern's meta-model is complete, consistent, but also flexible so that designers may use the pattern under varying circumstances.

Most architectures include one or two thematic patterns to seed the system's design. Even with these thematic patterns, there are still many details to sort out. As we add new concepts to the meta-model, it is possible that could undermine the patterns in our architecture's foundation.

Reconcile Inconsistencies

Combining meta-models—for example, by merging patterns—may introduce inconsistencies in the combined meta-model. For example, two meta-models might define a *worker* element, but the responsibilities for the worker and rules for its use are radically different. Reconciling inconsistencies involves merging similar concepts and renaming different concepts with the same name so that they remain distinct. Rules may also need to be adjusted. Failure to resolve these inconsistencies can undermine our design efforts.

As we add new concepts to the meta-model, the rules for using those concepts should also be updated. Rules describe how elements and relations interact in the system. They must reflect reality. For example, many programming languages have strict type systems. If we implemented a pipe-and-filter system (introduced on page 84) using a language with strong types, then the meta-model should include rules about types. If the language we choose doesn't enforce types, then we'll need to define message descriptions or protocol headers.

Rules also describe *conceptual constraints* we choose to place on the architecture. Conceptual constraints allow us to promote specific quality attributes. For example, in the layers pattern (introduced on page 80), an element within a *layer* is only *allowed to use* other elements in the same layer or the layer directly below it. We created this rule to promote maintainability. Violate this rule, and we'll end up with an unmaintainable bowl of spaghetti.

We create rules the same way as other concepts. Ask a question. Test the model. Update the model by amending or adding rules. Repeat until the model sufficiently answers your questions.

Use Good Names

Naming things is hard. Naming things is also surprisingly important. Since naming is a design tool, many of the principles you already know from writing good code apply to architecture too.

In *Good Naming Is a Process, Not a Single Step,*[2] Arlo Belshee describes seven stages of naming. The names we choose reflect how well we understand what we're designing. As our understanding improves, so too do the names we give the concepts. Here are Belshee's 7 Stages of Naming applied to software architecture.

Stage 1: Missing
> No name. We don't know enough about the system or context to extract a named element.

Stage 2: Nonsense
> Name has absolutely no meaning. We have identified a chunk of ideas as being somehow related.

Stage 3: Honest
> The name describes at least one of the element's responsibilities.

Stage 4: Honest and Complete
> The name directly describes *all* of the element's responsibilities.

Stage 5: Does the Right Thing
> The name reflects a conscious decision to evolve the element's responsibility. This only happens as we gain more knowledge about the element's role in the context of the architecture.

Stage 6: Intent
> The name describes the element's responsibility but also its purpose. Understanding purpose requires that we understand *why* the element exists in addition to what it does.

Stage 7: Domain Abstraction
> The name transcends individual elements to create a new abstraction. This is where new concepts for the meta-model are born.

2.　http://arlobelshee.com/good-naming-is-a-process-not-a-single-step/

Here's an example of one naming progression. In this project, we were attempting to name a set of elements responsible for fetching data from a web service and transforming it.

Stage	Name
1. Missing	The thing that does the thing
2. Nonsense	Cranberry
3. Honest	Job Starter Process
4. Honest and Complete	Data Fetcher, Checker, Transformer, and Job Starter
5. Does the Right Thing	Data Transformation Job Runner
6. Intent	Data Preparer
7. Domain Abstraction	Data Preparation Agent

The final name emerged from the realization that there are several *Agents* with similar responsibilities and interaction rules across the system. The concept of *Agents* was a powerful idea that let us create clean abstractions and an improved meta-model. Now the name *Agent* carries meaning and communicates intent for architectural elements bearing that name.

Use names as a litmus test to determine how well you understand the concepts in the architecture. If your names are nonsense or simply honest, then you may have more work until you understand the concepts you're designing.

⚒ Get Your Hands Dirty: Create an Architecture Flipbook for Conway's Game of Life

Conway's Game of Life is a zero player simulation in which the universe consists of a two-dimensional grid of cells.[3] For any given iteration of the game, a cell may be either alive or dead. There are four rules that determine a cell's state:

1. Any live cell with fewer than two live neighbors dies (under-population).

2. Any live cell with two or three live neighbors lives on to the next generation.

3. Any live cell with more than three live neighbors dies (over-population).

4. Any dead cell with exactly three live neighbors becomes a live cell (reproduction).

---

3. https://en.wikipedia.org/wiki/Conway%27s_Game_of_Life

Individuate the concepts in a meta-model that might describe Conway's Game of Life by making an Architecture Flipbook, described on Activity 12, *Architecture Flipbook*, on page 228.

Here are some things to think about:

- What are the nouns and verbs in the game's description and rules?
- Looking at the names you choose, where do they lie on Belshee's 7 Stages of Naming?
- What questions do you need to answer with your model?
- What elements and relations are in your diagram's legend?

Build Models into the Code

Models allow us to reason about the architecture, but they suffer from a fatal flaw. Most models are a *representation* of the architecture, inherently divorced from the code. Without care, the ideas discussed in our models will never make their way into the code we write. Alas, all our thinking and reasoning about quality attributes is for naught!

Despair not. With some thought, we can build many of our architecture models directly into the code. There are many benefits to building architecture models into the code. When the architecture is self-evident within the code, it's easier to maintain conceptual design integrity and promote desired quality attributes. Building models into the code decreases the chances of architectural drift since models and code move nearly in lock step. We also alleviate the need for some documentation since we've embedded design intent into the software system itself.

Unfortunately, in *Just Enough Software Architecture: A Risk-Driven Approach [Fai10]*, George Fairbanks shows us that it is not possible to directly realize all design concepts from the architecture's conceptual meta-model in code. It is possible to shrink this *model-code gap*, but we can't close it completely.

To shrink the gap between our models and the code, we can use what Fairbanks calls an *architecturally evident coding style*. With this approach, we embed hints about our models, their rules for use, and the rationale behind the design into the code. Doing this lets us close enough of the gap to make our mental models of the architecture come alive in the code we write.

Apply the Vocabulary of the Architecture

Terminology mismatch is a common source of confusion when moving from architectural abstractions to code. The architecture talks about *layers*, *services*, and *filters*, but the code implements *packages*, *classes*, and *methods*. The simplest way to embed a model is to use the vocabulary of the architecture.

If we're using layers, then let's call our code packages layers. If we've adopted a pipe-and-filter pattern, our classes should be named *pipes* and *filters*. If we talk about *pilots* and *navigators* in our system metaphors, then we should use these words as names for types and instances.

Embedding the domain model into the code is another way to shrink the gap between models and code. Modeling code after domain concepts is a common practice in object-oriented programming. Many frameworks, including object-relational mappers and actor-based systems, assume (or at least strongly encourage) a domain model as part of the implementation. Modeling the domain in this way is a core tenet of domain-driven design and several other design methodologies. Similarly, event-based and reactive patterns lean heavily on insights derived from event models derived from domain workflows.

Organize Code to Make Patterns Obvious

Good naming is just the beginning. How we organize the code dramatically affects architectural structures in code. A compiler will happily build your Java application whether every class is in the same file or classes are logically organized around thematic packages. The following example shows how to organize layers into their own code packages:

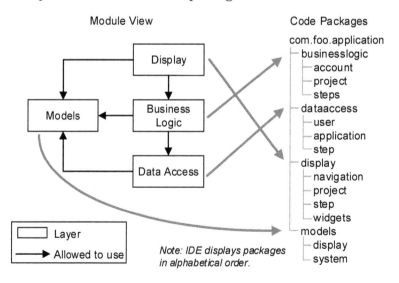

There are other ways to organize this code. Instead of using traditional layers, we could have created functionality-oriented modules. With this pattern, all classes required to complete a functional area are contained within a single package. Classes external to the functional package would not be able to access the business logic or data access classes.

Organizing code so that it matches the designed module structures should be a standard best practice. Patterns on a whiteboard don't promote quality attributes. The code does. If you can't see the pattern in the built system, then it doesn't exist. If the pattern wasn't implemented, then desired quality attributes can't be satisfied as designed. Simon Brown has done a lot of work in this area and shares several examples in *Software Architecture for Developers [Bro16]*.

Organizing code into packages that correspond to architectural elements is the least we can do. Even better is to enforce the relations so that it becomes virtually impossible to violate the architecture.

Enforce Relations Among Elements

The problem with most architectures is that they rely on discipline and vigilance to maintain conceptual integrity. Instead of relying on discipline alone, look for ways to enforce the architecture in code. It is impossible (or at least *really* difficult) to disobey design decisions enforced by the code.

The degree to which we can enforce the architecture depends on the type of structures we're dealing with, the programming languages, operating environment, and the other technical factors.

Module Structures

Module structures are the simplest to see in the code but often the most difficult to enforce. In most modern programming languages, we can enforce an *allowed to use* relation by limiting access to specific modules. If that fails, it's usually possible to distribute modules as a library with decent documentation.

When we can't enforce relations, we can at least monitor them. Use static analysis tools to identify violations of the *uses*, *allowed to use*, or *requires* relations. In some programming languages, you might use types creatively to render relations among elements visible and easy to monitor.

Component and Connector Structures

One approach to enforcing component and connector models is to design the system to fail fast when the architecture is violated. Design by contract, first defined in *Object-Oriented Software Construction [Mey97]*, is an approach where pre-conditions, post-conditions, and invariants are added to the code and checked at runtime. When a developer violates the contract, the application throws an error and execution ceases. Contracts work at many granularities of abstraction, including objects, services, and processes across threads.

Another common approach to enforcing C&C models is to prevent connections between components that should not be connected. One example is to require authentication between components, a common practice when connecting to a data source from a data access tier.

The swift rise in popularity of microservices architecture is in part due to the fact that the pattern makes domain models visible and enforceable at runtime. Enforcing *allowed to use* relations within module structures can be challenging. Turn those modules into components, and we can enforce interaction rules at runtime.

Allocation Structures

Expressing the intent behind allocation models in the code used to be extremely difficult. It is not possible to describe and enforce allocation models in the code thanks to the rise of technologies and paradigms such as platform-as-a-service, container technologies (for example, Docker), infrastructure as code, and distributed version control systems.

Treating infrastructure as code creates opportunities for static analysis. Automating build and deployment pipelines to take advantage of cloud-based platforms means we can introduce automated architecture checks into the deployment process. Most platform-as-a-service products can test hardware allocation limits. We can also use configuration and automation to enforce hardware scaling and platform provisioning.

Containers are lightweight and disposable compared to physical hardware and traditional virtual machines. With containers, it is possible to adopt simple and easy-to-enforce allocation patterns such as installing one process per container.

Distributed version control combined with web-based tools such as GitHub makes it easy to allocate teams to specific architectural components while maintaining an open, social development culture. Workflows such as *fork and pull* or *upstream repository* limit access without preventing collaboration.

Add Hints as Comments

Code itself can only take our models so far. We might be able to enforce design decisions, but code constructs won't tell us why those decisions were made.

We can infuse some rationale into the code with good naming and an appropriate use of known patterns. For everything else, there are comments.

Descriptive prose within the code can take many forms. Comments that describe rationale are essential, and you should link liberally to existing design documentation. Even exception messages can contain design hints. We can avoid generic errors by briefly explaining the design rationale behind the error. For example, an *UNKOWN* error is less helpful than *ASSUMPTION _VIOLATED: Document ID required for validation.*

Generate Models from Code

Even when models cannot be seen or enforced in the code, sometimes we can automatically generate models of the system we've built. Depending on the programming language, technologies, and patterns, it may be possible to use models to verify compliance and monitor design evolution automatically.

Any modern object-oriented language can generate UML class and package diagrams. Most programming languages have a dependency analysis tool. Use this generated models to analyze module structures.

Component and connector structures are harder to generate automatically. To generate C&C structures, add instrumentation so that runtime models can be observed. Use the recorded data to generate models and perform other architecture compliance analysis. See Activity 33, *Observe Behavior*, on page 295 for further thoughts on this topic.

Project Lionheart: The Story So Far...

Development has started, though things got off to a rocky start. The team chose to go with conventional tiers pattern for the runtime structures and layers for the code, but there are still many decisions to make. Many team members use different words to describe the same elements in the architecture. As a result, our design discussions end with everyone nodding heads in agreement only to learn later that each person took away a different conclusion.

The code is already a wreck. It reflects the team's lack of understanding of the design decisions made so far. The patterns you thought the team selected for the architecture are nowhere to be found within the system.

After realizing the problems, you call an impromptu whiteboard jam (described on page 255) in an attempt to build consensus around the design decisions and extract a common meta-model. During the whiteboard jam, you encourage teammates to describe the system precisely. Eventually, we settle on some good names for the concepts, elements, and relations in the models. After the meeting, you formalize the team's conclusions by capturing the meta-model in our wiki.

Now that we have a common meta-model, it's time to refactor the code so that it matches the models we want. Knowing that pair programming is an excellent opportunity to teach architectural principles, you pair with teammates as you fix structures in the code. Luckily it is still early in the system's life, so the refactoring is straightforward.

As you pair with different teammates, you learn that not everyone agrees with or understands the current architecture. Before we get much further along, you decide it would be wise to explore our architecture options in a collaborative workshop.

Next Up

Models help us manage complexity by providing abstractions that we can use for reasoning and communication. There is a conceptual meta-model behind every model. When we know what that meta-model is, we can use it for analysis and communication, and to help us design the architecture.

In this chapter, you learned where models come from and how to describe them, but that doesn't make it any easier to individuate concepts or identify the rules within a meta-model. In the next chapter, you'll learn how to facilitate a group workshop called a design studio that harnesses the power of the group to explore the design space and arrive at good candidate models.

Host an Architecture Design Studio

In nineteenth-century France, architecture professors collected students' projects in wooden carts so they could be easily transported for grading. Of course, nobody was ready for the professor to take their project when the cart came around, but that didn't stop the professor from taking it anyway. As a result, students followed after the cart, feverishly working *en charrette*, in the cart, to finish their bridges and buildings, attaching bits of balsa wood and twists of wire as the professor wheeled the cart off to pick up the next student's project.

In the twenty-first century, *charrette* is a style of workshop inspired by the idea that more time does not necessarily lead to better designs. Architecture professors in nineteenth-century France knew this, and it's a great lesson still today. The user experience (UX) community popularized the charrette as the *design studio*. A design studio encourages group collaboration and has strict time constraints to help the team see a broad range of ideas in a short time frame.

In this chapter, you're going to learn how to plan and facilitate an architecture design studio. We'll start with an overview of the design studio method. From there you'll learn how to facilitate a design studio. Good facilitation, after all, isn't just good manners—it's good business. We'll wrap up the chapter with some tips and hints to ensure your design studio is a huge success.

Plan an Architecture Design Studio

In an architecture design studio, we take advantage of the group's collective wisdom and experience. During a design studio you'll place a strict time constraint on exploration activities so that the group generates as many different ideas as possible, as quickly as they can. We accomplish this by guiding the group first to explore and then quickly narrow down the field of ideas to a few likely candidates.

A design studio creates buy-in for design decisions and improves team communication by letting everyone have a hand in designing the architecture. We achieve this by keeping the workshop fast, effective, and fun—the *three "Fs"* of design exploration. Fun amplifies engagement, which in turn acts as a force multiplier for the speed and effectiveness of exploration activities.

Our job as a design studio host is to plan a workshop that results in a strong set of actionable ideas. Three types of ideas come out of a design studio:

Ideas for things to make. Some ideas will seem promising. The next step for these ideas is to flesh out details by making models or prototypes.

Ideas that need more research. Some ideas will seem right but consist of broad assumptions or miss important information. Plan to investigate these ideas further by running experiments or performing research. Depending on what you learn during the investigation, some ideas might be scratched whereas others become candidates for the architecture.

Ideas that open new questions. Sometimes you might only end up with new questions about the problem we're solving. This is a fantastic outcome for a design studio workshop. It's better to have these questions now than when we've been heads down coding for a few weeks. Take these questions back to stakeholders to improve our understanding of the problem.

A typical workshop lasts anywhere from a few hours up to a day. It's also possible (and in some cases preferable) to let the spirit of your design studio guide your work over the course of several days. No matter how much time you spend, all design studio workshops follow the same basic structure.

Architecture Design Studio Stages

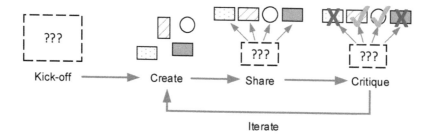

1. *Prepare*—Do research to understand the problem you're going to explore.

2. *Kick-off*—Describe the workshop goals and problem context to the group.

3. *Create*—Make models, draw sketches, and build prototypes. Usually a time-boxed activity.

4. *Share*—Present what you've created to the group and describe specifically how your design achieves the goals.

5. *Critique*—The group provides feedback about what you shared relative to how well they think the design satisfies the goals.

6. *Iterate*—Repeat steps 3–5, refining your models and creating new ones. Plan to iterate at least three times for each set of goals you are exploring.

7. *Follow-up*—Decide on next steps for the most promising ideas, risks, or questions.

Let's take a closer look at each stage of the workshop.

Before the Workshop: Prepare

Before kicking off a design studio workshop, we'll need to choose goals and decide who to invite (see *Invite the Right Participants*, on page 120). Gathering a group to design architecture is not a good use of anyone's time until you at least partially understand the problem you'll to explore.

Preparing for a workshop can take serious time and should not be underestimated. Talk to stakeholders. Do your research. Work to define the business goals. Refine quality attributes and other architecturally significant requirements (ASRs). Before starting the workshop, you should understand enough of the problem and context so that you can articulate useful workshop goals.

Define one or two workshop goals that clearly describe what the group will explore during the workshop. You don't want one person designing a database while someone else is working on deadlock problems. It's OK if you only partially understand the problem before starting the workshop. Exploring solutions is one way to gain a deeper understanding of the problem.

Workshop goals tell participants how they will spend their brainpower during the workshop. There are a few examples in the table on page 116.

Preparing for the workshop might take a few days or even weeks. You should at least have draft business goals and architecturally significant requirements before starting. Once you have a handle on the project context and a reasonable workshop goal, you're ready to run the workshop.

If your goal is to explore...	You might say...
A specific set of quality attributes	"Scalability and reliability are our top two quality attributes. How can we promote these at the same time?" (You'll share the specific scenarios with everyone.)
Interfaces between components	"We've decided to use REST for our APIs. Let's figure out what that really means for our system." (Assumes everyone knows what is involved with RESTful architecture)
Domain models	"Based on our stakeholders' business, we need to define some common abstractions that we'll use throughout the system."
How to get out of a jam	"We're seeing a size and scale of data we didn't anticipate ten years ago when we first designed the system. Let's figure out as many options as we can."
Allocation structures	"We need to partition the system so we maximize parallel development effort."
Pattern selection	"We need to decide how we're going to get data from point A to point B. Before we go into pros and cons, let's understand the options."
Many different ideas	"Today we want to see as many different ideas as possible. Everyone should try for at least 5 ideas."

Kick Off the Workshop

Start the workshop by setting the stage for a successful collaboration. Make sure everyone has the proper context by sharing what you know so far about the problem and the architecture. Review anything relevant to the area you plan to explore. The amount of workshop time devoted to sharing context should be commensurate with the group's background knowledge. If this is the first time some people have seen business goals or ASRs, spend more time describing the context.

After reviewing the context, outline the workshop goals. These goals are used throughout the workshop and keep the group focused. During the workshop, everyone will create designs to satisfy the goals. We'll also critique design ideas with these goals in mind.

Iterate through the Create-Share-Critique Cycle

We'll spend most of the workshop in the create-share-critique cycle.[1,2] Each iteration through the cycle explores more of the design space and improves the group's understanding of what is possible. We'll talk about specific activities we can plug into this cycle in *Choose Appropriate Design Activities*, on page 119.

Create

During the create step, participants work alone or in small groups to address workshop goals by sketching and modeling their design ideas. Keeping it analog works best during a workshop. Using pens or fat markers and paper encourages people to focus on ideas rather than precision. At this stage of the game, you value ideas, not perfection.

The create step is always time boxed. Short workshops might spend only 5–7 minutes in the create step. Longer workshops can allow for more time. Keep in mind that more time does not always lead to more or better ideas! Architecture exploration requires deep thought, so adjust time relative to your goals. Anything less than 5 minutes is not enough time for most software architecture topics.

Share

After everyone has created something, it's time to share it with the larger group. This step is sometimes called *pitch*, as in *make a pitch* for your idea. Give each group 3–5 minutes to share what they created and describe how their design satisfies the goal. Groups should hit only the main points and avoid giving a full briefing. Participants will learn quickly not to create more than they can share.

During the share step, workshop participants listen and may not ask questions. Everyone will have a chance to ask questions and share comments during the critique step.

Critique

Immediately after a group shares their design, give the other participants an opportunity to critique the ideas. Feedback during the critique should focus on the merits of the design relative to the workshop's goals. The idea is to lay the foundation for a constructive dialogue. How does the design fall short of satisfying a goal? Why does the design not meet the specified need?

---

1. https://vimeo.com/37861987
2. http://www.madpow.com/~/media/files/designstudio-webinar.ashx

During the critiques, encourage everyone to be specific and focus on facts.

Do this	Avoid this
Do: Focus on the goals the designers said they addressed.	Don't: Get defensive about your design.
Do: Be specific; focus on facts.	Don't: Share personal opinions—"I like XYZ, it's my favorite."
Do: Ask clarifying questions.	Don't: Get sidetracked by problem solving.
Do: Point out risks and new problems introduced by the design.	Don't: Be a jerk (your turn is next!).
Do: Point out benefits about the design.	Don't: Focus only on downsides.

Critiques should point out good things about a design as well as things that can be improved. Even terrible designs have a few good ideas, and there is always room for improvement even in the best designs. Every design should receive a mix of positive feedback and constructive criticism. Once all groups have shared their ideas, do it all over again.

Iterate

The purpose of the create-share-critique cycle is to promote rapid divergence and convergence of thinking as described in *Diverge to See Options, Converge to Decide*, on page 63. During the create step, we generate new ideas. During the share step, we create opportunities for cross-pollination and serendipitous inspiration. During the critique step, we eliminate dead ends and nudge people toward better (or at least different) solutions.

Iteration allows participants to build on what they collectively learn. Move through the create, share, and critique steps as quickly as you can while remaining effective.

With each iteration, tweak the group dynamics. Tweaking group dynamics between iterations encourages broader exploration while simultaneously building a sense of shared ownership. If participants are working alone, have them work in pairs or small groups. If they are working in groups, try mixing up the groups. Plan for at least three iterations of the full create-share-critique cycle for each set of goals in the workshop.

Close the Design Studio and Decide on Follow-up Actions

A strong finish can mean all the difference between a productive workshop and a fun waste of time. Allow time at the end of the workshop to reflect on emergent themes and discuss general observations as a group. Also, decide on specific action items. Which ideas seem promising and should receive more attention? Were any significant risks raised that should be addressed? Are there any experiments that should be started?

Take pictures of all the material produced during the workshop. Create write-ups in a shared repository while the ideas are still fresh in everyone's minds. Most importantly, record the action items and follow up with individuals to make sure they take the next steps.

Choose Appropriate Design Activities

As the design studio host, we're responsible for choosing activities that guide everyone through the create-share-critique steps in a fast, effective, and fun way. There are many design activities we could use, though not all design activities are appropriate for architecture design. Try to select activities that are architecturally focused and effective when thinking about the system as a whole.

Here is an example workshop agenda based on the round-robin design activity. The workshop itself might run anywhere from 90 minutes if we're only exploring initial ideas to a whole day if we're well prepared and plan to explore multiple parts of the system deeply.

Activity	Timing	Purpose
Introduce the context and goals	15 minutes	Arm everyone with the knowledge they'll need to be an active, contributing participant in the workshop.
Round-robin design activity, described on page 252	30 minutes	Promotes rapid divergence and convergence to get the workshop rolling. This agenda plans for only one round, but you could do more with more time.
Group Poster Activity, described on page 249	30 minutes	Summarize findings as posters so they can be shared more easily among the group. Start building consensus.
Present and critique posters	15 minutes	Allow about 3 minutes per poster for presentations. Use dot voting for the critiques.
Reflect and review action items	10 minutes	Review how the workshop went and define next steps to ensure strong follow-up. Allow about 10% of the workshop time for this.

To customize the workshop, use different exploration activities. Instead of a round-robin design, try a whiteboard jam, described on page 255. If your aim is to arrive at a better system metaphor, try telling stories by pretending the architecture has human qualities, outlined on page 226. The activities you choose for the design studio should help you achieve your goals.

Get Your Hands Dirty: Sketching Practice

During a design studio, we ask participants to sketch quickly and share big ideas under extreme time pressure. Sketching and sharing can be difficult if you haven't practiced. Practice sketching architectures so you are well prepared to help participants who freeze up during a workshop.

Here are some things to think about:

- How many different ways can you draw a line? An arrow? What meaning might the different lines and arrows convey?

- Try to draw the most precise architecture diagram you can. Now draw the same views and see how much precision you can remove without creating ambiguity.

- Draw as many different types of people as you can. Find a style that works for you.

- Try filling a whole page with shapes, arrows, people, and doodles.

- For real practice, purchase a pocket notebook and fill it with sketches.

Invite the Right Participants

With any group exercise, the quality of the workshop is determined by the participants. Too many people in a workshop makes for an expensive meeting. The wrong people in a workshop can limit how wide you explore and might even bump constructive discussions off course. As the host, you need to balance two variables: size and diversity.

Right-Size the Workshop

Effective collaboration breaks down in groups larger than about seven people. Large groups are difficult to manage, require more time for communication, and are impossible to coordinate for scheduling. One way to manage a large group is by dividing it into smaller ones. Even then, a single facilitator can realistically handle only three or four subgroups at a time.

Depending on what you want to achieve and whether you have a co-facilitator available, limit the size of an architecture design studio to about ten people. As a rule of thumb, work with the smallest group that can still effectively explore. If you need to pair with only one other person to work through an idea, then work with just that one person. A group of about 3–5 people seems to be a good sweet spot for many software architecture design tasks.

Invite a Diverse Audience

The ideal architecture design studio always includes at least one person who can offer a dissenting opinion or who brings a different perspective. Including someone with a different background or a fresh perspective creates greater opportunities for eureka moments.

Start by inviting essential stakeholders. Also include someone who knows little about your particular problem and can attack it from a different perspective. If your team is programmer heavy, invite a tester or product manager. If you are all systems developers, invite someone knowledgeable in front-end development. Bring in people who are good at asking questions or thinking about complex ideas. Ensure you have a range of experience across a variety of topic areas.

Everyone has a unique perspective. These differences can help the group explore further and wider than if everyone thought the same about the design.

Harness the Power of Groups Wisely

While all design is social, this does not mean all design must be done in groups. Group collaboration does have a potential dark side. *Groupthink* is a phenomenon where the group loses its individuality and worries more about harmony and consensus than satisfying the goals of the workshop. When a workshop falls into groupthink, the decisions they make will be suboptimal and sometimes even be harmful.

Seasoned basketball coaches can tell how well their team is doing by listening to the squeaks players' shoes make on the court. Likewise, a healthy design studio workshop has an unmistakable *hummm* of collaborative brainstorming. There are some specific things to listen for to determine if your group is collaborating well in the table on page 122.

Proactive facilitation is our best tool for effectively harnessing the power of the group. Look out for the silent majority who seem to just go with the flow. Discussions lacking in disagreement may seem like positive progress but is

If the group...	It might mean...
Asks questions to clarify meaning, politely challenges ideas, and discusses implications of an idea	Everyone is collaborating well
Goes along with whatever seems to be the prevailing idea; hesitates to share their thoughts	Potential fear of conflict or lack of confidence in collaborating
Does not share a wide range of ideas; acts as an echo chamber; comes back to the same themes	The group didn't diverge their thinking widely enough
Always lets the same people do the talking	Not everyone understands the discussion; dominant personalities are overwhelming quieter individuals

more likely to be the opposite. Conflict defines the boundaries of exploration and highlights important concepts.

Manage the Group

Facilitation is more than just making an agenda and keeping time. Facilitation is an active role. How you share an activity has significant influence over how participants approach it. How you interact with participants can alter their behavior in the workshop. It's the facilitator's responsibility to keep the design studio moving and ensure the workshop produces useful outcomes.

Allow Enough Time for the Workshop

Running out of time or rushing through activities can undermine the workshop goals and decrease participants' confidence in the findings. You want to see a broad range of ideas in a short amount of time so that you can cheat bounded rationality (see *Find a Design That Satisfices*, on page 27).

It might be possible to complete a rapid exploration workshop with only one or two goals in an hour or two. Such workshops are ideal for exploring a small number of narrow goals or for building consensus when the group understands the high-level solution but needs to explore details.

A design studio with many goals might need one or two full days to complete. When the problem is not well understood, plan on having many smaller sessions over the course of several weeks. Remember that not every problem can be explored collaboratively in a workshop setting.

Set Expectations from the Start

Great workshops have some degree of mystery but also let participants know up front what they'll be doing and why you're here. State the workshop goals up front and ensure the group is on board before starting.

Start a workshop by sharing the general workshop agenda. It's not necessary to share every detail. Some details we'll want to keep secret to prevent participants from getting confused or "pre-fetching" designs. For workshops running more than a few hours, share estimated start times for agenda items so participants can self-select in or out of specific activities. This way participants will be present at the workshop and deal with distractions at times that won't disrupt the workshop.

Set ground rules at the start of the workshop. Here are some examples of ground rules:

Sample Workshop Ground Rules	
Everyone participates	When time is up, we move on
No "right" or "wrong" answers	Ask questions if you need help
Watch the clock (I'll help too)	Have fun (seriously) ☺

Introduce Activities with the Tell-Show-Tell Approach

When introducing a new activity to the group, always tell participants what they'll do, show them an example of what it looks like, then review the instructions you just gave them. Most people will miss important details the first time they see something new. Reviewing instructions after seeing a concrete example gives participants a second chance to ask questions about the activity.

It's best to use examples from previous workshops. When examples don't exist, create a mock-up by staging a picture of the activity or approximating an example.

Share Tips for Activities

Inevitably when you say *Go!*, someone will freeze up. For many participants, this workshop could be their first time working collaboratively like this.

To help participants get started, share tips for each activity. A simple reminder or nugget of advice is an excellent way to help participants avoid blank page syndrome. Keep an eye out for groups or individuals staring at a blank page—they may need help getting started.

Set Deadlines

All activities in the architecture design studio are time boxed. Set realistic but aggressive time constraints to keep things moving. Participants should feel rushed but somehow manage to finish the activities just in time. Ideally, every activity is a buzzer beater with groups putting finishing touches on their sketches as you call *Time's up!*

Educate Participants Just-in-Time

Unless you've collaborated with all the participants in your workshop before, set aside some time to teach people critical software architecture and design concepts just-in-time during the workshop. The goal with just-in-time education is to ensure participants have just enough information to be successful in the particular design activity you're doing. A quick review of important architectural concepts or an introduction to quality attribute scenarios might be all that's required.

Participation is essential to a workshop's success. It's why you gathered a group in the first place! Ensure participants have the knowledge they need to participate effectively.

Use Parking Lots

Design is a journey that often takes a winding road to reach a destination. During a design studio, you may happen upon interesting ideas and useful discussions that you don't have time to explore at that exact moment. Keep a running list, a parking lot, of discussion points to be visited at the end of the workshop. Using parking lots keeps the workshop moving and assures interested parties there will be time to discuss topics that interest them.

Work with Remote Teams

It's not always practical to gather a group of people for a design workshop. Luckily, design studios and other collaboration-focused workshops work great for remote teams. Here are a few tips for facilitating a remote workshop. These tips apply to any of the activities discussed here as well as the activities described in Part III.

Use remote collaboration tools. This is an absolute prerequisite. Find a combination of remote collaboration tools that allow your group to work together and share the fruits of your exploration. Depending on the specific activities in the workshop, you will need tools that allow screen sharing, collaborative document editing, collaborative drawing, brainstorming, group chat, and voice communication. Many tools are available on the web for each of these options.

Add time to the agenda. Distributed groups need more time to complete collaborative design activities. Remote meetings always experience technical problems. Plan ahead and you won't be surprised.

Create breakout opportunities. Only one person can talk on the phone at a ftime. When only one person can speak at a time, group work becomes nearly impossible. Create a back channel for communication using group chat software. If group work is part of the workshop, decide which teleconference phone numbers they'll use and set clear deadlines for when the large group should reconvene.

Provide a focal point. It's easy to get distracted in a remote meeting. Facilitators don't have the ability to sketch notes on a whiteboard—only the people in the room with you will see it. Prepare presentation material that participants can use on their own or share your screen. Invite everyone to contribute to a shared document during group discussions to keep everyone engaged.

Make it face-to-face. Nothing beats face-to-face interaction. When possible, use video conferencing software that allows participants to see one another for at least parts of the workshop.

Take it off line. Workshops aren't the only way to explore ideas. You can run many design activities in *slow motion*, over the course of several days. For example, a round-robin-like activity can be accomplished via email just as effectively as in person.

Here's an example of what a remote architecture design studio looks like. Marie, our facilitator, arrived early, started her screen sharing software, and dialed into the meeting's teleconference number. Once all participants were dialed in, Marie kicked off the meeting by presenting slides containing the workshop's agenda and goals. Marie would usually write these things on a whiteboard, but she wanted all participants to be able to see them.

The team was doing a round-robin design activity. Marie instructed participants to sketch a view of the architecture and take a picture with their phone to share it. Each participant shared their sketch via a Slack private message. For the second round, participants annotated the picture they were assigned using drawing software, took a screen shot of it, and added the original and annotated images to a shared Box.com folder.

After some brief discussion about the sketches, Marie divided participants into groups. Each group used Google Hangouts and shared Box.com documents to create a presentation with their ideas for the architecture. At the requested time, everyone rejoined the workshop teleconference to share their presentations. During the critiques, Marie and other participants took notes together in a shared document. Instead of a rapid-fire 90-minute workshop, the design studio ended almost on time after a little more than two hours.

Project Lionheart: The Story So Far…

The team is at a crossroad. Some team members feel we should use a service-oriented approach using microservices. Others feel we should play it safe and stick with a tried-and-true multi-tier pattern. You need to resolve the conflict and create buy-in for the design decision. Since either pattern would probably work out fine, you host a design studio to help the team decide.

Your goal for the workshop is to explore the nuances of each pattern and flush risks into the open for the team to discuss. You start the workshop with small-group exercises to generate ideas. The microservices and multi-tiered patterns come up, but a few other interesting and unexpected ideas are raised as well.

After the initial round of presentations and critiques, you have us create group posters. Unexpectedly, as the team works through the different ideas, microservices fall completely out of favor! By the end of the two-hour workshop, the team explored a half dozen design options and arrive at a great solution. More importantly, everyone had a say in the final decision and there seems to be a genuine sense of shared ownership among the team that didn't exist before the workshop.

Next Up

A design studio is a fantastic method for quickly exploring ideas. Perhaps even more important is the journey your team takes to arrive at a decision. Everyone who participates has a stake in the design they helped create. A sense of shared ownership encourages greater autonomy and a sense of responsibility. This shared ownership permeates all aspects of design from code to architecture.

Collaborative design workshops are a powerful tool, but as we've seen so far, there is more to architecture design than group work and sticky notes. A design studio alone is not sufficient for designing an amazing architecture.

Its effectiveness depends greatly on the context in which it's used. We still need to think and do the work.

So far you've learned how to define the problem in a way that aides architecture design, how to explore design concepts, how to create models, and how to make design decisions. In the next chapter, you'll learn how to visualize design ideas so you can share them with your stakeholders and team.

CHAPTER 10

Visualize Design Decisions

The best way to share an idea is to make it tangible. Tell me about your architecture and I may not understand you. Show me your architecture, and I can explore it at my own pace, using my preferred cognitive style. Developers intuitively know this. Need to talk about an abstract idea? Find a whiteboard and start sketching. If we can draw the idea we're trying to share, then we'll know our imaginations are in sync.

Anyone can draw. Architecture diagrams don't need to be pretty, but they do need to share ideas effectively. In Chapter 8, *Manage Complexity*, on page 99 you learned how to create accurate models so you can reason about how well the architecture promotes desired quality attributes. In this chapter, you will learn how to draw architecture diagrams to enhance communication among developers.

Show the Architecture from Different Views

It's impossible to capture every interesting detail about the architecture in a single picture. Instead of trying to put everything into a single diagram, we'll create multiple views of the architecture. A *view* is a story about the architecture told from the perspective of a particular stakeholder or set of related concerns.

Think about how we use a mapping application like Google Maps to plan a road trip. Zoom in and we can see city streets. Zoom out and whole cities become just dots along interstate highways. Apply an overlay and we can see real-time traffic or weather. We can even swap maps of streets for satellite images or topography. Some applications offer street-level perspectives, which allow us to see the world at eye level from a snapshot in time.

We can use these different views of the world in our mapping application to plan a road trip. What's the best route from Pittsburgh to Albuquerque? How do we avoid that thunderstorm? Where is a good place to eat chicken chow mien along our route?

Just like a map, each view of the architecture helps stakeholders answer questions about the system. How is development progressing? Who is working on which components? How will we support our quality attribute scenarios?

There isn't a fixed set of views for every software system, but there are several views that are useful for most software systems. Let's explore some of these useful views in more detail.

Tell Us What Elements Do with an Element-Responsibility View

Lines and boxes are the architect's most used tool and her least trustworthy companion. Box and line diagrams make complex relationships among elements easy to see, but their architectural meaning is never self-evident. Recall this overview diagram of the Project Lionheart services:

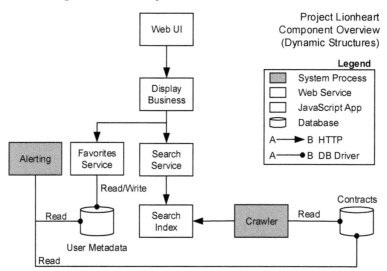

This diagram is missing vital information. We know every element serves a specific purpose, but a picture alone is not a view. The element-responsibility catalog shown on page 73 for this diagram fills in the missing pieces. Depending on the information we need to share, we can express responsibilities as diagram annotations, in a table, or as descriptive prose.

Element-responsibility views are extremely common. In some cases, this might be the only view you need. If you can list the elements and their responsibilities, then you stand a chance of building a working system.

Zoom In or Out with a Refinement View

I always love that scene in a television crime show when the hero cracks the case by enhancing a blurry image. *I can't see his face. Zoom in. Enhance!* The cool thing about software, unlike blurry images, is that we actually can zoom in and enhance nearly infinitely.

Refinement is the process of increasing detail in a model over a series of views. It's like zooming in on a structure to show the elements' inner workings, enhancing, and then zooming in again.

Let's zoom into the Lionheart Display Business component to take a closer look at some of its static structures.

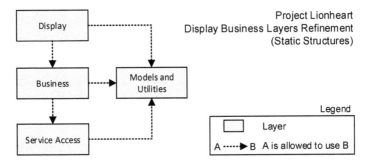

At one level of refinement, we can see the Display Business component uses a typical layered pattern: one layer for display, business, and service access logic, with a sidecar layer to organize data models and utility classes. This diagram establishes context, but we might learn more about maintainability if we refine further.

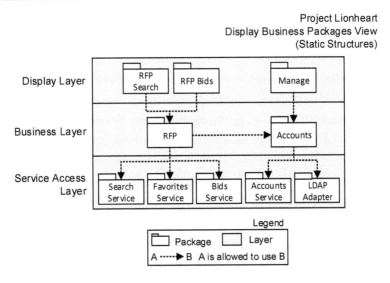

In this refinement, we show packages inside the layers and how they interact with one another so we can reason about maintainability quality attribute scenarios. Looking at this refinement, it's clear that the *RFP Package* might be too interconnected, which makes testing and debugging difficult.

Notice that the *Models and Utilities Layer* is not shown in this refinement. Everything is *allowed to use* classes in the *Models and Utilities Layer*. Including all the relations would make the diagram too cluttered for analysis, so we eliminated some relations from this view. Slicing and dicing views is useful but can make the architecture models harder to understand.

Refinement views help us focus on the details needed to answer specific questions about the architecture. Coarse-grained refinements provide a big picture view of the world. After we've established the context, we can show finer-grained refinements by zooming in to show important details needed by specific stakeholders.

Use the principles of architecture minimalism described in *Preserve Ambiguity*, on page 16 to decide when to stop refining a model. Only refine to a level of detail necessary to demonstrate specific quality attributes and reduce high-priority risks.

Show How the Architecture Promotes Quality Attributes

A *quality attribute view* demonstrates how the architecture achieves specific quality attributes. Quality attribute views might hide details not relevant to the current discussion, or highlight details relevant only to the given quality attribute. For example, consider this availability scenario for Project Lionheart from the table on page 54.

> A user searches for open RFPs and receives a list of available RFPs 99% of the time on average over the course of the year.

To satisfy this quality attribute, we introduced a redundancy pattern. Let's create a view as shown in the figure on page 133.

Promoting availability means our Lionheart services must be resilient in the face of failures. To accomplish this, we'll need multiple instances of the *Display Business*, *Search Service*, and *Search Index* components. Since the *Display Business* and *Search Service* components are stateless microservices, we can easily deploy multiple instances in any container management system such as Kubernetes[1] or Marathon.[2]

---

1. http://kubernetes.io/
2. https://mesosphere.github.io/marathon/

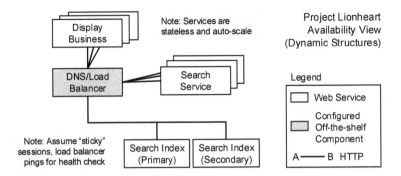

The *Search Index* is stateful and a potential performance bottleneck for our system, so we'll need to be more careful about data storage. We'll also need to think through routing when there is a fault to avoid downtime and data partitioning. To keep things simple, we'll use a load balancer and Domain Name System (DNS) to route requests.

Let's use the diagram to determine whether we satisfied the quality attribute scenario. Pretend one of the *Search Index* components fail. The load balancer detects the failure with a health check and routes requests to the secondary *Search Index*. So far, so good.

This view is moving in a good direction but needs more work. How often does the health check occur? What are the requirements for a ping? What happens if the load balancer goes down? What happens when a failed *Search Index* comes back online? These questions and more should be described in explanatory prose accompanying this diagram. One diagram might not be enough to thoroughly explain how the architecture satisfies our availability scenario.

Connect Elements from Different Views

With many views in play, it's useful to see how elements in different views are related to one another. A *mapping view* serves just this purpose by combining two or more views into a new view that shows how the elements are related.

Two useful mapping views are *work assignment* and *deployment*. In a work assignment view, we show who works on different parts of the system by mapping teams with the elements they'll build. Deployment views show where runtime elements from a component and connector view will be installed and used.

Here's an example of a work assignment view for Project Lionheart:

Component	Team Assigned	Notes
Web UI	Honey Badgers	Team consists of front-end web development pros
Display Business	Honey Badgers	Component is tightly coupled with Web UI
Search Service	Red Shirts	
Search Index	Red Shirts	Team of experienced Solr developers
Favorites Service	Honey Badgers	Team has capacity; component directly impacts user experience
Alerting	Open/Unstaffed	First team available
Crawler	Red Shirts	Team has expertise
DNS/Load Balancer	Tron	Infrastructure experts
User metadata and contracts databases	City of Springfield	They own the databases

Notice that this view is not a diagram. Our objective is to communicate design decisions by any means necessary. Sometimes a simple table is all that's needed to get the job done.

Mappings create connections between stakeholders with different concerns. This work assignment view is perfect for a project manager who needs to create a schedule or staffing plan.

Mapping views provide a layer of context that can be difficult for stakeholders to piece together on their own. Consider a product manager's needs. Maybe they want to know when certain features will be ready to ship. A mapping between architectural components and value-adding features would help everyone understand which parts of the software support different features. This tiny smidge of knowledge enables team self-organization and helps developers prioritize work with the product manager's needs in mind. Now you're empathizing with stakeholders!

Let Ideas Breathe with a Cartoon

All the views we've seen so far have been rather precise. Precision has a cost. Precise models require exacting details and are time-consuming to create. Sometimes precision gets in the way of communication, especially when you're exploring ideas. As we're getting to know the system, it's sometimes useful to create accurate models with less precision.

An *architecture cartoon* is a fast-to-create, imprecise model that favors communication over analysis. Use cartoons for rapid iteration and informal communication. They are perfect for exploration workshops and impromptu discussions.

Cartoons capture the essence of the idea you want to share. Here is a cartoon of a horse and an anatomically precise diagram of a horse. A horse has four legs, a bushy tail, and a mane. A more precise drawing might help if we need details about the musculature or anatomy. But if we just need a placeholder for a horse, then my cartoon works fine.

A Horse! drawn by M. Keeling,
Sharpie on recycled printer paper, 2017

From 1. Arabian Horse. 2. Zebra. 3. Ass engraved by T. Dixon, published in An History of the Earth and Animated Nature by Oliver Goldsmith, 1822

Architecture cartoons use simple notations and ignore many of the best practices we'll discuss throughout this chapter. Using loose notations is OK, especially while you're working through an idea. Once design decisions start to converge, then it's time to create a more precise model.

Bringing this back to architecture, here's a cartoon of the Project Lionheart Overview. Compare it with the more precise views we've seen so far.

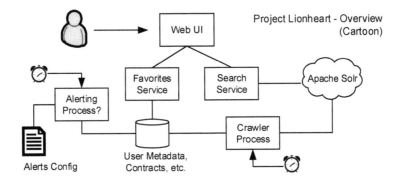

Create Custom Views to Show Exactly What You Need

Any view of the architecture that helps you effectively tell a story about the system to stakeholders is a view worth having. Get creative and make custom views for your particular purpose.

Views always combine multiple variables. Elements and responsibilities. Quality attributes and patterns. Elements and project schedules. Inventing a new view can be as simple as combining new variables with architectural elements. Need to show performance bottlenecks in the system? Start with a component diagram that shows information flow, color-code components based on execution time, and voilà, we've created a performance view.

Remember, all views, even custom views, are governed by an underlying meta-model as discussed in *Design the Meta-Model*, on page 101.

Draw Fantastic Diagrams

Great diagrams are not just beautiful pictures. Great diagrams are accurate models that reflect the conceptual underpinnings of the architecture. Architects may be infamous for drawing box and line diagrams, but there's more going on in these diagrams than just coarse-grained abstractions.

As you learned in *Show the Architecture from Different Views*, on page 129, you can show many different design ideas with diagrams. Visualizing the architecture with a diagram makes it tangible in a way that other mediums cannot. Fantastic diagrams make the architecture accessible to everyone.

Here are some tips for creating fantastic diagrams:

Do this	Avoid this
Do: Create a legend that summarizes parts of the meta-model relevant to this diagram.	Don't: Assume your readers know your notations (even with the UML).
Do: Add a descriptive title and tell what kinds of structures are in the diagram.	Don't: Try to include everything in a single diagram.
Do: Add text annotations to enhance clarity.	Don't: Use notations that lose meaning when printed in black and white.
Do: Use a consistent notation across all diagrams.	Don't: Go overboard with superfluous flourishes or an excessive variety of shapes and lines.
Do: Make the patterns visible.	Don't: Skip descriptive prose.

Let's explore these tips in more detail.

Use the Legend, Don't Just Include a Legend

What do the symbols in this diagram represent?

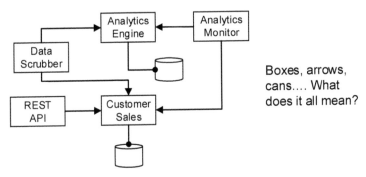

Boxes, arrows, cans…. What does it all mean?

Without a legend, it is impossible for us to know what's happening. Here is the same diagram, this time with a legend:

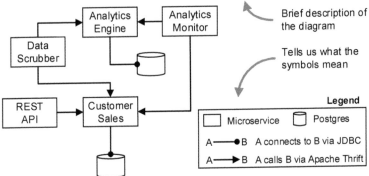

We can see immediately that we're dealing with fine-grained web services and that the communication mechanism relies on Apache Thrift.[3] Downstream designers responsible for implementing a component in this architecture will want to know these details. Other stakeholders can use this information as the basis for further conversations.

The legend introduces the architecture's conceptual meta-model (introduced on page 101) to our audience. Draw the legend first and use it to keep our diagrams consistent with reality and turn them into tools for analysis.

Now that we have a common understanding of the meta-model, we start to notice mistakes and have questions about the diagram. Should the *Analytics*

---

3. http://thrift.apache.org/

Monitor and *Data Scrubber* be microservices? What if I told you the *Analytics Engine* service provided a REST interface and not Thrift? Is this a mistake, gap in knowledge, or plan for the future?

No matter what notation you use, every diagram should have a legend. This advice applies to standardized notations such as the UML as well as custom notations. Not everyone who sees our diagram will be familiar with the dialect of UML you use. Legends enhance meaning.

Highlight the Patterns

The previous diagram is hiding a secret. Look what happens if we move some of the components around. Notice that we only changed the elements' positions.

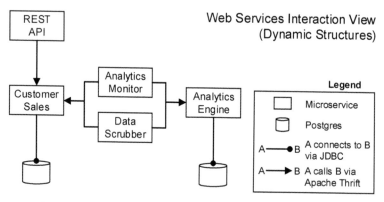

Rearranging the services reveals that services in this architecture are allocated using a multi-tier pattern! This rearrangement might seem inconsequential, but making the patterns visible communicates the intent behind the architecture to downstream designers. For example, knowing this is a multi-tier pattern, I would not expect the *REST API* to communicate directly with a database from the *Data Tier*.

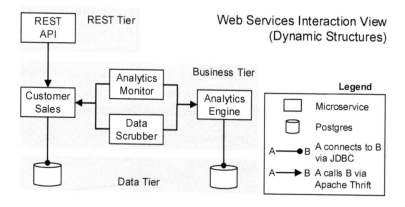

Simon says:
Keep It Simple and Complete

By Simon Brown, independent consultant and author of Software Architecture for Developers [Bro16]

Having run diagramming workshops for more than 10,000 people around the world, I can say with some confidence that software developers struggle to communicate software architecture using diagrams. Many of the diagrams I see focus on the decomposition of software into logical building blocks, although they usually do this at the expense of information about technology. After all, we've been taught to keep the "logical view" of a software system separate from the "development view." Unfortunately, this tends to result in a collection of diagrams that make little sense when viewed individually, with neither diagram providing an accurate reflection of the code.

One solution is to merge the logical and development views of a software system, treating the combined diagrams as a collection of zoomable maps on top of a code base. This is the concept at the core of my *C4 model*—a collection of diagrams that show varying levels of abstraction. A *System Context diagram* shows your software system and how it fits into the environment around it, in terms of users and other software systems. A *Container diagram* zooms into your system boundary to show how it's made up of containers (applications and data stores). A *Component diagram* zooms in to a particular container to show the components inside it. Optionally, a UML class diagram zooms into a particular component to show the code-level elements it's built from.

Although UML is still useful, I prefer a simple *boxes and lines* notation to describe software architecture. To avoid confusion, my advice is to keep the notation as simple and self-describing as possible, adding a key/legend where necessary. Finally, adding more text to boxes is a great way to add information about responsibilities, providing a nice, at-a-glance view and removing ambiguity from what is usually just a collection of named boxes.

We want the patterns to be visible in the diagrams we draw. We can accomplish this in a variety of ways. Choose names that reflect the pattern. Create views that highlight the patterns we've selected. Arrange the elements so you can *see* the pattern. Above all, use patterns as part of your vocabulary for sharing designs.

Strive for Consistency and Simplicity

Every drop of ink in our diagrams means something. Color, shape, orientation, font choice, and position convey meaning. Avoid superfluous details to help readers focus on the ideas you want to share. Choose different colors or shapes to highlight different ideas, not simply to make the diagram look pretty.

When sharing ideas, consistency is king. If an idea from the conceptual meta-model is present in two different diagrams, use the same shapes and colors to represent it. Readers will find meaning behind every change in color and font, even if you didn't mean anything by it.

Likewise, too many details will overwhelm and confuse readers. Sometimes we'll need multiple arrow heads to express an idea. Other times, too many arrows obfuscate meaning. Work to create the simplest diagrams as possible that still provide meaning.

Provide Descriptive Prose

The stories that accompany the picture are the most interesting part of a view. The story explains how elements in the view come together to promote or inhibit quality attributes and why we designed the system the way we did. Sometimes the diagram is the least interesting part of a view. All the action is in the story!

We'll use *descriptive prose* to tell the stories about our architecture. Descriptive prose can be a simple table, paragraphs of text, bullet points, or even a verbal narrative. Think of diagrams as visual aides for stories about the architecture: where the architecture came from, how it works, where it's going.

In Chapter 11, *Describe the Architecture*, on page 143 you will learn how to share the stories that accompany views. Diagrams are a vehicle for communicating design decisions and context, but diagrams can't speak for themselves. It's up to you to provide the story.

Get Your Hands Dirty: Critique Some Diagrams

Find some diagrams from a recent software system you helped build. Knowing what you know now about how to visualize the architecture, what would you change about these diagrams? If this project is still in progress, try to improve the view and share it with your team.

Here are some things to think about:

- What does the diagram help you to reason about?

- What are the essential patterns in the diagram? Are there hidden patterns?

- What is the underlying meta-model? Can it be discerned from the diagram alone?

- Is the diagram complete? Could it be simplified and still be effective?

Joe asks:

Should I Use an Architecture Description Language?

We're not going to cover formal Architecture Description Languages (ADLs) in this book, but you should be aware that such a thing exists. Most architects use simple drawing tools such as PowerPoint, Visio, and Graphviz for day-to-day work. Some people even use pencil, paper, and a phone camera to great effect.

Simple diagramming tools are easy to use and produce shareable diagrams, but pictures don't easily facilitate in-depth analysis. ADLs solve this problem by restricting and enforcing the vocabulary used to specify models. ADLs are usually implemented in tools, which can run automated checks against the models. Some ADLs can even generate or reverse-engineer code.

ADLs sound awesome but in practice don't always make life easier. The ADL you select will limit expressiveness of the design. Software tools that support ADLs will often save models in proprietary formats. In my experience, most tools are immature and have a steep learning curve.

My advice is to use an ADL only if you really, really want to use one. You can peruse an up-to-date list of ADLs at http://www.di.univaq.it/malavolta/al/.

Project Lionheart: The Story So Far...

Software development is in full swing and progressing nicely. Every day we learn something new about the problem we're solving. The architecture is becoming more mature with every detail. The team draws pictures regularly to bounce ideas off each other and work through alternatives.

Teammates frequently sketch the same diagrams during design discussions. You take a picture of some whiteboard sketches with your phone and add the pictures to your source code repository along with with a brief write-up. You also start to build out element responsibility views so it's easier to explain how everything works together. So far these views have been most useful when we add new elements to the architecture.

Up to this point in the project we've only shared design decisions informally. And we've had a few misses because of this. You decide it's probably time for us to improve our documentation and rely less on tribal knowledge.

Next Up

When trying to share an abstract idea, just start drawing. Do not hesitate. As you sketch, the abstract becomes tangible and new insights will emerge. Teammates will join you as you reason through the complex. Use these visual aides to tell stories about how your design decisions promote quality attributes. As the stories and diagrams coalesce, a view of the software system will emerge. Every view is a window into the architecture.

In the next chapter, you're going to learn more about telling stories with your diagrams by creating architecture descriptions. Architecture descriptions start with a picture but also include design decisions, history, and the rationale for why you designed the system the way you did.

CHAPTER 11

Describe the Architecture

Software architecture documentation has a reputation for being notoriously awful. It takes time away from writing code. It always seems to be out of date. It's usually written in some proprietary binary file format that you can't edit. And on top of all that, nobody reads it anyway! It's no wonder some people call software architecture descriptions SAD!

Bad architecture descriptions make us sad. Great architecture descriptions give our team clarity of vision. Great architecture descriptions are a planning asset, a communication aide, and a collaboration tool. They improve the quality of the software we build by helping our design decisions reach everyone.

In this chapter, you'll learn how to create amazing software architecture descriptions that people love. Why will people love them? Because you'll give your audience the exact information they need in a humane and easy-to-learn format. Love is a strong word to apply to software architecture descriptions. I mean it. Creating an amazing software architecture description is easier than you may realize.

Tell the Whole Story

In *Build Models into the Code*, on page 107 you learned that there will always be a gap between the models in the architecture and the code we write. We can close the model-code gap somewhat, but we can't express every architectural design decisions in code. Nevermind that few stakeholders can read code and no code exists at the beginning of a system's life when design planning is most needed.

We need architecture descriptions for several important reasons.

Get organized. Building software is as much about working with people as it is working with technology. Architecture descriptions show how everything comes together. Whether we are assigning responsibilities to teams or letting people self-organize, everyone needs to know how components in the system work together so they can align themselves accordingly.

Establish the lingua franca between technical and business stakeholders. Every stakeholder has a right to understand the architecture. While models establish the vocabulary of design, the architecture description translates those models into ideas different stakeholders can understand. One of the most important jobs of an architecture description is to show how the business goals and quality attributes are addressed in the architectural design decisions.

Put a spotlight on quality attributes. Quality attributes are often out of sight and out of mind. The architecture is the one place we treat quality attributes as first-class citizens. Keep quality attributes at the front of everyone's mind by making the architecture a real thing that people can see, read about, and talk about.

Clarify thinking. It's easy to believe you have everything figured out if nothing is written down. When you put pen to paper, you'll realize how mushy the ideas in your head really are. Writing an architecture description forces us to confront our knowledge and come to terms with what we know, what we think we know, and what we don't know.

Create something you can evaluate. We can't reason about things we can't see, touch, or share. We also can't afford to wait for every design decision to be realized in code before critically evaluating it. Architecture descriptions give us a way to analyze our design decisions while it's easy to make changes. Spending the afternoon explaining a dumb idea to someone is much better than spending a month implementing it.

Show it off. Software architecture is cool! You poured your heart and soul into designing a beautiful software system. The whole world should appreciate it! Architecture descriptions are the best way to brag about the software systems you've built. A good architecture description projects confidence for customers and upper management. It shows leadership by clearly articulating a purpose, plan, and vision.

Architecture descriptions are supremely valuable. The trick to getting the most bang for the buck is to choose the appropriate description methods for your current project and team context.

Match the Description Method to the Situation

There is no one-size-fits-all approach to creating software architecture descriptions. Less mature systems might change their architecture several times in a single conversation. A co-located team working on a smaller system can get by with whiteboards and storytelling. A system built for a regulated industry may be legally required to document design decisions in a specific way.

There are two questions we need to answer to decide how to document our architecture. How likely are our design decisions to change? And how far must we share our design decisions? Depending on how you answer these questions, you'll arrive at one of four types of description methods: tribal, communal, formal, or wasteful.

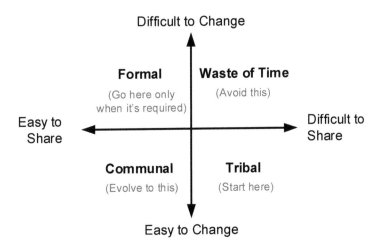

Which architecture description approach should I use?

Create an Oral History with Tribal Methods

Tribal description methods rely heavily on oral tradition and cultural artifacts. Storytelling, metaphors, and informal sketching are all examples of tribal architecture descriptions. Always start here. Tribal descriptions are easy to change, which is perfect for the rapid design churn young architectures face.

While tribal methods are easy to create and change, they are also difficult to share. A system metaphor, described in Activity 29, *System Metaphor*, on page 281, might work well when your whole team is within earshot of your conversation, but oral histories are only alive when someone can tell the story.[1] Constantly telling stories can be exhausting, even on small teams of only half a dozen people.

Reach Further with Communal Methods

Not all aspects of an architecture evolve at the same rate or require the same kinds of description. As a rule of thumb, if you find yourself telling the same story to more than a few people, then it's time to evolve the style of architecture description to increase reach. Enter communal methods.

Communal architecture description methods are shared by the community, not just individuals of the tribe. Architecture haiku (Activity 21, *Architecture Haiku*, on page 263), architecturally evident coding styles (described on page 107), and architecture decision records (Activity 20, *Architecture Decision Records*, on page 260) are all examples of communal description methods. Communal descriptions are still easy to change, but they are also easy to share compared to tribal methods.

Most teams will evolve from tribal descriptions to communal descriptions naturally as the architecture matures and the rate of change decreases. Communal description methods are good enough for many teams. In some situations, we want something more permanent. We can get this permanence with formal architecture descriptions.

Invest in Formal Descriptions Only When Required

Formal description methods include traditional architecture description documents and formal models. These tend to be larger documents and require more effort to create. Formal models (the sort that defines the architecture with a mathematical model) require a higher degree of accuracy and precision.

High-risk systems or architecture decisions requiring a high degree of coordination are good candidates for formal description methods. Depending on your industry, you may be required to create a formal document. Even then, it pays to start with tribal methods and progress to communal methods before building formal descriptions.

---

1. Michael Keeling. *Creating an Architecture Oral History: Minimalist Techniques for Describing Systems*. SATURN 2012. http://resources.sei.cmu.edu/library/asset-view.cfm?assetID=20330

Instead of starting with a traditional document, start with whiteboard sketches and a system metaphor. Record ADRs one at a time as you make decisions. Once you've made some decisions, bring everything together as an architecture haiku and continue refactoring code so that it reflects the models in your design. After the architecture starts to coalesce, if desired (or when a stakeholder asks for it), create a traditional document.

Create a Traditional Software Architecture Description

The *traditional software architecture description*, or SAD, is a classic design document that every architect should know how to write. While these documents are time-consuming to create, they are worth their weight in gold. This does not mean you should make the document as large as possible! What I mean is that a traditional SAD is well worth the effort.

Most stakeholders—developers included—have probably never seen the architecture as a whole. The SAD is the one artifact that brings everything together to tell the whole story.

Traditional architecture documents might run 10 or 20 pages depending on the template used. I've written only a few SADs that have run 70 pages or more. Keep in mind these page counts include all the pomp and circumstance that goes along with a formal document. Even not counting the fluff, a traditional SAD is an investment.

Start a traditional architecture description by building or finding a template. You'll find many templates available online.[2] Your organization may even have a template. I strongly recommend the Software Engineering Institute's *Views and Beyond* [3] and the ISO/IEC/IEEE 42010 standard templates.[4]

All traditional architecture descriptions include the same basic parts:

Introductions and preamble information This includes the title page, update notes, signature page, table of contents, a list of figures, licensing and legal boilerplate, and other information required of a formal document. The table of contents and figure lists help readers navigate the document more easily. The rest is meant to convey the importance of the information held within the document. Some stakeholders find these preambles impressive. Remember, you may be required by your organization to include some of this information.

---

2. http://www.iso-architecture.org/42010/applications.html
3. http://www.sei.cmu.edu/architecture/tools/document/viewsandbeyond.cfm
4. http://www.iso-architecture.org/42010/templates/

Overview and introduction to the SAD Briefly describes the purpose of the document as well as the methodology used to organized and create it. Your SAD could be the first time some stakeholders have read an architecture description. Take this opportunity to educate them just-in-time so they can appreciate the architecture designed for them.

Summary of stakeholders, business goals, and architecturally significant requirements Since all decisions in our architecture flow from stakeholders' concerns, list them before describing the design. I like to summarize key constraints and quality attributes here as well. If you've created an ASR Workbook (introduced on page 60), then add a reference to it. Strive to keep the architecture description DRY (Don't Repeat Yourself), just like your code.

Context view Provides an overview of where the software system fits in the world. See Activity 22, *Context Diagram*, on page 265 for details.

Relevant views As we discussed in *Show the Architecture from Different Views*, on page 129, architecture is too big and complex to show in one diagram. We need to create multiple views of the architecture to explain how it satisfies quality attributes and other requirements. A list of views is not very consumable, so to help our readers we'll organize views around a related set of stakeholder concerns. Each *viewpoint* shows views needed to reason about something a stakeholder cares about, such as a set of related quality attribute scenarios. You'll learn more about using viewpoints in *Organize Views around Stakeholders' Concerns*, on page 152.

Risks, open questions, future work Include a section for known risks and open questions. The purpose of these sections is to shine a light on the land mines you already know about so downstream designers can hopefully avoid them.

Appendices At a minimum include a term glossary and list of acronyms with expansions. I recommend you include a quality attribute taxonomy as an appendix as well. Some formal documents will also include change procedures and change request templates.

Creating a SAD can be exhausting. Work as a team to complete the document. Designate one person as the *Master of the SAD*. The Master of the SAD creates the template and decides who will write each section of the document. The Master of the SAD is also responsible for making sure the document is complete and has a consistent style.

Avoid Wasting Time

For the sake of completeness, there is a quadrant on our grid made up of difficult-to-change, difficult-to-share description methods. If you find yourself here, it's time to try something different. Let's look at two examples of waste-of-time description methods.

One example of a possible waste of time is the *slideware architecture description*. Presentations are a powerful tool for architects. The problem with slides is that they rarely stand on their own and can be difficult to change. Someone must present them to make sense. Someone spent hours getting all the transitions and layered boxes and connecting arrows to look just right. After so much work, people hesitate to change their beautifully laid-out diagrams, even when the world has changed. Compared to tribal methods, slides are etched in stone.

The best way to avoid wasting time is by creating great architecture descriptions. All great descriptions, no matter what method you use, have four traits:

1. They are custom built with the audience in mind.

2. They show multiple views of the architecture.

3. They clearly define the elements and their responsibilities.

4. They explain the rationale for design decisions.

In the next sections, you'll learn what these traits mean and how to put them into practice to create fantastic architecture descriptions.

Respect Your Audience

As you learned in *The Four Principles of Design Thinking*, on page 15, all design is social. Who will use your architecture description? What do they need to get out of it? How can you best provide the information they need most? When empathizing with our stakeholders, we identified and recorded their key concerns. We've come up with a plan for addressing their concerns in the architecture and now our job is to share that information.

When you know your audience, you'll be able to create an architecture description that gives them exactly what they need. The better we do this, the more likely people are to read the architecture description, which in turn further amplifies the impact of our design decisions.

George says:

Tell a Story at Many Levels

By George Fairbanks, software engineer at Google and author of Just Enough Software Architecture: A Risk-Driven Approach [Fai10]

We've all dropped into a project and struggled to understand the code. Perhaps you are browsing the repository of an open source project and find just one folder with hundreds of source files. It takes a lot of effort for you to infer how things work and you probably make mistakes.

It doesn't have to be that way. You can organize your code as a *story at many levels* so that it makes sense and tells a story as you zoom in or out. Consider what you ate yesterday evening. You recognize it as dinner, and zooming in you also recognize courses, then dishes, then ingredients.

The levels help you think clearly. If you're wondering how long dinner will last, thinking about the number of courses is helpful and thinking about allergies is best done by ingredients. But the reverse doesn't help at all.

People have been thinking about dinner for a lot longer than software, so it's already baked into our language. You will have to invent your story and levels, though you can lean on developers who have come before you. Architecture patterns give you general names to use like *connectors* and *layers*, and specific ones like *reduce stage* and *broker*.

Your story at many levels won't come for free, so you will spend time gardening, making minor refactorings as you go so that the story stays clear. Today you might have just three connectors, so they all go in the same folder, but some well-timed gardening should catch it before it grows to dozens. As with most things, a stitch in time saves nine, plus it makes you look like you knew what you were doing the whole time.

It's easy to focus your attention on the source code only, but the system's runtime deserves similar attention, as does how it is allocated to hardware or containers. If you want to think about it clearly, structure it as a story at many levels.

Think about your stakeholders and what they value. What are their roles and responsibilities on the project? How do they like to process information? How will this person use the information you give them? Sometimes it helps to create an empathy map of your audience to help you get started (see Activity 2, *Empathy Map*, on page 195). There's a sample empathy map on page 151 for a developer on my team.

By studying the example empathy map, we can see that this person needs a thorough document with a clear rationale since he likes to argue both sides of any decision. We can also see that this person is interested in properties related to deployment and wants technical details.

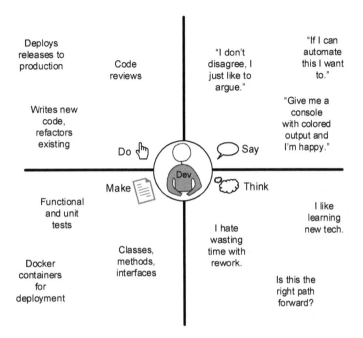

Now that we know what kind of information our audience wants and how they might consume it, let's talk about how we can make the most understandable architecture description for them.

Focus on Understandability

Communication is king when it comes to architecture descriptions. Your audience wants to understand you. Speak the language of the domain in which you're working to make your architecture description understandable. If your stakeholders talk about *material master numbers*, use their terms instead of introducing new words like *product IDs*.

How you choose to describe complex, abstract ideas is also important. Use plain speak and avoid jargon. Briefly define architecture concepts to ensure your reader has required background knowledge. Unless it is completely wrong, favor design terminology stakeholders already use. For example, if stakeholders prefer to discuss *nonfunctional requirements* then use that term instead of *quality attributes*. Err on the side of effective communication.

Understandability also extends to notations. Not everyone will know every design notation. This advice goes double for the Unified Modeling Language (UML). There are several flavors of the UML, and though it can express architectural ideas well, it's not always direct or obvious. You may know exactly how to use all of UML's 16 or so diagrams, but not everyone in your audience has studied UML as intensely. As you learned in *Draw Fantastic Diagrams*, on page 136, always define your notation and the meta-model behind it by including a legend on all diagrams.

Finally, organize your description so it's easy to consume. Use a standard template for written documents and make it look good. Fix the alignment so it's easy to read. Use text formatting to your advantage. Think about how the information looks in print, digital, and presentation formats. A great-looking document tells readers the content is trustworthy and was created by a professional.

Do this...	Avoid this...
Do define architectural concepts the first time you use them.	Don't unnecessarily introduce new concepts.
Do speak the language of the problem domain.	Don't assume everyone intuitively understands diagram notations.
Do include a legend on diagrams.	Don't use jargon.
Do use a common template if one exists.	

You've learned a few techniques for documenting design decisions. You've also learned how to think about your audience to design an architecture description that is right for them. Next, we'll combine these two ideas together by organizing the architecture description relative to stakeholders' concerns.

Organize Views around Stakeholders' Concerns

Different people want to know different things about the software system you are building. Developers on your team will want to know about code organization, deployment, and component interaction. Testers on your team will want to know about the interfaces and communication protocols. The product owner on your team wants to know about technical dependencies and get a sense of the overall progress. New teammates might be overwhelmed by the existing documentation and could benefit with some help getting started. At a minimum, architecture descriptions should describe design decisions, design rationale, and structures in the design.

How we organize this information is important too. The Human rule of design applies equally to how we share details *about* the design just as much as it applies to the design itself.

When we organize views of the architecture and the various design documentation that goes with it with our stakeholders in mind, then it's far easier for others to understand the architecture. Doing this requires that we think about what stakeholders want to know. We can then create a view of the architecture unique to that set of related stakeholder concerns. Designing usable documents is how we get people to love our architecture descriptions.

Establish the Viewpoints

A *viewpoint* defines an approach for describing the architecture from the perspective of a related set of stakeholder concerns. Viewpoints define not only what views you should show but also who the views are for, as well as the notations, vocabulary, and rules to use when creating it. They are a part of the ISO/IEC/IEEE 42010:2011 standard defined in *ISO/IEC/IEEE 42010:2011 Systems and software engineering – Architecture description [Int11]*.

Viewpoints were designed for use with traditional architecture descriptions, but the general principles apply to any architecture description approach we've discussed. Let's look at an example.

We've identified several components in Project Lionheart. Eventually, we'll need to deploy these components somewhere. The development team needs to know where to deploy them, and the city IT department will need to be told what systems to monitor. It sounds like we need a deployment viewpoint. Here's one possible view from that viewpoint:

Component	Deployed to
Web UI	Runs in user's browser, served by Display Business (accessed through load balancer)
Display Business	Tomcat on a Linux VM, hosted by cloud provider
Favorites Service	Tomcat on a Linux VM, hosted by cloud provider, VM is independently deployable from Display Business
Search Service	Same VM as Favorites service
Search Index	Cloud-provided Solr service
Alerting Process	Process initiated by cloud scheduler, independent container (depends on cloud provider)
Crawler Process	Local server maintained by City IT
Contracts and User Metadata DB	Cloud-hosted Postgres

Additional views for the deployment viewpoint will flesh out dependencies among components, platform or third-party software requirements (for example, a particular Linux version), areas of risk, costs, or network topology. The viewpoint itself can consist of both graphical and textual views.

In practice, the information in this example view can be captured in a few ADRs or summarized in an architecture haiku. For the Project Lionheart team, it might be enough to capture the tribal knowledge in the deployment scripts themselves. Add some comments to the scripts to capture design rationale. While this is OK for the development team, a summary table like the one shown will help with the project hand-off to City IT. Always consider the audience when deciding how to document the architecture.

Create Custom Viewpoints

There are several established viewpoint sets you may use to guide your architecture description practices.[5] I can personally recommend the *Software Engineering Institute's views and beyond approach [BBCG10]* as well as *Phillipe Krutchen's 4+1 view model [Kru95], Rozanksi's and Woods's viewpoints and perspectives [RW11]* approach and Simon Brown's *C4 model [Bro16]*.

We often organize viewpoints around quality attributes. Viewpoints can also be constructed to satisfy specific stakeholder needs. Here are a few examples:

- A *scalability, security,* or *maintainability viewpoint* will demonstrate how the architecture satisfies specific quality attribute scenarios.

- A *regulatory viewpoint* might provide a particular stakeholder group concerned with regulatory requirements information needed to perform an audit.

- A *teachability viewpoint* or *welcome to the team viewpoint* might walk a new teammate through your architecture and development practices with the goal of getting them to commit code on day one.

- A *business impact viewpoint* might show how different parts of the architecture contribute business value.

Viewpoints are a must in traditional architecture descriptions. With tribal and communal approaches, create viewpoints opportunistically and keep them lightweight. For example, once there are several ADRs in your code repository, create a viewpoint page that connects decision records together to provide overarching context. Mountains of documentation are not required to organize architecture descriptions for human consumption. Be kind to your readers and they will be delighted.

---

5. http://www.iso-architecture.org/42010/afs/frameworks-table.html

Views help us organize ideas so we can share the architecture effectively. There's more to an architecture description than just views and design decisions. Why you made the decisions in the first place is just as important.

Explain the Rationale for Your Decisions

Design rationale describes why we made each design decision. Maybe you chose a pattern to promote a certain quality attribute. Maybe you picked a technology the team is familiar with or one that had the right cost. Every decision had alternatives, pros, and cons. We weighed trade-offs among properties and justified our conclusions through some logical thought process.

The better downstream designers understand the rationale for your decisions, the better they can embrace the *intent* of your design. The better others understand the intent behind your decisions, the more likely they will be to uphold the architectural integrity of the system as it evolves.

Rationale in an architecture description comes in many forms. It might be prose, a story, or a couple of bullet points. Sometimes your pile of rejected decisions can be more telling than a lengthy explanation.

Describe the Paths Not Taken

Developing software is a journey. The path is winding and there are dozens of roads leading to the same destination. Every fork in the road, every decision you make, is an opportunity to help others understand why the software architecture is the way that it is. One method for helping people understand the decisions you made is to enumerate all the options you rejected.

Consider the paths not taken in the Project Lionheart architecture. See the table on page 156.

Not everyone can be in the room when we make a decision. Reading the paths not taken lets you play back decisions so others can get a feeling for the architecture's journey. Without this knowledge, it's like watching the last five minutes of a movie. You missed all the character development and anything the characters do at the end will seem random. When you have the background, Darth Vader's decisions at the end of the *Return of the Jedi* hold a deeper meaning. Without the background, you might think Vader is just fickle and annoyed.

You will always reject many more ideas than you keep. Humans can dismiss dozens of options in the blink of an eye without even realizing it. Formally record any decision you discuss as a team. If you notice you're having an intense inner monologue, try to externalize your thoughts so others can benefit.

Path not taken	Discussion
One huge web application	Doesn't allow us to schedule computationally intensive operations
Java for Display Business service	Several teammates know Node.js, promote maintainability with JavaScript in the client and server
Index RFPs in SQL database, search service reads the database directly	Doesn't give an expressive enough query syntax required by stakeholders
MongoDB for data storage	While it seems like a good fit, no expertise on the team
Isolate services to their own containers	Not enough familiarity with technology. We can ship sooner putting everything on the same VM. This decision is not binding. We can change strategies later.

Get Your Hands Dirty: Describe the Paths Not Taken for a Project

Think about a recent project. Write down some of the alternative architecture choices that your team considered and why you rejected each option. Of these decisions, who on your team can describe the rationale for the decision?

Here are some things to think about:

- Were there any major discussions you had as a team?
- What decisions did your team struggle to make?
- What decisions were made under uncertainty?
- Were there any *point of no return* decisions that forced you down a particular path?

Project Lionheart: The Story So Far...

The team has done a good job of making diagrams and sketching during design discussions, but pictures of whiteboards are not a replacement for a good old-fashioned architecture description.

Since our team is small and co-located, you decide to continue using whiteboard sketches and system metaphors, but you encourage us to also start recording design decisions as architecture decision records. Metaphors and whiteboard drawings let us thrash quickly and cheaply. Recording ADRs as we make decisions creates a public record that is easier to share among the team and with future developers.

You decide to delay creating a formal architecture description. A more official document should be easier to write later in the life cycle. The ideas it contains will also be less likely to expire before we finish preparing the document since most design decisions will be set in code by then. Our primary audience is the next team after us. When the time comes, you think it will make sense to create teachability, deployment, and strategic change (extensibility) viewpoints.

Next Up

Architecture descriptions can be great. It's up to you to design them for awesomeness. Think about what your audience needs to know and organize views of the architecture to help people see the whole picture. Describe the elements, their responsibilities, and why you chose them for this architecture. Take advantage of the breadth of description methods. Stuffy, big documents are not the only way to explain design decisions. The most important thing is to communicate effectively and explain your vision for the architecture to the world.

Creating an architecture description also creates our first opportunity to test the system's design, even before we've written much code. The ability to test the architecture early is great news since, as you'll see next, the earlier you can evaluate the architecture, the less pain you'll have down the road.

CHAPTER 12

Give the Architecture a Report Card

School report cards are an important feedback loop for students, parents, and teachers. Instead of waiting until the end of the year to learn if you pass or fail a subject, a quarterly report card can tell you if you're on track to get the grades you want and show you where you can improve before it's too late. Taking the time to evaluate our architecture, like school report cards, can help us catch problems early so we can stay on track to deliver.

Instead of thinking of evaluations as taking away time from programming, think of them as a way to make the time we spend programming even more powerful. Evaluations can take as little as an hour, and we can even fold them into existing development processes without anyone being the wiser.

In this chapter, you'll learn how to give the architecture a report card. The feedback from an evaluation can be used to educate the team, create buy-in for design decisions, reduce delivery risks, and improve the architecture.

Evaluate to Learn

Architecture evaluation is a process by which we learn the extent to which an architecture is fit for purpose. A common fallacy when designing software architectures the belief that we should check the architecture only once, at the end of a design phase. If the whole architecture isn't correct, then everything fails and the implementation can't start. This thinking is wrong, wrong, wrong.

Architectures are never wholly good or wholly bad. Just like we can't see the entire architecture in a single view, we also can't evaluate the whole architecture in a single go. It's possible for a single component to be well designed, or one area of the architecture to be well understood while others are filled with risk. Not everything is required to be fully baked to begin implementation.

One way to use architecture evaluations is as a ceremonial sign-off. In cases where components must strictly meet specific criteria, such sign-offs can be extremely valuable. For example, a sign-off evaluation can avoid costly rework for systems with many integration points or significant hardware needs.

While sign-offs are sometimes important, using evaluations only as a phase gate check is a missed opportunity. The world constantly changes around us. The only way to know whether our architecture still satisfies our stakeholders' needs is to evaluate it.

During our evaluations we want to learn two things: *How good is the architecture?* and *How is the architecture good?* To answer these questions, we'll use what we know about the architecturally significant requirements (ASRs). The better the architecture satisfies the ASRs, the better the architecture fits its purpose.

Test the Design

Test early, test often. This idea is as true for code as it is for architecture. Even when the architecture is only in its infancy, before we've written any code, there's always something we can test.

There are three things we'll need to evaluate an architecture. First, we need an artifact, a tangible representation of the design. Next, we need a rubric, a definition for *better* or *worse* from the stakeholders' perspective. Finally, we need a plan for helping reviewers generate insights so they can form an opinion about the goodness of the architecture.

Make Something to Evaluate

Before we can evaluate anything, we need to have something to evaluate. We can evaluate real things, not ideas. We need to prepare a tangible artifact to evaluate. The artifact could be as simple as a whiteboard sketch or as detailed as a full architecture description.

Tangible things to evaluate are easy to find. Here are some ideas:

- Write some code.
- Sketch a model on paper or a whiteboard.
- Draw a model in a diagramming application.
- Prepare a slide-based presentation with different views of the architecture
- Summarize the results of an experiment in a presentation or whitepaper.

Ipek says:

Lines Are Also First-Class Citizens!

By Ipek Ozkaya, senior member of technical staff at the Software Engineering Institute at Carnegie Mellon University

My work involves helping organizations and teams improve their systems' quality from the perspective of the fitness of its architecture. An unavoidable and obvious request in these engagements is "Show me your architecture." Over the years, based on the responses I get, I've developed a personal catalog of misconceptions about architecture and architecting.

A printout of all of the sequence diagrams for all the use case scenarios you thought of so far is *not* your architecture! While the collection of all your use cases and their behavioral traces, such as those you capture in sequence diagrams, are useful and important to your system, they do not provide the right level of abstraction to reason about classes of behavior of the system.

Code review can *not* replace an architecture review! The bottom line of any architecting effort is to design and implement a system that meets its business and stakeholder goals. Working code is the inevitable reality. However, architectural concerns cross-cut many elements in the implemented system. An effective architecture review is bound by those architecturally significant requirements and all the elements they touch. Traditional code review practices do not cover this end-to-end perspective.

Boxes are *not* the only architectural elements! In cases when a team does have an artifact, often called the Software Architecture Document, and sadly referred to as SAD, the document contain depictions of ad hoc box-and-line drawings. This is a great start, but discussions are long on the boxes while the lines are completely forgotten. This is unfortunate because many times the lines carry the most critical aspects of the architectural decisions.

Of these three misconceptions, the most significant one is to appreciate the importance of lines in software architecture diagrams. Think about it. If you aim to increase performance, then you focus on the frequency and volume of the inter-element communications. If you want to increase modifiability, you limit interactions between elements. If you want to optimize security, you protect the inter-element relationships. All of these are represented by the lines!

Many architectural decisions are carried on those thin, often forgotten lines. Since so many architectural decisions are carried by the inter-element relationships, one of my first recommendations to teams is to get a better understanding of the relationships between the elements. Treat the lines as first-class citizens in your architecting journey!

- Create a traditional architecture description (introduced on page 147), architecture haiku (see Activity 21, *Architecture Haiku*, on page 263), or set of Architecture Decision Records (Activity 20, *Architecture Decision Records*, on page 260).

- Build a utility tree showing which quality attributes are promoted by different components.

In *The Four Principles of Design Thinking*, on page 15 you learned to make things tangible to facilitate communication. The artifact used during an evaluation will communicate our best intentions for how we plan to (or in some cases, already have) addressed the ASRs.

Prepare artifacts that are likely to solicit the type of feedback we want. For example, if we want reviewers to focus on a specific quality attribute, then the artifacts should include views relevant to that quality attribute. If the architecture is young and we want general feedback, consider using *sketchier* diagrams to show that the design is in flux. If the design decision is about something high risk and high cost, favor greater precision and formality to communicate the seriousness of the matter at hand.

Define a Design Rubric

Every architecture exhibits shades of *right* and *wrong*. One reviewer may conclude the architecture is a masterpiece whereas another proclaims it a dumpster fire. A *design rubric* defines the criteria reviewers should use when judging the fitness of the architecture.

Rubrics consist of two parts. *Criteria* describe the characteristics used to evaluate the design artifacts. *Ratings* describe the scale used to interpret the characteristics. Typically, rubrics take the shape of a matrix.

In the example on page 163 from Project Lionheart we're using quality attribute scenarios as the criteria, listed on the left. On the right, reviewers enter their ratings using the provided scale, which is described at the bottom.

Let's explore how we arrived at this rubric and define some general advice for creating rubrics.

Select Criteria Based on Architecturally Significant Requirements

Architecturally significant requirements define the software's purpose from a stakeholder's perspective. In Chapter 5, *Dig for Architecturally*, on page 49, you learned how to specify ASRs in a way that enables analysis and evaluation. If we define ASRs in a precise, unambiguous, and measurable way, then we can use them to help define a rubric for evaluation.

Criteria →   Reviewers' → scores go here

Quality Attribute	Scenario	Rating (1 - 4)
Availability	Lionheart responds even when the index is unavailable.	
Availability	Results are always returned except during maintenance.	
Performance	Results are visible within 5 seconds under average load.	
Scalability	The system can expand to handle 5% annual data growth for the next 7 years.	

Rating Scale

1 = Does not meet expectations for scenario or unable to evaluate
2 = Partially satisfies scenario or satisfies the scenario but with unacceptably high risk, technical debt, or cost
3 = Satisfies scenario with acceptable risk, technical debt, and costs
4 = Satisfies scenario with little or no risk or technical debt and within budgets

 Defines how to score the criteria

Using the ASRs as a guide, we can select a rubric's criteria. The best rubrics meet the following conditions:[1]

Important and essential The criteria in a rubric defines what we think a good architecture should look like relative to the ASRs. Criteria should not include ideas that are *nice to have* or frivolous details not required for the architecture to be fit for purpose.

Distinct Criteria within the same rubric should not overlap with one another. Each criterion is one facet of the overall fitness of the design. Ideally each criterion can be assessed and scored independently.

Observable and measurable Reviewers must be able to assess and score the criteria in the rubric. The artifacts we prepare for the evaluation will make criteria visible. The activities we perform during the assessment will collect data that lets us measure the criteria.

Precise and unambiguous Every reviewer should interpret the criteria in the same way.

Quality attribute scenarios should already meet these recommendations and always make for good criteria.

---

1.   http://www.ucdenver.edu/faculty_staff/faculty/center-for-faculty-development/Documents/Tutorials/Rubrics/index.htm

Decide the Rating Scale for Criteria

During the evaluation reviewers will judge the criteria using a provided rating. Rating scales define what *needs improvement, good, better,* and *best* looks like. The size of the scale depends on the goals of the evaluation. Here are some different rating scales and when they might be appropriate to use:

Scale Size	Examples	Use it when...
2	yes or no; condition satisfied or not satisfied	Acceptance is all or nothing for a condition, standard, or presence of an item; single or few reviewers
3	fail, pass, or awesome; never, sometimes, or always; low, acceptable, or high	There is a minimum acceptable threshold but also a preferred expectation for the design; multiple reviewers are involved
4	never, sometimes, usually, or always; fail, fair, pass, or exceed	Detailed feedback is desired; expectations can be *nuanced* or involve multiple pieces
5+	choose a number 1–10	Avoid using. Too many options in the rating scale lead to inconsistent reviews.

In our example from Project Lionheart on page 162, we chose to use a simple 1–4 scale so reviewers could offer more feedback about the design. To use the rubric, multiple reviewers will score the criteria and we'll average the results. We'll also highlight any criteria that scored a 1 for further discussion, even if the criteria have an acceptable average score.

This example rubric captures scores well but doesn't have space where reviewers can explain *why* they scored criteria the way they did. Scores are an easy way to assess the design quickly, but knowing what reviewers were thinking when they scored different criteria is invaluable information.

We have artifacts. We have a definition for *better* and *worse*. The last step is to help reviewers score the rubric by helping them generate insights about the architecture.

Generate Insights

Design rubrics contain answerable questions as shown in the figure on page 165. We find the answers by helping reviewers generate insights about the

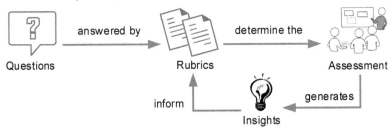

Key Components of an Architecture Evaluation

design, which reviewers use to form opinions about how well the design satisfies the ASRs.

We can generate insights in a number of different ways, such as questionnaires, directed explorations, risk elicitations, or code analysis. To help decide which activities will bear the most fruit, we'll need to figure out what information is required to answer our rubric. Here are a few examples:

Rubric Criteria	Insights to help score the criteria
Amount of Risk	Identify risks with risk storming (described on page 301) or a general risk elicitation workshop; examine the number and severity of risks identified
Amount of Uncertainty	Generate open questions with a question-comment-concern workshop (described on page 298); examine the number of open questions and estimate how difficult they are to answer
Reviewer Consensus	Use multi-voting, surveys, thumbs up/down, and ratings
Design Completeness	List known components and their current design state; define a threshold for *complete* and *more work needed*
Fit for Problem	Walk through quality attribute scenarios (described on page 307) and identify sensitivity points, problem areas, risks, and questions
Technical Debt	List value adding use cases that cannot be implemented with the current architecture; estimate the cost to prepare the architecture for the use case
Quality	Count the number of defects by architectural component and define a threshold for *high* and *low* quality

The bulk of the effort in an architecture evaluation is spent generating insights. Since insights are often generated collaboratively during workshops, let's learn more about how to plan and facilitate an architecture evaluation workshop.

⚒ Get Your Hands Dirty: Ask Seven Good Questions

Good evaluators ask the right questions. Learning to ask the right questions takes practice. Write down seven or more questions about the architecture of a recent project for which you don't know the answer. Why seven? We want to move past the obvious to find interesting things others might have missed.

Here are some things to think about:

- Be specific. General questions only provide general insights. The more specific the questions, the more actionable your insights.

- What do you know (or not know) about the relations in the architecture?

- Are there one or more views of module, component and connector, and allocation structures?

- What worries you? Playing *what if...* is not a fun game, but worries are often the seed of real engineering risks.

Host an Evaluation Workshop

The goal of an *architecture evaluation workshop* is to gather and analyze the data necessary to assess the architecture. By the end of the workshop, we should be in a position to qualify how well the architecture satisfies desirable quality attributes and other ASRs.

While there are many ways to run an evaluation workshop, all workshops follow the same basic formula:

1. *Prepare*—Find or create required artifacts. Define rubrics. Select methods to gather data and invite reviewers.

2. *Prime the Reviewers*—Share the artifacts and rubrics with reviewers. Explain the goal of the evaluation and answer reviewers' questions. Reviewers should fully understand the artifacts, rubrics, and purpose of the evaluation before starting the assessment.

3. *Assessment*—Lead reviewers through activities to explore the artifacts and generate insights needed to score the rubric. Activities can be collaborative or solo.

4. *Analyze*—Compile the data provided by reviewers. Summarize the results and look for trends.

5. *Follow-up*—Decide on next steps based on what you learned during the workshop.

Let's take a closer look at each of these steps.

Prepare for the Evaluation

As a part of our preparation, we must decide the goals of the evaluation and develop whatever artifacts we need to meet those goals. Here are some examples:

If you want to evaluate...	You might need artifacts like...
How well a specific quality attribute is promoted	Views relevant to the quality attributes of interest, test results, use cases, quality attribute scenarios
Technology or pattern options	Technology or pattern descriptions, experiment overviews, experiment results, quality attribute scenarios
Likelihood of hitting cost or schedule targets	Component overview, component estimates, technical dependencies, team capacity
Design evolution path	Overviews of the current and to-be architecture, list of evolution steps
Architecture description completeness or correctness	An architecture description, questions that should be answerable by looking at the description, description quality checklists
Security	Abuse cases, misuse cases, threat models, data stores, views needed to identify sensitivity points and attack vectors
Release Readiness	Quality attribute scenarios, relevant views, release checklists, test results

In addition to preparing artifacts, we'll need to create rubrics and decide what data is required to score them. If you plan to run the assessment as a workshop, then prepare the agenda and any materials needed to host the workshop.

When selecting reviewers, look for stakeholders and non-stakeholder experts who are detail-oriented and care about the system being designed. Ideal candidates will have relevant domain knowledge or expertise in the technologies and patterns used in the architecture. They will also be prepared to offer an objective assessment. As few as two reviewers can perform an assessment, but it's possible to involve dozens of reviewers if required.

After the reviewers have committed to participate in the evaluation, we'll need to prepare them to do a good review.

Prime the Reviewers

All reviewers should have the information needed to provide good feedback. Present necessary background information to reviewers, such as the system's context, architecturally significant requirements, and the artifacts under review. Answer any questions the reviewers have about the context, rubrics, and goals.

A slide deck or whiteboard talk works well for this. When conducting an evaluation within your team, consider creating artifacts and reviewing context together, just-in-time at the start of the workshop.

Once the reviewers are primed and ready, it's time to perform the assessment and generate some insights.

Facilitate the Assessment

During the assessment part of the workshop, we'll generate insights by guiding reviewers through a series of activities designed to illuminate inconsistencies in thinking or highlight potential problem areas. Many activities can be used to generate insights. Here are a few examples, which are described fully in Chapter 17, *Activities to Evaluate Design Options*, on page 285:

- Many evaluations will use some form of a scenario walkthrough as described on page 307. This activity is the most basic and reliable architecture evaluation tool.

- The Question–Comment–Concern activity described on page 298 is a form of visual brainstorming that helps reviewers quickly surface facts and questions about the architecture.

- Risk storming, described on page 301, is also a form of visual brainstorming, which focuses exclusively on risks in specific views of the system.

- If the goal of the evaluation is to compare and contrast alternatives, we might use the Sketch and Compare activity as described on page 311 to pit two or more ways of promoting the same quality attributes against one another.

- Code review, described on page 289, is not reliable on its own for finding architectural problems but it can identify misalignment between detailed design and the architecture. Code review is also an excellent tool for keeping tabs on static structures as they emerge.

- If we've recorded ADRs for our system (see Activity 20, *Architecture Decision Records*, on page 260), then we can replay the design decisions and decide whether those decisions still hold true. Proposed ADRs can be evaluated for fit as well.

Choose evaluation activities based on what we need to learn, the time available, and the stakeholders' familiarity with architecture evaluations. A small, experienced evaluation team of only 3–4 people can generate interesting insights with a simple question–comment–concern activity in as little as 60 minutes. A less experienced group might yield better results by walking through scenarios or design decisions explicitly.

During an evaluation workshop, we want to determine whether the architecture passes our criteria, but this shouldn't be the only outcome from the workshop. We also want to learn how to improve the architecture's design, not just that it needs improvement.

Analyze Data and Reach Conclusions

No matter what criteria we use during the evaluation, we want a clear and definitive conclusion. Explicitly state how well the architecture stood up to the criteria used to evaluate it and make concrete recommendations for how the architecture can be improved. The conclusions from an architecture evaluation should not be a simple pass or fail.

Whether the architecture is fit for purpose is only half the story. It's just as important to understand why the design is fit (or not) for purpose. Great designs can always be improved. Even a poor design will get some things right.

Use the insights generated during the evaluation to look for trends and opportunities. To decide *how* the architecture is good, look for risks and open questions. Risks show where the design might allow bad things to happen relative to criteria assessed in the workshop. Open questions shine a light on gaps in communication or knowledge about the architecture.

Use the data from the workshop to take advantage of reviewers' different perspectives. Share the data and ask reviewers to look for trends. Ask reviewers what worries them. Collect their questions. Even if we know the answer to a question, the fact that someone asked implies there is room to improve communication.

Once we've analyzed the data and reached some conclusions, it's time to decide what to do about it.

Decide on Follow-up Actions

We don't have to address every issue, risk, and open question identified during an evaluation. We won't have time to fix everything. Prioritize the work that must get done and separate it from the issues that are interesting but not essential. Assign someone to decide what to do about each high-priority item.

To close the evaluation workshop, create a summary of the findings and follow-up actions and share the list with all participants. For smaller workshops, a simple email with action items works great. For larger workshops, a brief write-up with links to raw notes ties a nice bow around the evaluation.

The concluding write-up is an excellent way to summarize findings for stakeholders and acts as a visible sign of progress for the architecture. Summaries are an excellent resource both for future architects of this system and architects who want to run evaluation workshops for a different system.

The Gold Standard: Architecture Trade-off Analysis Method (ATAM)

The *Architecture Trade-off Analysis Method* (ATAM) is among the first and certainly the most comprehensively defined and studied architecture evaluation method created to date. The method is described in detail in *ATAM: Method for Architecture Evaluation [KKC00]* and *Software Architecture in Practice [BCK12]*. The ATAM heavily influenced the basic evaluation workshop outline discussed in *Host an Evaluation Workshop*, on page 166.

By the book, the ATAM is a multiday, multiweek process that recommends using a trained facilitation team. If you're designing a highly complex system such as missile guidance or autonomous vehicle navigation systems, then the traditional ATAM is highly appropriate. For everyone else, we can usually get away with less process. Use the evaluation workshop structure from this chapter as a starting point.

The ATAM is thorough and well defined. If you've never hosted an architecture evaluation, consider trying an ATAM. It is the gold standard of evaluation methods.

Evaluate Early, Evaluate Often, Evaluate Continuously

If the first mistake is skipping architecture evaluations, the second mistake is waiting too late to start. The sooner you start testing your designs, the sooner you'll be able to improve them. Better still, make evaluation a regular part of your development routine.

There are dozens of opportunities every day to confirm (or amend) design decisions. Every day we walk through the architecture and tell stories about how it promotes quality attributes. We submit code for peer review. We pair program as a regular part of our everyday workflow.

Balance Cost and Value with the Evaluation Pyramid

The test pyramid is a concept introduced by Mike Cohn in *Succeeding with Agile: Software Development Using Scrum [Coh09]*. The premise is straightforward. Different kinds of tests find different kinds of defects, but some tests are easier to create and maintain than others. The test pyramid proposes that the majority of tests should be fast to run and cheap to maintain unit tests. Since unit tests can't catch everything, we should also create a small number of slow, brittle full-stack integration tests.

The premise behind the *evaluation pyramid* is similar to the test pyramid. The vast majority of architecture evaluations should be fast and cheap *quick checks*. Quick checks won't find every kind of design issue so we'll also want to perform a few thorough but costly *deep evaluations*. To provide for some consistency between quick checks and deep evaluations, we can perform *targeted evaluations*.

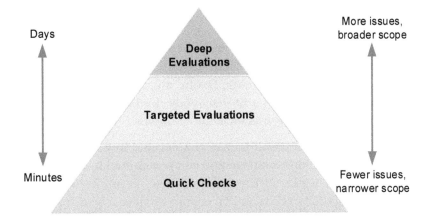

On a typical system, we might perform only one or two deep evaluations, dozens of targeted evaluations, and hundreds of quick checks. Deep evaluations will always be a major milestone in the system's life. Targeted evaluations might happen as part of a regular cadence, perhaps as often as every 2 to 4 weeks. Quick checks occur daily—sometimes multiple times each day—and become a seamless part of the development workflow.

Here are some examples of each type of evaluation from the pyramid:

Evaluation Type	How many?	Description	Examples
Deep Evaluation	1–3	Considers the whole system and interplay of several ASRs	Architecture Trade-off Analysis Method
Targeted Evaluation	dozens	Considers a single decision, component, or ASR	Risk storming, Question–Comment–Concern, Architecture Briefing
Quick Check	countless	Considers discrete design decisions as they are made, often used to reinforce understanding or evaluate details	Code review, storytelling, whiteboard jam, sanity check

Just because we evaluate the architecture continuously, it does not mean we are doing a good job of it. We also need to look for a variety of issues during our evaluations to ensure we have good coverage.

Look for Different Kinds of Issues

Eat the rainbow is something I tell my son to make sure he eats a variety of fresh fruits and vegetables. Fresh foods are different colors because they have an abundance of different vitamins. Eating different colors ensures he gets all the vitamins and minerals a healthy body needs. Variety is as important for healthy architectures as it is for healthy bodies.

Most of the methods discussed in this chapter and in Chapter 17, *Activities to Evaluate Design Options*, on page 285 can be adapted to draw out different kinds of issues. An issue, in the general sense, is any topic that requires additional investigation or thought. To ensure we have a healthy architecture, look for issues from across the *architectural issues rainbow* as shown in the figure on page 173.

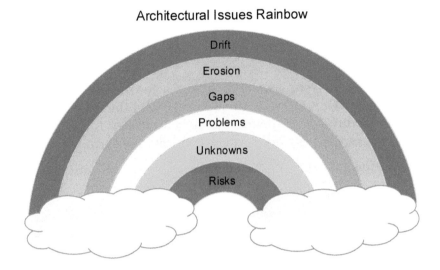

Architectural Issues Rainbow

Every issue from the rainbow can tell us something different about our architecture.

Risks (Red)

A risk is something bad that *might* happen, but it hasn't happened yet. As you learned in *Let Risk Be Your Guide*, on page 32, risks have two components: a condition and a consequence. The condition is something currently true about the architecture. The consequence is something bad that might happen as a direct result of the condition.

Risks can be mitigated or accepted.

Unknowns (Orange)

Sometimes we simply don't have enough information to say whether or not the architecture satisfies ASRs. Identify unknowns by looking for open questions about how things work and how specific ASRs will be addressed. Architecture evaluations can turn unknown unknowns into known unknowns. You can deal with the latter. The former can kill your architecture.

Unknowns require further investigation.

Problems (Yellow)

Problems, unlike risks, are bad things that have already come to pass. Problems arise when you make a design decision and it just doesn't work out the way you hoped. Problems can also arise because the world changed around you so that a decision that was a good idea at the time no longer makes sense. If the architecture already exists in code, we think of problems as technical debt.

Problems can be fixed or accepted.

Gaps in Understanding (Green)

When you zig and your team zags there is a gap in understanding. Gaps in understanding arise when what stakeholders think they know about the architecture doesn't match the current design. In rapidly evolving architectures, gaps can arise quickly and without warning.

Gaps in understanding can be addressed through education.

Architectural Erosion (Blue)

The implemented system almost never turns out the way we imagined it. This gap between the designed architecture and the as-built architecture is called *architectural erosion*, sometimes called *architectural drift* or *architectural rot*. Without vigilance, the architecture drifts from the planned design a little every day until the implemented system bears little resemblance to the plan.

Architectural erosion can be addressed by paying attention to the little details—in code or documentation—on a regular basis.

Contextual Drift (Violet)

Sometimes the world changes without us noticing. Software takes time to build. Over the months, facts that were true can become untrue. New facts come to light. Circumstances change. *Contextual drift* happens any time the business drivers or context driving our decisions changes after we've made a design decision.

Contextual drift can be addressed by occasionally revisiting business goals, architecturally significant requirements, and other things we think we know about our stakeholders and their needs.

A common mistake new software architects make is to look for the same kinds of issues all the time. A simple way to take your architecture evaluations to the next level is to ask questions that haven't been asked before. Look for a variety of issues and you won't be surprised by what you don't know.

Start with Low Ceremony Evaluation Methods

The amount of ceremony in a method refers to how much formality is required to apply the method. High ceremony methods are filled with rituals and can be costly to use. High ceremony methods are easy to repeat and produce consistent results. Low ceremony methods, on the other hand, are informal and have few rituals. As such, they are faster and cheaper to apply but narrower in scope, and more likely to produce inconsistent results.

If your team is new to architecture evaluations, starting with a high ceremony method such as the ATAM can be off-putting and might scare teammates away from evaluations for life. Instead of diving into high ceremony methods first, ease your team in to evaluations by starting with low ceremony methods. You might choose not to tell your team they are doing an architecture evaluation.

Here's an example of how this could play out. After a whiteboard jam (introduced on page 255) but before the group disbands, kick off an evaluation. Grab the whiteboard marker and say, *This looks like a good start. Are there any issues you see with our ability to promote <insert quality attribute here>?* Write down what they say on the whiteboard next to the diagrams. Help the team summarize findings and decide on next steps. Boom. Impromptu architecture evaluation completed in 10 minutes or less.

Low ceremony evaluation methods reinforce architectural thinking among the team and build a culture that challenges design decisions. As your team becomes comfortable with low ceremony approaches, strategically introduce targeted evaluations and, eventually, a deep evaluation.

Project Lionheart: The Story So Far...

We're about two months into the project and we've accomplished quite a lot. We populated our backlog, completed an architecture spike, and completed several iterations of development. Continuous integration is running, we finished several value adding stories, and we made our first internal releases. The planned architecture is sketched on whiteboards around the office and several important design decisions are recorded as architecture decision records. You think now seems like a good time to reexamine our planned design based on what we've learned so far.

You schedule a question-comment-concern workshop on page 298 during the next iteration. You start the workshop by reviewing the top five quality attribute scenarios. Next you ask us to draw some views of the architecture related to those quality attributes. Walking us through each scenario, you invite us to add sticky notes to the whiteboard drawings, capturing our questions, comments, and concerns. After 50 minutes we have a long list of issues that needs our attention.

To finish the workshop, you help the team *think* about next steps. We spend the last 10 minutes of the workshop creating an action plan to address the major issues we identified. Some of the actions include refactoring code that has drifted from our planned design and running an experiment to verify that we can correctly do phased deployments with no downtime.

You schedule another evaluation workshop two iterations as another checkpoint. We discuss design issues daily and everyone decides we should continue encouraging this practice.

Next Up

The architecture is a living part of the team's culture. Every day we choose to live with the architecture we've designed. Living with a poor design can become unbearable. Architecture evaluations help us understand how to make our architecture better.

In the next chapter, we're going to pull together everything you've learned so far and focus on how to lead a team of architectural thinkers to develop awesome software.

CHAPTER 13

Empower the Architects on Your Team

It takes a village to develop a modern software system. Technology advances such as containerization, super cheap computers, and on-demand cloud infrastructure put tremendous power and flexibility directly in developers' hands. In response to these new technologies, emerging architecture patterns such as microservices and function-as-a-service assume developers have a greater awareness of how their decisions influence quality attributes and other system properties.

On modern software systems, there is little difference between a *developer* and an *architect*. This isn't to say that modern software development teams don't have technical leaders. They do, though today's software architects don't always self-identify as architects. Modern software development teams need a different kind of leader than the traditional, top-down architect.

Modern software architects design with their team, not for their team. Today's architects are equal parts coach, mentor, and technical guru. We started this book by discussing essential architecture and design principles. Throughout Part II you learned how to put those principles into practice. In this chapter, you'll learn how to grow and empower your team as you design awesome software architectures together.

Promote Architectural Thinking

Teams who embrace the idea of *software architect* as a way of thinking instead of as a role on the team produce better software. When the majority of the team is an architect, the team can explore more design decisions faster. Software quality increases since more eyes can critically evaluate design decisions. Documentation is leaner and conveys more knowledge with less effort.

When everyone on the team can design architecture, everyone feels a greater sense of shared ownership over the design. The software becomes *our system*, not *the system*. Change becomes easier to manage since everyone understands the intent behind the design and feels a sense of responsibility for maintaining design integrity. Development velocity increases thanks to less rework, improved quality, and more efficient communication.

With a greater sense of ownership comes increased happiness, which in turn amplifies engagement in the whole software development process. When we design software together, we create force multipliers that accelerate our ability to ship amazing software. The benefits are amazing, but it's important to remember not everyone is ready to accept more design responsibilities.

It is our job to nurture our team's design skills while at the same time designing an architecture with them. We must empower our team while at the same time ensuring we design an appropriate architecture that lets us ship value-adding software for our stakeholders.

We accomplish this by providing just enough guidance to keep the team on track without requiring that we oversee every design decision. We build skills. We improve trust. We make it possible to recover from mistakes. We try to stay a few steps ahead of our team so we can shepherd them away from traps and pitfalls.

Programmers Make Architectural Decisions Every Day

In the early 2000s I read a software horror story about a developer who managed to take down all phone switches on the Eastern seaboard with a single line of code. *That'll never happen to us!* I told a coworker. We laughed. Fifteen years later the joke is on me.

These days I don't have to read case studies to find software horror stories. I only need to talk to fellow developers. I have met a developer who accidentally spent over $20,000 on Amazon Web Services for a university project. Another who spent a weekend recovering terabytes of data after a script did not behave quite as expected. Me? I once took out a cluster of servers used by over 100 developers with one line of code.

Today's programmers make design decisions about the architecture every single day. When one line of code can tank a required quality attribute, then you are a software architect whether you identify as one or not.

Facilitate Decision Making and Foster Skills Growth

For the team to truly own the architecture, the software architect must support them fully. Instead of acting as the sole design authority, we'll infuse our teams with the knowledge and skills they need to make design decisions for themselves. When things are going well, architects look more like coaches or mentors than authoritative leaders who make all the design decisions. Above all else, when possible, we let the team design the architecture instead of making the decisions ourselves.

Here are some examples of how architects can make this happen:

OK Software Architects	Great Software Architects
Select patterns and technology without input	Collaboratively select patterns and technologies with input from the team
Write detailed documents, release only once, fully complete	Create document templates for the team to use, build and review documents with the team incrementally
Make or approve all design decisions	Teach the team how to decide, provide design guidance, delegate decision making, provide reviews and feedback
Dictate who builds specific elements	Help the group self-organize and choose work
Avoid changes to the architecture	Embrace the inevitability of change and make the architecture easy to change
Mandate technology decisions	Build consensus for technology decisions

It's never easy to replace a great software architect, but great software architects can leave their team when the time is right. Software architects can safely move to a new team, not because they finished all the hard design work, but because the team has learned what it takes to be great software architects themselves. The only way this can happen is with practice.

Create Opportunities for Safe Practice

We want to give our team more design authority, but this is only possible if they're prepared to handle it. Teammates can't gain experience unless they practice. We're on a tight deadline, and taking time away from development for training is asking a lot. What do you do? Find safe ways to practice design.

Pair Design

Pairing is one of the simplest and safest ways to practice design. Start by working one-on-one with teammates while you're doing design work. If you need to think through a model, invite a teammate to join you for a whiteboard jam, introduced on page 255. If you have a meeting to talk to stakeholders about quality attributes, take a teammate with you. Ask a teammate to review a document filled with decisions before you share it with the whole team.

Create Scaffolding

In education theory, *instructional scaffolding* refers to support structures given to individual students to promote and reinforce learning. In school, you likely experienced many scaffolding techniques such as detailed feedback on a test, handouts, rubrics, and homework templates. We can use similar techniques when teaching our team about architecture. Here are a few examples:

- Build templates to support commonly delegated design work.

- Provide constructive criticism during peer reviews. See Activity 31, *Code Review*, on page 289.

- Create a code skeleton for new components. The code skeleton should sketch the module patterns planned but still require work to put meat on the bones. Bonus: Pair with someone to create the skeleton.

- Describe expectations for a particular artifact and share an example of what *better* and *worse* versions of that artifact look like.

- Create checklists for different design mindsets and tasks to help teammates internalize architectural thinking.

Introduce Architectural Guide Rails

An *architectural guide rail* restricts design options to ensure detailed design stays within the bounds of the desired architecture. Guide rails are a form of constraint we choose for ourselves. We can use guide rails to make design simpler (see *Limit Design Options with Constraints*, on page 49), but we can also use guide rails to create opportunities for safe practice. Imposing guide rails decreases the chances that we'll mess up the architecture.

Guide rails come in many forms and varying strengths. A *design policy*, instructions that describe something to do or avoid doing, is a simple guide rail but difficult to enforce. We can temporarily impose design policies when we delegate design work or put policies permanently in place to reduce risk, promote quality attributes, or overcome team weaknesses.

The strictest architectural guide rails are built into the code and make it impossible to do the wrong thing in the architecture. We discussed several approaches for creating guide rails in *Build Models into the Code*, on page 107. One example of a guide rail is to require the use of a specific library. Imposing this constraint might make development easier and help you avoid simple mistakes.

Host Information Sessions

If your team is keen on software architecture, consider hosting information sessions so you can dive deep into specific topics. Always be prepared to teach relevant information just-in-time before the knowledge is required to be applied. Dozens of micro-lessons are just as good as a single long training session.

As the team's skills increase, they'll start to share more feedback about the architecture's design. Be gracious with feedback and encourage it. When the team is willing to tell you how to improve the architecture, then you'll know you're doing something right and can think about delegating more design authority.

Delegate Design Authority

As we include more of the team in the design process, we must decide how much design authority to keep and how much to delegate. Our goal is to give away as much design authority as possible without putting essential quality attributes at risk or otherwise endangering the architecture. In *Management 3.0: Leading Agile Developers, Developing Agile Leaders* [App11], Jurgen Appelo describes seven levels of authority. We can use these levels to help us decide how much design authority to keep and what we can leave to the team.

Level 1: Tell You make the design decision and tell the team what will happen, usually by producing an artifact.

Level 2: Sell You make the design decision and show the team why it is the right call.

Level 3: Consult You ask the team for input before making the design decision. Ultimately the decision is still yours.

Level 4: Agree You collaborate with your team and reach consensus about the design decision as a group. Everyone has an equal voice.

Level 5: Advise You influence the team by sharing your opinions and insights but let someone else make the design decision.

Level 6: Inquire You let the team make the design decision and ask them to show why their decision is the right one.

Level 7: Delegate You leave the design decision to someone else. In this capacity, you might help gather information as a facilitator but someone else is responsible for the decision.

The level of authority you use will vary from decision to decision and team to team. Delegate the right level of design authority for the situation and you'll increase the team's confidence, happiness, and agility. Delegate too little design authority and you may undermine trust and make some people feel micromanaged. Delegate too much design authority and you'll end up with an anxious, unhappy team and a poor design.

In the best case, when you delegate too much design authority to a team that is not ready to handle it you'll have to try again at a lower authority level. When the team fails under these circumstances, it undermines trust and creates waste through rework, assuming you catch the decision early enough. Although that situation is not ideal, you can still recover. In the worst case, a bad design decision might go unnoticed until it's too late to recover easily.

Choosing the appropriate level of design authority is not an exact science. It takes some trial and error to figure out how your team likes to operate. The easiest way to check that you're choosing the best level of authority is to talk it over with your team and decide together.

When to Keep Design Authority

When the risks of failure are high, it's better to be conservative with how much authority you delegate. Stick to the first three delegation levels when the team is inexperienced. This approach is proven to work and improves your chances of producing a useful design. Unfortunately, the first three delegation levels don't come with as many bonus multipliers in quality, happiness, speed, and agility.

Simultaneously designing an architecture and skilling up a team is one of the most challenging times to be an architect. You're under pressure to deliver and unblock development. It'd be so much easier just to design it yourself! In the short term this may be true, but then your team will not grow and you will never be able to delegate design decisions. If you are the only architect on your team, then your skills, knowledge, and time will constraint the types of systems your team designs.

If you are in doubt, keep design authority until an appropriate opportunity presents itself.

Patrick says:
Architect as a Technical Leader

by Patrick Kua, principal technical consultant at ThoughtWorks

An architect's role is tough. Amongst their many responsibilities, an architect aims to reduce technical risk, plan for future change, and ensure that systems meet their quality attributes. However, for an architect to be truly successful, they also need to act like a technical leader.

Effective architects cannot always rely on their authority to make decisions. In today's ever-changing technology landscape, it's impossible for an architect to know all the details about the latest tools and technologies and how to apply them well. Instead, the effective architect must draw upon the wider experience of their development team and organisation. As a technical leader, the architect builds a shared technical vision for the team and focuses on amplifying the effectiveness and growing the skillsets of team members.

If architects are measured by the quality of decisions, they should also be interested in helping developers make better decisions. After all, each line of code represents a choice and, ultimately, each choice is a decision that has been made. The architect can improve developers' decision making by articulating operational or environmental constraints and agreeing with the team on architectural principles to gently guide future decisions.

Each of these activities—building a technical vision, describing constraints, and applying architectural principles—requires completely different nontechnical skills. These skills, often classified as "soft skills," are often the hardest to build. To be successful in this role, architects should draw upon deep communication skills such as explaining technical ideas in non-technical terms, using diagrams and models to build a common understanding and telling stories to motivate, excite, and challenge team members. Another essential leadership skill worth developing is the ability to listen. Not only will good listening skills improve the knowledge of the architect, but they will also grow the commitment of the team and organisation to the final technical vision.

Those architects who solely focus on deep technical expertise and owning all technical decisions are destined to build and live in their own ivory tower. You can avoid this situation by developing technical leadership skills and use them to build stronger bridges with the team and the rest of the organisation.

When to Give Away Design Authority

If your team already has some experience, then look for opportunities to consult, decide together, or only share advice before letting others decide. Delegating design authority is of particular importance for decisions that strongly influence the team's day-to-day-work or for design decisions in which there is passionate interest.

As the team learns more about architecture and as you gain confidence leading the team, incorporate collaborative workshops into your practice. Collaborative group sessions work well when you're able to agree, advise, inquire, or fully delegate decision making. Your role as a participant will decrease as you give more authority to the team. Instead, you support your team as a knowledgeable facilitator.

Many activities in Part III describe ways to include multiple stakeholders in the decision-making process. Here are a few examples:

- Tell stories with your team and encourage them to tell stories about the architecture too. Check out Anthropomorphize the Architecture on page 226 and System Metaphor on page 281.

- Encourage active participation with collaborative workshops such as Design Studio on page 113, Question-Comment-Concern on page 298, Risk Storming on page 301, and Scenario Walkthroughs on page 307.

- Check that the team is engaged and understand what's happening with an Architecture Briefing on page 286 or Sanity Check on page 304.

- Delegate artifact creation when good examples are available. A few artifacts that are easy to delegate and review include Architecture Decision Records on page 260, Architecture Haiku on page 263, and Inception Deck on page 269.

Get Your Hands Dirty: Delegation Poker

In *Managing for Happiness: Games, Tools, and Practices to Motivate Any Team* [App16], Jurgen Appelo introduced *Delegation Poker*, a game you can play with your team to practice choosing a delegation levels. Print or buy *Delegation Poker* cards from the Management 3.0 website[1] and play this game with your team. The game's rules are available on the website.

---

1. https://management30.com/product/delegation-poker/

Here are some things to think about:

- Before playing, each player should write down a few brief case studies related to areas you want to agree on a delegation policy. Try to have at least one case study from each teammate.

- Use the chapters in Part II to guide topic areas. Does the team feel confident in their skills for some topics?

- Are there decisions the team does not feel comfortable owning? Why?

- What areas will benefit most from giving the team more design authority? How can you help your team prepare for the additional responsibility?

Design Architecture Together

You learned in *Build Amazing Software*, on page 12 how software architecture improves our ability to ship awesome software. The architecture, not the architect, provides these benefits. It's the architect's job to guide the team to design an architecture so we can get these benefits. In *What Software Architects Do*, on page 3 you learned how software architects go about this task, and we've expanded on these ideas throughout the book.

Let's revisit the architect's key responsibilities from the perspective of our new knowledge:

Define the problem from an engineering perspective. Architects are responsible for defining the architecturally significant requirements, especially quality attributes. We prefer to use human-centered design methods to gather these requirements so we don't lose touch with stakeholders' true needs.

Partition the system and assign responsibilities to elements and teams. Architects guide the team to identify patterns that will promote desired quality attributes. We prefer to minimally design the architecture to ensure key quality attributes are achieved, leaving all other decisions to downstream designers.

Keep an eye on the bigger picture and ensure design consistency of the whole. Architects monitor the design as it emerges and shepherd the team as they implement the architecture. We strive to capture design decisions as accurate models using the lightest-weight documentation methods that work for the team and stakeholders. We use these models to reason about the system, evaluate our decisions, and identify risks in our ability to achieve business goals.

Decide trade-offs among quality attributes. Architects help the team reconcile trade-offs as design decisions are made and as the architecture evolves over time. We use risk to determine how much design work is required and where to focus the team's attention.

Manage technical debt. Architects deal with the reality of shipping software by identifying technical debt and devising strategies for paying it back. We recognize that technical debt is an unavoidable consequence of success and work to manage debt strategically over the life of the software system.

Grow the team's architecture skills. Architects empower their teams to take ownership of the system by ensuring the team has the knowledge and skills required to understand, explore, make, and evaluate an architecture. We prefer to design the architecture with our team instead of designing the architecture for our team.

For many teams programming is the easy part. Understanding what the problem is and deciding how the broader system comes together to solve that problem can be tough. The better everyone understands the architecture, the more prepared your team will be to tackle the challenges of software development. Designing the system together creates this deeper understanding.

Project Lionheart: The Epic Conclusion

Mayor van Damme is pleased. We completed the project only a few weeks behind our original schedule despite the constant stream of changes that occurred nearly from the start. We satisfied all the high-priority quality attributes, though there were a few hiccups during load testing before the official public release. Other than that everything went well.

The team strongly feels that the foundation provided by our architecture made it all possible. Our decision to do less architecture design up front worked out fine. The team had prior experience with most of the frameworks and technologies we used. In the beginning, we focused on the areas of greatest risk and worked to build consensus around the architecture. We had a few lucky breaks, such as stumbling upon a major problem with two web services, but we found the problems early enough that we had time to rewrite them from scratch. The final iterations of the project were stressful but not unbearably so.

Our last official work on Project Lionheart is to create maintenance documentation for the city's IT department. The team is writing a *moth ball* document, a user's guide, and cleaned-up versions of relevant architecture views. The original architecture driver's specification maybe only 50 percent accurate at this point. We never created a formal architecture description. We'll retain these documents for historical purposes and create a new *teachability viewpoint* to walk new developers through the architecture as it exists in the code.

The mayor's office estimates the application we built will save the city nearly $1 million in the first year. It feels good to see how our design decisions help the city meet its goals in the real world.

Next Up

Architects are leaders. This fact does not mean architects choose every element and relation in the architecture by themselves. Software architects strengthen their influence over the design by enabling others. Grow your team's architecture skills by collaborating with them and by creating safe opportunities for practices. This growth is just as important as making good design decisions.

The principles and practices you learned in Parts I and II give you most important things you need to know about software architecture design. Master this information and you will be an amazing software architect. What we covered here is far from the whole story. Many excellent resources are available that go deeper into documentation, viewpoints, patterns, evaluations, and specific technologies. As you grow as an architect, never stop going deeper, learning more.

Your next step? Use what you learned to build amazing software! To help get you started on your journey as an architect, Part III includes a collection of practical design methods organized around the four design thinking mindsets. I call it the *silver toolbox* as an homage to Fred Brooks's seminal *No Silver Bullet [Bro86]* essay.

No single software engineering practice provides an order of magnitude improvement in productivity, reliability, or simplicity. Although there are no silver bullets, we all have a *silver toolbox*, a collection of software engineering methods that, when used together, make vast improvements possible. I hope you have already found a few useful tools in this book that you can add to your silver toolbox.

The state of software design practice ten years ago looked very different than it does today. Ten years from now the way we design software systems will be different still. You're now a part of the community who will shape the future. Don't worry—it'll be fun. And we'll build some awesome software along the way.

Part III

The Architect's Toolbox

Every architect has a collection of design methods he or she uses to get stakeholders talking and teammates thinking. Use the methods in Part III to start your own architect's toolbox.

CHAPTER 14

Activities to Understand the Problem

In the understand mindset we actively seek information from stakeholders and work to define (or redefine) the problem. Understanding is more than just specifying requirements. We also need to figure out who our stakeholders are, identify business goals for the system, and ensure requirements specified with an eye toward the architecture.

As you'll recall from Chapter 5, *Dig for Architecturally*, on page 49, there are four kinds of architecturally significant requirements. All of these requirements will influence the architecture, but quality attributes are the most influential and a key concern for architects.

Constraints Unchangeable design decisions, usually given but sometimes chosen

Quality Attributes Externally visible properties that characterize how the system operates in a specific context

Influential Functional Requirements Features and functions that require special attention in the architecture

Other Influencers Time, knowledge, experience, skills, office politics, your own geeky biases, and all the other stuff that sways your decision making

The activities in this chapter help teams empathize with stakeholders and dig for architecturally significant requirements. Use them when you need to get a better grasp on the real problem.

Choose One Thing

Discuss priorities with stakeholders by presenting them with an extreme choice: if you only get one thing, what will it be? This activity can help stakeholders make decisions when facing difficult trade-offs.

Benefits

- Clearly communicates, *this is more important than that.*

- Starts a conversation about why a certain choice was made and what would need to change for stakeholders to change their mind.

- Makes it obvious when stakeholders disagree.

Participants

All stakeholders

Preparation and Materials

- List of alternatives, such as quality attributes, or other difficult trade-offs, such as cost, schedule, and features.

Steps

1. Explain the rules of the game. Stakeholders may choose only one of the presented options. Remind participants that this does not mean you will do only one thing, but instead the point is to have tough conversations early to avoid trouble down the road.

2. Present a set of options to stakeholders. Discuss what each option means and make sure everyone understands the options.

3. Force stakeholders to pick one option. All stakeholders should agree that this is the most important thing. In this activity we want consensus.

4. Briefly discuss why the option was selected. This discussion is often more important than the option picked.

5. Pick another set of architecturally significant requirements that are in tension with one another and play again.

Guidelines and Hints

- Play this game before things get too difficult. This conversation is easier when it's hypothetical than when it's real.

- Quality attributes that are in tension with one another should be pitted against one another.

- Use this activity to prioritize influential functional requirements.

- This technique works well as an informal conversation to help get better understanding of stakeholders' true need.

Example

Here are a few scenarios one team posed to some stakeholders and how things played out when stakeholders were asked to choose one thing:

Matchup	Stakeholder's Choice
Faster performance or greater accuracy	Faster performance, assuming accuracy met a required minimum threshold.
Cost vs. time-to-market	Time-to-market; stakeholders were willing to accept greater technical debt to get required features by a specific date.
Usability vs. security	Security; this was the number one quality attribute and surprisingly beat several other important quality attributes.
Availability vs. cost	Availability; achieving high availability on this particular system required potentially expensive redundancy for which stakeholders would willingly pay (up to a point) if required.

Alternatives

Instead of pitting one alternative against another, use *trade-off sliders* to let stakeholders make multiple comparisons. To use this activity, identify 3–5 related alternatives. Each item can receive a number 1 – N, where N is the number of items in the list. No two items can have the same number. This activity is often presented visually using sliders.

	1	2	3	4
Performance	**1**			
Scalability	1	2	**3**	4
Agility	1	2	3	**4**
Reliability	1	**2**	3	4

Empathy Map

Brainstorm and record a particular stakeholder's responsibilities, thoughts, and feelings to help the team develop a greater sense of empathy with stakeholders' goals.

Benefits

- Discover your audience's needs before developing an architecture description
- Help decide what information to include or exclude
- Create a rubric for evaluating the effectiveness of an architecture description

Activity Timing

10–30 minutes

Participants

Software architect, development team

Small groups of 3–5 or as a solo exercise

Preparation and Materials

- Before the activity starts, choose which stakeholders, systems, or users will be the focus of the activity.
- Flipchart paper or a whiteboard, markers, and sticky notes
- This activity can be adapted for remote participants with screen-sharing or remote collaboration software.

Steps

1. Draw a grid on a whiteboard or piece of paper. Label each quadrant—do, make, say, and think.

2. Pick a specific stakeholder and write his or her name in the middle.

3. Brainstorm tasks this person does, artifacts this person makes, things this person says, and feelings this person may have.

4. Write each idea on a sticky note and place it in the corresponding quadrant.

5. Review the empathy map and highlight insights.

Guidelines and Hints

- Be specific. Pick a person to empathize with, not a general role.

- Validate the findings from your empathy map with stakeholders.

- Mention quality attributes, risks, or other concerns this person may find relevant.

- Adapt this method for understanding application end users, external systems (for interface design), or for use with proxy stakeholders to understand quality attributes.

- Use software such as Mural[1] when participants are distributed.

Example

There is an example empathy map for a developer stakeholder persona on page 197.

Alternatives

The quadrants of an empathy map can be changed. Another common schema is hear, see, do (or say), and think (or feel).

Empathy maps are also useful for quality attribute analysis.[2] This approach is especially useful when your stakeholders are unable to participate in other workshops, such as the Activity 7, *Mini-Quality Attribute Workshop*, on page 210. Instead of focusing on what the stakeholders do, say, or think, we focus on how stakeholders react to specific quality attributes. Obviously, it's better to ask stakeholders directly. When they are not available, this is a good substitute.

---

1. https://mural.co/
2. Thijmen de Gooijer. *Quality Requirements on a Shoestring*. SATURN 2015. http://resources.sei.cmu.edu/library/asset-view.cfm?assetID=436426

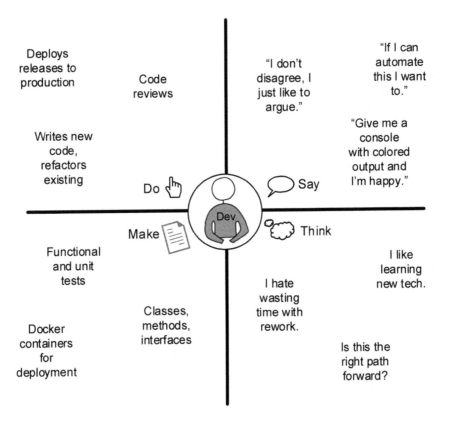

To use this variant, pick a stakeholder and brainstorm at least two quality attribute scenarios or general concerns for each relevant quality attribute. Use dot voting[3] to estimate how this stakeholder might rate the quality attributes. Ideally, you should validate the outcomes of this exercise, but this is not always practical. These insights can be used during other workshops to help ensure a stakeholder's perspective is represented even when that stakeholder is not present.

---

3.   http://dotmocracy.org/dot-voting

In the following example, from a workshop facilitated by Thijmen de Gooijer, sticky notes represent raw quality attribute scenarios. The lines in the center of the chart show how different absentee stakeholders might have felt about different quality attributes shown on a quality attribute web on page 207. The quality attribute web helps us visualize the importance of different quality attributes during structured brainstorming activities. During the workshop, different participants were asked to play the role of an absentee stakeholder by using the empathy map as a guide.

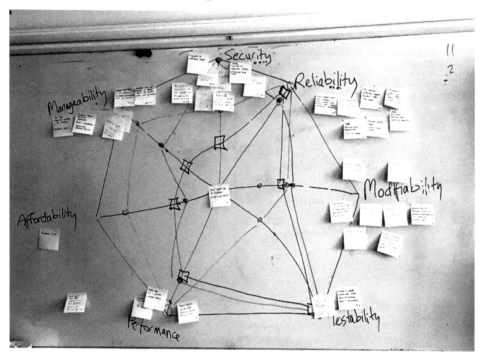

Goal-Question-Metric (GQM) Workshop

An approach for identifying metrics and response measures so that we can connect data with business goals. The *Goal-Question-Metric approach* (GQM) was introduced by Victory Basili, Gianluigi Caldiera, and H. Dieter Rombach in *The Goal Question Metric (GQM) Approach [BCR94]*. The goal of GQM is to identify measures we can use to determine whether a goal has is satisfied.

There are three parts to the GQM approach. The goal defines conceptual requirement that must be met. Goals can describe quality attribute scenarios, general software quality, business goals, or other topics. Questions illustrate the means by which we can characterize one or more goals. Metrics defines the measures needed to answer one or more questions.

Benefits

- Emphasizes using stakeholder goals as the basis for measures

- Shows clear lineage from data to stakeholder goals by way of the questions that must be answered to decide whether a goal is satisfied

- Flexible approach that can help teams think about metrics in a variety of situations

Activity Timing

15–90 minutes

Participants

This activity can be done solo or in a small group of 2–5 people. Any mix of stakeholders will work.

Preparation and Materials

- Whiteboard or flipchart papers, markers
- Goals to be explored can be optionally identified before the workshop

Steps

1. Write a goal at the far left of the whiteboard.

2. Prompt participants to provide questions. *What questions would you need to answer to know if we've met this goal?* Write each question to the right of the goal. Draw lines from the goal to the questions to create a tree.

3. Explore each question to identify metrics needed to answer the question. Write each metric to the right of the questions. Draw lines from each question to the metrics required to answer it.

4. Repeat the exercise for any related goals that might reasonably use the same questions or metrics. The end result should be a tree that connects metrics to questions and questions to goals.

5. Identify data required to compute each metric. Write the data needs to the right of the metrics. Draw lines from each metric to the data needed to compute the metric.

6. For each piece of data identified, determine where you can get the data. Write down each data source for each bit of data. Describe the cost of gathering data from each of the data sources.

7. The last phase of the workshop is to prioritize data and metrics. Clearly identify *must have* metrics. Look for data sources that can provide data needed to compute multiple metrics or metrics that can answer multiple questions.

8. Record the results of the workshop by taking pictures and writing down the discussed goals, questions, metrics, data, and data sources.

Guidelines and Hints

- Be sure to have plenty of space for drawing the GQM tree.

- Look for opportunities for reuse. Metrics can be used to answer more than one question. Likewise, the same data might help compute multiple metrics.

- Data sources and data are likely to influence the architecture, but also look for opportunities to gather data outside of the architecture.

- Record results in a table or spreadsheet to validate with stakeholders later. The identified metrics are revisited throughout the life of the software system.

Example

In this example, the goal is written on the far left, questions are captured in the middle column, and metrics are written in the column on the far right. Data used to compute the metrics was omitted from this particular GQM sketch.

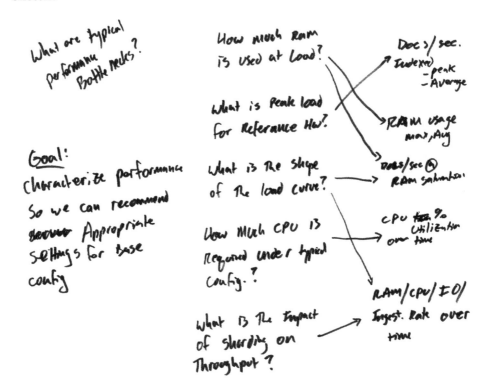

Interview Stakeholders

Sometimes the easiest way to learn about stakeholders' business goals is to ask. When we *interview stakeholders* we ask about their plans for the software, uncover the problem context, get a feeling for looming risks, and dig for details about quality attributes and other requirements.

Interviews may be either structured and follow a set script or unstructured. Unstructured interviews are more conversational and often easier for the subject, but you should still go into the interview with a planned set of topics. Interviews can also be either face-to-face or conducted offline via question-naires or surveys.

There are many stakeholder interview resources with checklists and question templates. I recommend *Designing for the Digital Age: How to Create Human-Centered Products and Services [Goo09]* by Kim Goodwin if you are looking for further depth regarding this technique. An extensive excerpt from the chapter on stakeholder interviews is freely available on the web.[4]

Benefits

- Focus on general information gathering

- Format allows for open back-and-forth discussion

- Provides background information that can be used to prepare for other workshops or activities

- Quickly validate quality attribute scenarios and other ASRs

- Creates a direct connection between stakeholders and architects

Activity Timing

A single interview should last no more than 30–60 minutes.

Participants

This activity can be done one-on-one or in small stakeholder groups. The architect leads the interview. Stakeholders are the interview subjects.

---

4.   http://boxesandarrows.wpengine.com/understanding-the-business/

Additional team members may observe an interview, but the interview group should be small—no more than one or two active interviewers—to avoid overwhelming the subject.

Preparation and Materials

- Interview goals and questions
- Pen and paper or laptop for taking minor notes during the interview
- Voice recorder to record the session so you can focus on the conversation. Write detailed notes after the interview. Most teleconference software has options for recording.

Steps

1. Explain the goals of the interview and how the results of the interview will be used. *We're going to validate some requirements we've gathered so far to make sure we capture your real needs.*

2. Ask the subject questions from your planned interview checklist.

3. Follow up with clarifying questions as needed to be sure you get the information you need.

4. Conclude the interview by thanking the subject for taking time to meet with you.

5. Directly after the meeting, jot down your general impressions of the interview, including any themes, technical asides, and design thoughts. If others observed the interview, collect their notes and general impressions.

6. Once all interviews have been completed, analyze the data collected. Update or create architecturally significant requirements as appropriate. Summarize any new risks or concerns that may require further action.

7. Once all interviews have been completed, hold a debrief meeting with the team and stakeholders to share insights.

Guidelines and Hints

- Avoid interviewing stakeholders about architectural concerns too early. There is often a significant amount of general design work that must happen before diving into architectural concerns.

- Phrase questions so the subject can share their true thoughts. Avoid leading the subject.

- When possible, use the subject's words when summarizing ideas.

- Talk to real users and primary stakeholders of the system being designed. For example, it's better to interview Eunice, who trains the hamsters herself, than Beatrice, who only oversees hamster trainers but doesn't train the little critters.

- Use data to help jump start conversations. See Activity 9, *Response Measure Straw Man*, on page 219 for a method that can gently encourage interview subjects to be more specific.

- Record the session or have a designated note taker so the interviewer can devote his or her full attention to the subject.

Example

Here is an example of how an unstructured interview might go. In this exchange, the architect is attempting to clarify a business constraint.

> **Architect:**   *You mentioned earlier that this new system replaces an existing one. What is the plan for the old system?*
>
> **Stakeholder:**   *Once the new system is on line we'll start the deprecation time line for the old system. The deprecation process can take up to nine months since we have to give current customers time to migrate off the old system.*
>
> **Architect:**   *Nine months is a long time. When do you hope that process will complete?*
>
> **Stakeholder:**   *The earlier the better, but I'm hoping by December of next year.*
>
> **Architect:**   *OK, working backward, to be able to deprecate by December the new system needs to be live by the end of March. Does that sound right to you?*
>
> **Stakeholder:**   *That's probably about right, yes.*
>
> **Architect:**   *Can you tell me a little more about the deprecation requirements? I want to verify that we aren't missing anything that could put deprecation at risk.*
>
> **Stakeholder:**   *Sure, there are four must-have features we need in the new system before we can deprecate the old one...*

With that last statement, the architect immediately begins thinking about influential functional requirements.

List Assumptions

Assumptions are truths about the system we simply take for granted. Hidden assumptions kill projects (or at least cause significant pain). With the *list assumptions* activity, we take assumptions out of the shadows by writing down as many assumptions as we can. Use this information to plan further design work, prioritize next steps, improve ASRs, and improve the team's shared knowledge about the architecture.

Benefits

- Head off misunderstandings about the true goals and requirements.
- Great for ad hoc analysis. Does not require a formal workshop or agenda.
- Avoid missing important requirements.

Activity Timing

15–30 minutes

Participants

Whole team working in pairs or small groups (no more than 3–5 people).

This can be done as a solo exercise, but you would need to share your assumptions list with someone; otherwise, your assumptions will remain hidden!

Preparation and Materials

- Any writing surface and writing tool: pen and paper, marker and whiteboard, or sharpie and sticky notes

Steps

1. Kick off the activity with the adage *You know what happens when we assume too much, right? It makes an ass out of you and me!*

2. Explain the goal of the activity. *Over the next 15 minutes we're going to write down all the assumptions we have about the system.*

3. Prompt participants by focusing on an area where assumptions need to be flushed into the open.

4. Write down the assumptions mentioned so everyone can see them.

5. As the pace slows, move on to the next topic or end the session by planning follow-up actions.

Guidelines and Hints

- Start by asking, *what do we think we know about X?*

- Write down everything mentioned, even if it seems like common knowledge.

- Pause to discuss assumptions that are surprising or generate a reaction from one or more participants.

- Record the assumptions in your team wiki.

Example

Here is an assumptions list drawn up immediately following Activity 19, *Whiteboard Jam*, on page 255:

Assumptions - Query Parse

- parsing is needed By Many Services
- WE eventually want a Shared Service
- We don't have time to create and Test a service for our deadline
- Everyone we care about right now uses Java/JVM
- A Library can Be used to Build a service in The future
- Current case is simple → we'll need More complex/Advanced capabilities in The future

Activity 6

Quality Attribute Web

The *quality attribute web* is a brainstorming and visualization activity to help elicit, categorize, refine, and prioritize stakeholder concerns and raw quality attribute scenarios. A quality attribute web captures stakeholders' concerns. We write each concern on individual sticky notes. The web is drawn as a simple radar chart with relevant quality attributes written around the edge like this:

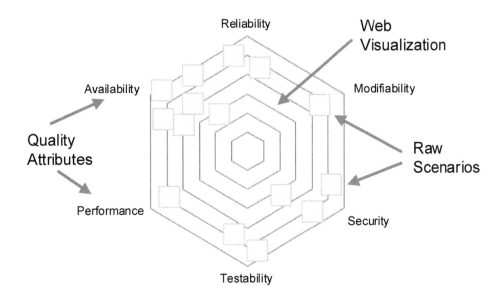

Benefits

- Guide stakeholders to think about quality attributes instead of features.

- Provide a visualization that shows how one system is different from another based on highly desirable properties.

- Help stakeholders prioritize quality attribute scenarios before refining them.

Activity Timing

30–45 minutes

Participants

Any stakeholders, including the team

Preparation and Materials

- If you are using a quality attribute taxonomy, prepare it ahead of time. You may find it helpful to print the web on poster paper instead of drawing it on a whiteboard.

- Sticky notes, markers

Steps

1. Draw or post a blank quality attribute web so everyone can see it. The web can be created ahead of time if you know which quality attributes to include. If you're not using a prepared web, brainstorm as a group to identify 5–7 quality attributes that are important to the stakeholders.

2. Brainstorm concerns and raw quality attribute scenarios as a group. Write each concern down on a sticky note and add it to the web near the quality attribute to which it most closely applies.

3. When time expires, write down the concerns and use the information to create quality attribute scenarios.

Guidelines and Hints

- Some stakeholders will need help getting started. Be prepared to help them phrase their concerns initially.

- Use dot voting to prioritize concerns on the web.

- Don't worry about getting perfect scenarios. A general thought, worry, response measure, or partial scenario is a great start.

- Combine with the mini-quality attributes workshop, described on page 210, for a more comprehensive workshop.

Example

In this example, quality attributes were brainstormed when the activity began and written on a whiteboard. In this particular workshop, you can see that availability and reliability tended to be on everyone's minds slightly more than other quality attributes. Of the twenty or so raw scenarios created during the hour long activity, only six or seven were prioritized highly by stakeholders. The remainder helped the team gain necessary context about the stakeholders' concerns.

Mini-Quality Attribute Workshop

The *mini-Quality Attribute Workshop* (mini-QAW) is a lean, facilitated workshop designed to help you talk about quality attributes with stakeholders early in a system's life.[5] During a mini-QAW, you'll collaborate as a group to quickly identify, develop, and clarify quality attributes with the help of a quality attribute taxonomy. By the end of the mini-QAW, you'll have a prioritized list of quality attribute scenarios and a wealth of contextual information about the system to be designed.

Benefits

- Walk through the essential steps of a traditional quality attribute workshop in only a few hours.

- Quickly identify raw quality attributes and prioritize them before refining into full scenarios.

- Provide opportunities for stakeholders to riff on each other's ideas.

- Create a forum for open discussion among stakeholders to discuss quality attribute concerns, risks, and other general concerns about the software system.

Activity Timing

Ninety minutes to 3 hours, depending on the size of the taxonomy and brainstorming method used

Participants

A facilitator, usually the software architect. A small group of stakeholder participants.

This workshop works best in small groups of 3–5, with a maximum size of about 10 participants. Host multiple workshops if necessary to keep the group size down. When hosting multiple workshops, review scenarios with all groups once the workshops have concluded.

---

5.   http://bit.ly/mini-qaw

Preparation and Materials

- Before the workshop, prepare a *quality attribute taxonomy*. The quality attribute taxonomy is a set of predefined quality attributes highly relevant to the type of system you are building. An example of a quality attribute taxonomy for service-oriented architectures is available from the Software Engineering Institute.[6] The taxonomy will be used to facilitate structured brainstorming.

- Prepare graphical quality attribute scenario templates in the style of the examples on page 53. Use these templates to capture scenarios during the workshop.

- If desired, prepare a quality attribute web, shown on page 207, on poster-sized paper for use during the workshop. If not using a pre-printed taxonomy web, draw a web at the start of the workshop.

- Sticky notes and markers for participants

Steps

1. Present the workshop goals and agenda.

2. Teach participants what they need to know about quality attributes. Describe the quality attribute taxonomy you'll use during the workshop.

3. Display or draw the quality attribute web so everyone can see it.

4. Brainstorm raw quality attribute scenarios using either structured brainstorming or a questionnaire. Instruct participants to write one idea per sticky note and place them directly on the displayed taxonomy web. Read the posted raw scenarios out loud as they are placed on the web. If this prompts participants to think of new scenarios, record and post them on the web too.

5. After the brainstorming phase, prioritize the quality attributes and raw scenarios using dot voting. Participants get 1/3 the number of identified raw scenarios. For example, if there are 25 sticky notes on the web, everyone gets 8 votes to spend however they please. Participants also get 2 votes for overall quality attributes. Everyone votes at the same time.

---

6. Liam O'Brien, Len Bass, and Paulo Merson. *Quality Attributes and Service-Oriented Architectures.* http://resources.sei.cmu.edu/library/asset-view.cfm?assetid=7405

6. Refine the top raw scenarios as a group until time runs out using the six-part scenario template shown on page 53. Remaining work must be done as homework.

7. As homework, refine the top raw quality attribute scenarios. Present the top refined quality attribute scenarios in a follow-up meeting to verify the scenarios and relative priority.

Guidelines and Hints

- Keep your taxonomy small, 5–7 quality attributes max.

- Use the web visualization to drive the workshop. Put the sticky notes close to related quality attributes.

- Don't worry about creating formal scenarios during brainstorming.

- Ask probing questions about the stimulus, response, environment.

- Pay attention when stakeholders sound worried about something. Stakeholders' worries are often the source of a possible scenario.

- Watch out for features and functional requirements.

- Do not skip the homework. This is the most important part!

- If workshop participants are not co-located, select screen-sharing software all participants can use or consider using a digital whiteboard application such as Mural. See *Work with Remote Teams*, on page 124 for more remote facilitation tips.

Example

Here is an example mini-QAW agenda:

Agenda Item	Timing	Hints
Introduce the Mini-QAW	10 minutes	
Teach participants about Quality Attributes	15 minutes	Set participants up for success
Brainstorm Raw Scenarios	30 minutes–2+ hours	Walk the System Properties Web
Prioritize raw scenarios	5 minutes	Use dot voting
Refine scenarios	Until time runs out	Finish as homework
Review the results	1 hour	Separate, future meeting

The mini-QAW is a very useful workshop with a few moving parts. Next, we'll look at some additional tips for each of the stages in the standard agenda.

Brainstorm and Prioritize Raw Scenarios

If workshop participants are relatively experienced, guide them through a simple brainstorming exercise. Set a time limit of 7–10 minutes for brainstorming and have participants work alone to come up with as many raw scenarios as they can. With less experienced participants (or facilitators), consider using the quality attribute web activity on page 207 with a prepared taxonomy and *quality attribute taxonomy-based questionnaire*. The taxonomy questionnaire is a list of questions based on a predefined quality attribute taxonomy designed to prompt stakeholders to think about potential scenarios. Questionnaires require more up-front work, but this approach is thorough and produces more consistent results than brainstorming without a questionnaire.

After brainstorming, prioritize the raw scenarios. Stakeholders will raise many concerns during a workshop, but not all concerns are worth the effort to refine further. After participants have finished voting, take a step back and look at the web. Are there areas of the web with a greater number of sticky notes than others? How does that compare with how people voted? Were the high-priority scenarios aligned with the high-priority quality attributes?

The example on page 214, is what the quality attribute web might look like after voting. Dots on sticky notes are a vote for a raw scenario whereas dots on the web are for the overall quality attribute regardless of the specific scenarios identified.

Start Scenario Refinement

After prioritizing raw scenarios, use the time remaining in the workshop to refine scenarios as a group. Show the quality attribute scenario template during the workshop and fill it in with stakeholders. The template can be printed on paper or shown as a presentation. The facilitator is responsible for refining any remaining scenarios as homework before the next meeting.

As you refine scenarios, keep an eye out for functional requirements masquerading as quality attribute scenarios. Everyone loves to talk about features, and it's easy for feature requests to come up during a QAW. When this happens, add the feature request to your notebook and redirect the conversation back toward specific quality attributes.

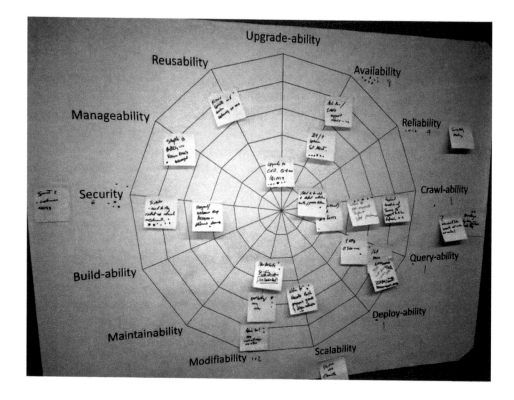

Verify Findings with Stakeholders

Hold a follow-up meeting to review the refined scenarios with stakeholders. Prepare a slide-based presentation of the findings or other appropriate write-up to share during the meeting.

During this follow-up meeting, check the accuracy of any straw man numbers you put into the scenarios (see Activity 9, *Response Measure Straw Man*, on page 219. Discuss information missing from scenarios and fill what you can. Finally, use this opportunity to double-check the priority of the top quality attribute scenarios. A simple *high* or *low* is usually sufficient. Any raw scenarios not refined are considered as *low* priority.

Alternatives

The mini-QAW is based on a more comprehensive workshop. The traditional QAW takes a few days to complete and is more appropriate for high-risk systems with many stakeholders. *Quality Attribute Workshops (QAWs), Third edition [BELS03]* describes the traditional QAW in detail.

Activity 8

Point-of-View Mad Lib

The Point-of-View (POV) mad lib summarizes business goals and other stakeholder needs in a memorable, engaging format. Here's a basic POV mad lib template. You can use this template as is or create your own.

The format should be familiar to anyone who has written agile stories, though the emphasis is on stakeholders' needs and how the overall system will provide value rather than specific features or functionality. You might think of it as a *user odyssey*, a statement that encompasses potentially multiple epics and stories.

Benefits

- Develop empathy for stakeholders' needs.
- Articulate business goals in a user-focused way.
- Use to start the conversation about business goals.

Activity Timing

30–45 minutes

Participants

Any stakeholders. This activity can be done alone or as a small group of 2–3 people. If necessary, a larger group can be divided into smaller subgroups of 2–3 people each.

Preparation and Materials

- Before the activity, identify the list of stakeholders for which you'll produce mad libs. This list can be created just-in-time with participants before introducing the mad lib activity.

- Markers and sticky notes for each group. Enough paper for each group to produce one mad lib per stakeholder.

Steps

1. Introduce the activity by sharing the goal of the exercise.

2. Describe the mad lib template and do a warm-up exercise to ensure participants understand the mad lib format. Everyone should participate in the warm-up.

3. Introduce the first stakeholder. Briefly share any information known about the stakeholder and discuss their needs as a group.

4. Give each group 90 seconds to create a mad lib.

5. Repeat steps 4–5 until all stakeholders have been covered.

6. Share the mad libs produced and briefly discuss as a group. Consensus is not required as a part of this activity.

Guidelines and Hints

- Be specific. Pick an actual person if you can.

- Don't worry about phrasing at first. It can be difficult to find exactly the right words. Getting the ideas out is more important.

- The impact of each mad lib should be outcome focused. Try the *5 Whys* technique[7] to help get to the bottom of stakeholders' real needs.

Example

The POV mad lib is meant to be filled in fast. Don't overthink it. Here are some example mad libs for the Project Lionheart case study:

- Mayor van Damme wants to reduce procurement costs by 30 percent because he wants to avoid cutting funding to education in an election year.

7.　https://en.wikipedia.org/wiki/5_Whys

- Mayor van Damme wants to improve city engagement with local businesses because it may improve the local economy when local businesses win contracts.

- The Office of Management and Business wants to cut the time required to publish a new RFP in half because it improves services and reduces costs at the same time.

Alternatives

Any of these approaches, and many others, may be substituted for the Point-of-View mad lib.

Design Hills

Design hills describe the impact stakeholders hope the software will have on end users.[8] Like other ways of specifying business goals, hills try to describe the value the software provides, not how the software is to be built.

Design hills have three parts: who, what, and wow.

Who? A specific stakeholder who is affected by the software to be built.

What? Something the stakeholder will be able to accomplish with the software that he or she could not do before.

Wow! A significant, measurable outcome that directly results from having used the software to complete the task.

Here's an example from Project Lionheart:

Who?
Specific person or role

What?
Specific task

Ron, Director of Parks and Recreation, can hire a temporary SCUBA Instructor within 3 weeks of submitting his request to the Office of Management and Business.

Wow!
Measurable, impactful result

---

8. http://www.ibm.com/design/thinking/keys/hills/

Traditional Business Goal Statement

Traditional business goal statements are plain and direct statements that describe how stakeholders derive value from the system. Business goal statements have three parts, often enumerated in a table.

Subject A specific person or role.

Outcome A specific and measurable description of how the world changes if the system is successful.

Context Describes the conditions around the goal so the team can develop empathy and a deeper understanding of the need.

Here's an example of the same POV mad libs written as traditional business goals:

Stakeholder	Goal	Context
Mayor van Damme	Reduce procurement costs by 30%	Strong desire to avoid making budget cuts to education in an election year.
Office of Management and Business	Cut the time required to publish a new RFP in half	Current publishing time is 9 weeks. Reducing time improves services across the city and reduces costs at the same time. Citizens suffer when city services go unfunded. Think: *no toilet paper at the girls' basketball game* or *not enough hypodermic needles for emergency medical crews.*

Response Measure Straw Man

The goal of a *response measure straw man* is to give stakeholders something to beat up until they arrive at their own answers. We do this by inventing a reasonable response measure for some quality attribute scenario as a way to kickstart discussions. The straw man technique works with other architecturally significant requirements discussed in Chapter 5, *Dig for Architecturally*, on page 49.

Benefits

- Provides an example of a measurable response and response measure
- Jump-starts thinking about quality attribute scenarios
- Overcomes blank-page syndrome by providing something to edit instead of creating response measures from scratch

Activity Timing

Varies, often combined with other activities

Participants

Architects will often create straw man response measures on their own and validate with stakeholders later.

Preparation and Materials

- A list of raw quality attribute scenarios as described in *Capture Quality Attributes as Scenarios*, on page 52

Steps

1. For each quality attribute scenario, make up a response and response measure. The response should be a reasonable, best guess based on your knowledge and experience. Response measures can be either outrageous or honest.

    - Choose an honest response measure when you think you can confidently estimate a good measure.

- Choose an outrageous response measure when your confidence is low to help find the boundaries around acceptable behavior.

2. Label the scenarios as having a *straw man response measure* to avoid potential future confusion.

3. Validate the scenarios and their response measures with stakeholders, such as during a stakeholder interview, described on page 202, or mini-QAW, described on page 210.

Guidelines and Hints

- Use a straw man to understand the boundaries around acceptable behavior.

- Responses should be correct for the scenario. The point is to zero in on an accurate and reasonable response measure.

- Listen to your stakeholders once you get them talking. When presented with a wrong answer, many stakeholders will react with useful information.

- Keep an eye out for anchoring. Anchoring is a cognitive bias where people let the first information they hear drive their decision making. The straw man should be a reasonable estimate or so outrageous it will be rejected outright. Exercise caution if your outrageous estimate is accepted.

Example

Here are some examples of response measure straw men created for a cloud-based information system:

Quality Attribute	Response	Straw Man Response Measure	Accepted Response Measure
Changeability	Time required to add a new algorithm	6 months	2 iterations
Portability	Effort required to move to new cloud provider	3 person-months	4 person-days
Performance	Average response time under typical load	1 minute	3 seconds max
Scalability	User load the system should be able to handle	10 requests per second	140 requests per second

Stakeholder Map

A stakeholder map is a network diagram of the people involved with or impacted by the software system. Use this method to visualize the relationships, hierarchies, and interactions between all the people who have an interest in the software system to be built.

Benefits

- Identify more stakeholders than just the usual suspects.
- Determine who to talk to about requirements.
- Help the team empathize with people and not just focus on technology.
- Create a snapshot of the system context and who's involved.
- Use as a document to bring new teammates up to speed or to assist with architecture validation.

Activity Timing

30–45 minutes

Participants

Whole team, known stakeholders

This activity can be conducted alone or with groups of 25 or more people depending how much physical space is available.

Preparation and Materials

- A drawing surface such as a large whiteboard or large sheets of paper. Tape paper to a wall or roll out on a large table. Provide markers of different colors so that most participants have a marker. When working with a group, be sure there is enough space and writing surface for all participants to contribute.

- If the participants are distributed, consider using a tool such as Mural.[9]

---

9. https://mural.co/

Steps

1. Introduce the activity by sharing the goal of the exercise. You might start by saying, *For the next 30 minutes we're going to explore who our stakeholders are. Once we have a better idea of who has a stake, we'll come up with a plan for who we're talking to first.*

2. Share the guidelines and hints for creating a stakeholder map.

3. Start the activity. Working together, everyone adds and annotates stakeholders collaboratively until time runs out or the map seems complete.

4. Once the map is complete, ask participants to share observations about the map. Are there interesting connections or unexpected stakeholders? Who are the *most important* stakeholders?

5. Take a picture of the map and store it in your team's wiki.

Guidelines and Hints

- Use simple icons to represent individual people; use multiple icons to represent groups.

- Be specific when naming stakeholders. Think about their roles or in some cases specific names.

- Use speech bubbles to represent stakeholders' needs or thoughts.

- Connect people using arrows to show relationships and influence. Label connections to describe relationships.

- Encourage participants to look beyond the obvious stakeholders if they stall out during the activity.

- Nudge wallflowers, participants who are just watching, to pick up a marker and add to the map.

Example

Here's an example stakeholder map created by three people in about 15 minutes:

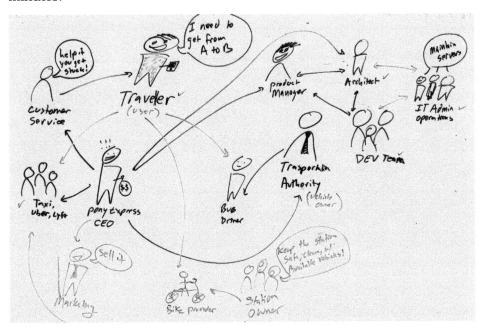

CHAPTER 15

Activities to Explore Potential Solutions

In the explore mindset, we work to discovery multiple design concepts and engineering approaches we think will solve specific problems. Architecture exploration focuses on the part of the world architects control—the software. We don't always get to choose the problem, but solutions are bound only by our knowledge, creativity, and skills.

Exploration may seem without bounds, but according to the redesign rule, introduced in *The Four Principles of Design Thinking*, on page 15, we rarely create new architectures completely from scratch. Since all design is redesign, exploration starts by considering solutions we already know, such as the patterns outlined in Chapter 7, *Create a Foundation with Patterns*, on page 79. We'll also explore knowledge codified in frameworks and experiences woven into our cultural fabric as rules of thumb.

Since architects are equal parts designer and engineer, there are a few other areas we'll want to explore. Construction methods enable real software to be built and can influence the architecture. Domain concepts from the problem space are a great starting point for solution ideation. Of course, we'll explore elements, relations, and their responsibilities too.

As we explore solutions, we'll gain a deeper understanding of the problem. Learning as we go is normal. In *Notes on the Synthesis of Form [Ale64]*, Christopher Alexander explains that we can only define a problem with a solution in mind. A problem will lead to a solution which in turn will redefine the problem. This is all part of the fun of design.

The activities in this chapter will help you generate options for the architecture. Use them to explore the structures that will become your architecture and figure out engineering approaches for making them real.

Personify the Architecture

To *personify the architecture* means to give it human qualities so that you can explore interactions among elements. Talking about the architecture as if it had human emotions helps us apply our experience with human relationships when designing the architecture. To use this technique, pretend elements in the architecture are people or animals and describe their emotions, motivations, goals, and reactions to stimuli.

Anthropomorphism is a fun, natural way to explore design concepts. Anthropomorphism is also problematic since applying fictional human qualities to a software system is imprecise and ambiguous. We're making up a story about our software and projecting human-like qualities onto the system! Trading precision for effective communication so that the architecture is easier to explain is usually worth it.

Benefits

- Make the architecture more relatable.

- Qualify desirable and undesirable properties and situations by thinking of how elements will "react" or "feel."

- Create memorable stories that help the team keep architectural concerns at the center of design conversations.

- Increase buy-in of design decisions by making the architecture almost feel like a teammate.

- Quickly try different emotions and reactions through simple story telling.

Preparation and Materials

- No preparation is required. This technique is often used during impromptu conversations about the architecture.

Steps

1. Pick a piece of the architecture for which you need to describe behavior. Think about a quality attribute scenario or functional requirement that element must satisfy.

2. Pretend the architecture has human qualities. How would the elements respond to the stimulus in the quality attribute scenario or functional requirement? Tell a story about what the elements do. Describe their motivation and reactions as if they were people.

3. Try different reactions and emotions for the same set of elements under discussion. Introduce variations into the architecture to see how elements might need to change their behavior.

4. After exploring different ideas, codify the options that look promising. Create a system metaphor, sketches, or other documentation for further analysis.

Guidelines and Hints

- Use anthropomorphism as a part of your team's regular design discussions.

- It's OK to feel a little silly. We are pretending the architecture is human, after all.

- Accompany stories with sketches to make the ideas discussed more concrete.

- Anthropomorphism is not a substitute for architectural views that describe the system using more precise language.

Example

Here are some of the human qualities one team gave their web services:

- Our services are *fickle*. They don't care where they live or which service instances they talk to from one request to the next.

- Most of our services are *stubborn*. They retry requests when the first request fails.

- Some of our services are *moody* and *impatient*. Moody services give up if they can't get what they want quickly enough. They'll *resentfully* make do with the data they have.

- Some of our services are *best buds*. They chat to each other often. We even discussed deploying them together in pairs so they won't be lonely.

Architecture Flipbook

In an *architecture flipbook*, we record every step of the design journey so others can follow along afterward. Every page of the flipbook includes a sketch and notes about incremental changes to a model. We use this record to think through options or backtrack to an earlier decision that might have led us astray. As a bonus, the resulting flipbook explains why the architecture looks the way it does.

Most people only see the final results of your design toils. All the wrong turns, goof-ups, and critical *aha!* moments become the designer's secret memories of their personal journey exploring design ideas. It's a shame these moments are lost since we can learn a lot by peeking into the architect's mind and seeing a model as it evolves.

Benefits

- Methodically think through a model.

- Externalize the branching and backtracking that happens naturally during design.

- Teach others how to think about design and modeling.

- Remove some of the mystery as to where the ideas for a model come from.

Activity Timing

A single flipbook session can take 30–45 minutes. This is brain-intensive work. Frequent breaks are helpful.

Participants

This activity can be completed alone or as a small group of 2–3 people.

Preparation and Materials

- Choose a simple diagramming tool you like to use. Microsoft PowerPoint or similar works well for this exercise. You can also draw on paper and take pictures as you go.

Steps

1. Pick a user story or quality attribute scenario to use as the motivation for the model you'll create.

2. On the first slide, describe the problem and any architecturally significant requirements relevant to the model you want to explore.

3. On the next slide, brainstorm and record interesting domain concepts from the problem and briefly describe them.

4. The next slide starts blank since we haven't created a model yet. Add a single element that you think is in the solution space for the system.

5. Copy the slide you just created and try to apply the user scenario or story you picked at the beginning. Can you achieve the scenario? Do any new questions arise that are specific to the solution space? Write down your questions and comments. Choose one thing to address and amend the model by adding a new element and required relations.

6. Repeat step 5 until you can successfully complete the user story or scenario, and all open questions have been answered. If you get stuck, backtrack to an earlier model and continue from that point. Indicate that the new slide is a *branch* of an earlier point.

7. Review the flipbook for inconsistencies and key moments. Use the history to help summarize the rationale for the final model.

Guidelines and Hints

- Start with the obvious concepts.

- Watch out for implied concepts or completely new concepts that are not explicitly named in the problem domain. These hidden concepts are the among the most interesting and important to get right.

- Make small changes with each step in the flipbook.

- Look for inconsistencies in the model relative to the scenario or user story to build the model.

Example

Here is an example flipbook showing a domain model for a system that trains predictive models from users' data. The prompt for the flipbook was simple but missing essential concepts. Here is the influential functional requirement used to seed the flipbook: *A trainer user can add queries with document references so that she can train a new predictive model.*

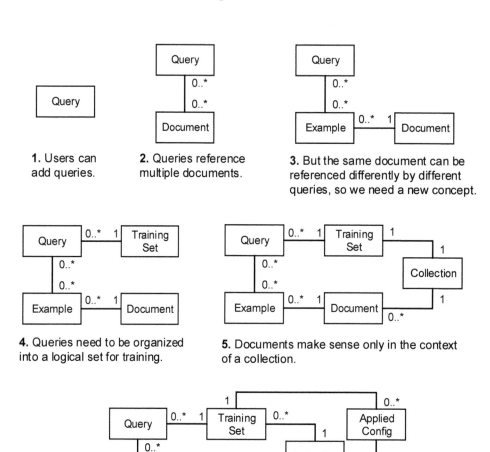

1. Users can add queries.

2. Queries reference multiple documents.

3. But the same document can be referenced differently by different queries, so we need a new concept.

4. Queries need to be organized into a logical set for training.

5. Documents make sense only in the context of a collection.

6. If instead we allow multiple training sets, then there must be a way to choose the set used at run time. How might the model change if we assume a training set can transcend collections?

This series of models shows a growing concept map (described in Activity 14, *Concept Map*, on page 236), which eventually formed the basis for a RESTful API. Notice how the example starts with concepts from the provided functional requirement but quickly uncovers hidden ideas not mentioned. At step 6, the example begins branching to explore alternative design paths for the model.

In *Building Models Quickly and Carefully*, George Fairbanks demonstrates this technique.[1]

Alternatives

Activity 26, *Paths Not Taken*, on page 274 is similar to creating a flipbook, though it emphasizes recording history rather than speculating about solutions. When listing the paths not taken, instead of thinking about the model up front we reflect on the current model and how we got here.

---

1.   http://georgefairbanks.com/blog/building-models-quickly-and-carefully/

Activity 13

Component Responsibility Collaborator Cards

Use *Component Responsibility Cards* (CRC cards) to propose architectural elements, describe their responsibilities, and show how they come together to form a view of the architecture. This exercise is an extension of the *Class Responsibility Collaborator* cards described by Kent Beck and Ward Cunningham in *A Laboratory for Teaching Object-Oriented Thinking [BC89]* and Scott Ambler in *The Object Primer: Agile Model-Driven Development with UML 2.0 [Amb04]*. This technique also works well for modeling domain concepts.

CRC Card Template

Component Name	
Responsibilities	Collaborators

Example CRC Card

Notices Service	Notices Index
Forward notices to index (façade)	Cluster management service
Validate notices	
	Unknown callers

Benefits

- Quickly iterate through design alternatives.

- Create group buy-in and shared understanding of the architecture.

- Create a connection between architecturally significant requirements and design alternatives.

- Identify potential gaps in the architecture.

Activity Timing

30–90 minutes

Participants

The development team works in small groups of 3–5 people. This is also a good exercise for solo work.

Preparation and Materials

- Index cards and markers for writing components and responsibilities. Host the activity at a large table where all participants can see the cards.

- Before starting this activity, you should know some of your system's functional requirements (use cases, stories, or similar) and quality attribute scenarios.

Steps

1. Introduce the goals for the exercise and share an example CRC card.

2. Read aloud a functional requirement or quality attribute scenario.

3. Create a card to represent the user or source for a quality attribute scenario. Write the user or source's name at the top of the card. Underneath write the trigger that initiates the use case or scenario.

4. Add a new card to the table to represent the architectural element with which the trigger card first interacts. Write the name of the element at the top of the card.

5. Evolve the architecture by adding cards for known elements or creating new elements as needed. Write the responsibilities of each element directly on the cards. Record relationships to other elements on the side of each card. During the session, physically arrange cards to visualize relationships.

6. As design alternatives emerge, keep all the cards on the table. Move cards to the side in case they are needed later. This lets you see and quickly evaluate alternatives.

7. Pick a new functional requirement or quality attribute scenario and walk through the architecture again. Add or change cards as needed. Alternatively, change assumptions about scenarios and see how that affects the architecture.

8. Repeat steps 4–8 until time runs out or the available functional requirements and quality attribute scenarios are addressed.

9. At the end of the session, record the elements and their assigned responsibilities. Also record key decisions and design principles that emerged during the session.

Guidelines and Hints

- Use index cards or sticky notes to represent elements.

- Keep the exercise fun and fresh by drawing pictures, not only text.

- It's OK to informally mix structures (static, dynamic, and physical) if it helps with reasoning.

- Use digital collaboration tools to work with remote teammates or create an instant digital record.

- Every card should have at least one responsibility by the end of the activity. Consider carefully whether cards without responsibilities have a place in the architecture. Are there cards with too many responsibilities?

Example

Here is an example of how CRC cards can be used to flesh out architectural elements and their responsibilities:

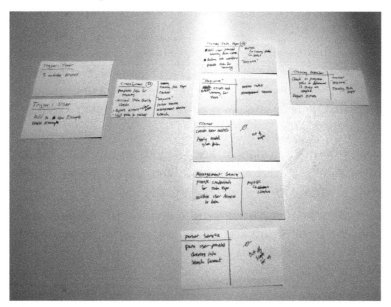

Once the cards were laid out, a few interesting things became apparent. First, the *Transformer* (second column from the left) seems to have a lot of responsibilities and collaborators. What would happen if we split those responsibilities into different elements? See the top figure on page 235.

We moved the original *Transformer* to the side and split the element in two pieces. The new *Transformer* will only transform data while a new element,

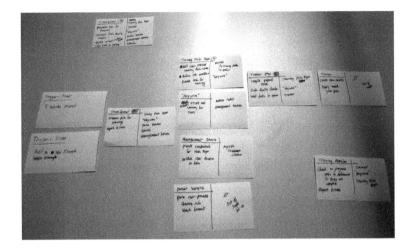

Training Prep, will prepare the transformed data for the *Trainer* element. We also identified a new element, the *Training Monitor*, but it's not relevant in this current flow.

Again examining the emerging model, the *Training Data Repo* (top of third column) appears to have overloaded responsibilities. Can those responsibilities be reasonably moved to new elements?

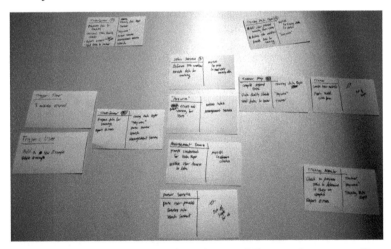

It turns out we can focus only on the jobs workflow and remove all responsibilities for writing user data from this element. We moved the old *Training Data Repo* card to the side and added a new element with fewer responsibilities named *Jobs Service* (top of the third column from the left).

Next we will record a snapshot of these models, introduce a new scenario, and adjust or create CRC cards to support the new scenario.

Concept Map

A *concept map* is a method for exploring domain concepts by visualizing how concepts in the domain are related to one another. Great software architectures are grounded in the problem domain. Concept maps help us uncover specific ideas from the problem domain as well as implicit ideas required to implement a solution. Every domain concept needs a home in the architecture. The relationships among domain concepts can help us pick the right patterns, interaction models, and information architectures.

Benefits

- Visualize domain concepts and their relationships.

- Try out different relationships among domain concepts.

- Uncover missing, hidden, or implied domain concepts required to implement a functional software system.

- Lay a foundation for partitioning architectural elements and for defining potential relations among elements.

- Provide a resource for evaluating an architecture's fitness. Is it consistent with the domain model?

- Outline a domain rich vocabulary for the software system.

Activity Timing

30–60 minutes

Participants

Create a concept map with technical stakeholders. Work alone or as a small group of 2–3 people. Verify a concept map with knowledgeable stakeholders.

Preparation and Materials

- Use drawing software for a digital map, or paper and pencil if you're going analog.

Steps

1. Choose a starting concept from the problem domain to *seed* the map. This will usually be a prominent noun from an architecturally significant requirement. Write the concept's name down and draw a box around it.

2. Record related concepts and connect them to each other as appropriate. Determine the cardinality of each relationship. Give each relationship a specific name. Relations should read like a sentence—*Concept A does something to or with Concept B.*

3. Choose a functional requirement or quality attribute scenario to help flesh out the domain concepts. Attempt to describe how the scenario would be satisfied by your current domain concepts. Pay close attention to concept gaps and omniscient concepts.

   A *concept gap* occurs when ideas are missing from the domain model. You'll know when this happens because you will not be able to complete a scenario without introducing new concepts.

   An *omniscient concept* is one that magically seems to know everything it needs to connect to other, potentially unrelated concepts. Identifying omniscient concepts requires a high degree of introspection over the domain and concept map.

4. Revise the concept map to introduce newly uncovered concepts. Repeat step 3 until the scenario can be fully satisfied.

5. Pick a new scenario. Refine the concept map as needed to address the new scenario.

Guidelines and Hints

- Use boxes to represent concepts. Use lines to show how concepts are related.

- Be specific when naming concepts and describing how they are related. See Belshee's 7 Stages of Naming on page 105 for naming advice.

- Label both ends of a concept relationship.

- Be prepared for concepts and relations to move as the map emerges.

Example

This example concept map from Project Lionheart shows several core concepts from the domain. The map reads, *City Department issues zero or many RFPs while an RFP describes the needs of one or more City Departments.*

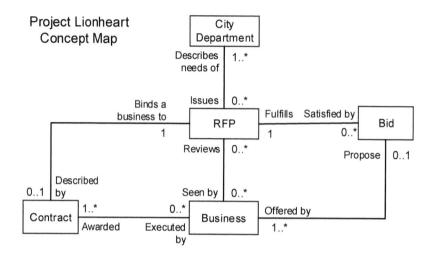

We can already start to see interesting ideas emerging from the map. The map itself captures several assumptions about business rules and valid states for the system. It also appears that RFP is a central concept. We should define that domain concept early to avoid running into problems.

Alternatives

Concept maps pair well with architecture flipbooks, described on page 228. To create a concept map as a flipbook, record each step of your design process as you explore the domain.

Context mapping from domain-driven design is similar but focuses more broadly on identifying contextual model boundaries across a large system. Concept mapping as described here is simpler and more narrowly focused. As a concept map evolves and grows, context mapping may become necessary. See *Domain-Driven Design: Tackling Complexity in the Heart of Software [Eva03]* for details on context mapping and more great design advice.

Divide and Conquer

In cases where you need to cover a lot of ground, break your team into small, independent groups dedicated to exploring a single problem. Divide the problem into smaller chunks and conquer them in parallel. Independent groups can use any exploration method they want within their group, but we still want some oversight to ensure everyone's time is well spent.

Dividing the exploration space into smaller focus areas increases the risk that you'll arrive at a fragmented and inconsistent design. The risk is especially high when you accidentally divide the exploration space in a way that prevents groups from exploring independently. You won't know this until after the groups have started their investigations, so you need to account for this in the method.

Divide and conquer works best with a tight feedback loop in which the broader group attempts to converge thinking regularly. The time between when the exploration space is divided and converges again can be as short as a few hours or as long as a week. Here's what the divide-and-conquer process looks like:

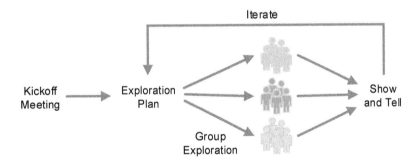

Benefits

- Explore more of solution space in a shorter period of time.

- See a range of design ideas that cover similar areas.

- Give designers the time needed to adequately explore solutions. Not every exploration should be time-boxed to a 90-minute workshop.

- Use a larger group effectively by exploring different areas in parallel.

Activity Timing

Planning the division can take as little as 20 minutes or as long as a few hours depending on the goals of the exploration and how well you know the topics you're exploring. The amount of time spent planning should be commensurate with the precision required for the exploration. If you're OK with some thrashing and overlaps, then spend less time planning. If groups must work on specific areas with clearly defined outcomes, then devote more time to planning.

Groups should work alone for no more than one week, with a preference for shorter periods on the scale of hours or days.

Participants

Divide the whole team and technical stakeholders into groups of 2–4. The architect leading the exercise may participate in a group, but it is beneficial for the lead architect to float among groups to resolve issues and offer coaching.

Preparation and Materials

- Before starting the exercise, you need to know enough about the lay of the land to divide the solution space for exploration. Create a prioritized list of open questions and risks to drive the planning.

- Decide how you will record group commitments. Prepare slides or notes for a kickoff meeting, which all participants will attend.

Steps

1. Hold a kickoff meeting. Explain the ground rules of the exploration and set expectations for what each group will share when the group reconvenes. The most important rule is that everyone shares what they have, whatever it is, when the groups reconvene.

2. Divide the exploration space and help participants self-organize into groups of 2–4 people. We do these things at the same time so participants can better adapt to an evolving situation. By the end of this stage, every participant should be in a group and every group should have a clear mission.

   When dividing the exploration space you may take either a breadth-first or a depth-first approach. In the depth-first approach, all groups explore the same general area. In the breadth-first approach, every group explores something different. Go depth first when you are confident in a general solution and need to refine it. Prefer breadth first when you need to quickly reduce risks across a variety of topics.

3. Establish the due date. Schedule the *show-and-tell* meeting. By scheduling the show-and-tell meeting during the kickoff, you create a social contract with each group. Everyone is expected to share something at the show-and-tell meeting.

4. Record each group's commitments for the exploration. This is the *exploration plan*. The general idea is to set clear expectations for what each group will accomplish during the exploration. At the show-and-tell meeting, groups are expected to show what they committed to exploring during the kickoff, or explain what prevented them from achieving their goals.

5. Begin the exploration. Groups divide and explore as they see fit. The architect should check on groups as they work.

6. Reconvene for the show-and-tell meeting at the agreed place and time. During the meeting each group shows their accomplishments relative to their exploration goals and briefly tells what they learned. Participants from other groups should have time to ask questions and provide constructive criticism. Note any new questions or risks raised during the show-and-tell meeting.

7. If there is more to explore, immediately plan another iteration of exploration. Go to step 2.

Guidelines and Hints

- All groups must share during the show-and-tell meeting. If the team completely missed their exploration goals, use this as a coachable moment to pivot or realign the group.

- To maximize exploration potential, encourage people to form cross-functional groups with people they don't work with every day. Consider occasionally mixing groups.

- Keep the groups small to avoid gold plating the designs and bike-shedding discussions in which the group focuses on trivial, tangential matters.

- Commitments made during exploration planning should come from the group. Some groups will need help scoping their commitments appropriately to the available exploration time.

- Remind groups that the exploration phase is ending so that they have enough time to prepare for the show-and-tell meeting.

Example

Let's look at the divide-and-conquer path one team took over the course of three one-week explorations. In this case, the team's general mission was to create a set of cloud-based microservices, which reused core legacy components where possible. The most important risks and open questions centered around the reusability of strategic components and choosing new technologies.

Here are the exploration goals for Week 1, with a summary of what was shared during the show-and-tell meeting:

Group	Exploration Plan	Show and Tell
One	Refactor plug-in framework to see if it's possible to extract from legacy codebase.	Showed primary interfaces and classes for the refactoring, which demonstrates the plan is feasible.
Two	Hello world gRPC[2] web service.	Demo of a Ruby-based client talking to a service implemented in Java.
Three	Create a concept map and draft microservice partitioning.	Draft concept map. Feedback from the group indicated that more work was needed.

Based on what group 1 learned in the first week, they chose to focus on the next risk for the legacy components. Groups 2 and 3 remixed their members.

Group	Exploration Plan	Show and Tell
One	Command-line invocation of legacy plug-ins.	This turned out to be more work than expected. Described roadblocks and remediation plans.
Two	Recommend database technology.	Three demos of different database technologies with a quick peek at the code.
Three	Revise concept map, draft microservice partitioning.	Concept map and microservice overview.

2.   https://www.grpc.io/

By the third iteration the groups were starting to get a good groove for the rapid, time-boxed nature of the work. The demos in Week 3 were tightly focused.

Group	Exploration Plan	Show and Tell
One	Command-line invocation of legacy plug-ins. This is the same goal as last week with the plan updated to reflect specific problem areas.	Demo of a single plug-in running independently of legacy system, list of next steps.
Two	Microservice discovery examples using Eureka.[3]	Partially working demo of Eureka with two simple microservices.
Three	Draft APIs for the first services.	Draft gRPC .proto files.

By the end of Week 3 the team had reduced risks enough to begin implementation and detailed design for specific microservices while they worked to refine the architecture as a whole.

---

3.   https://github.com/Netflix/eureka/

Event Storming

Event storming is a collaborative brainstorming technique used to identify domain events. Event storming can be used as a precursor to more in-depth domain modeling exercises, to assess the team's current understanding of the domain, and to identify risks and open questions in an existing domain model. Event storming is described fully in *Introducing Event Storming: An Act of Deliberate Collective Learning [Bra17]* by Alberto Brandolini.

Event storming helps teams better engage with subject matter experts who are knowledgeable about the domain but may have trouble pairing with developers directly. Event storming accomplishes this in two ways.

First, the format requires active engagement from all participants. Subject matter experts have no choice but to inject their knowledge into the process. Second, event storming encourages participants to be concrete and specific. If you have subject matter experts working with you, encourage them to describe their jobs and expertise in gory detail.

Benefits

- Visualize learning opportunities and facilitate a structured conversation about the domain.

- Uncover assumptions about how people think the system works. This allows you to identify misunderstandings and missing concepts.

- Create a shared understanding of the problem and potential solutions.

- Produce a highly visual, tactile representation of business concepts and how they relate.

- Enable diverse viewpoints to be represented.

- Allow participants to quickly try out multiple domain models so they can see where those concepts work and where they break down.

- Focus on concrete examples, not abstract ideas.

Activity Timing

An initial event map can be created in 30–45 minutes. Workshops should run at least 90 minutes to allow for setup and reflection. It's often useful to allow additional time to try different domain models.

Participants

Subject matter experts knowledgeable in the problem domain must participate. A few members of the development team should also participate to take advantage of the learning opportunity. If knowledgeable subject matter experts are not available, the workshop may not have great outcomes.

This workshop can be run with as few as 2–3 participants and as many as a dozen or more, depending on the workspace and facilitator's experience.

Preparation and Materials

- Large roll of paper, tape, lots of sticky notes (at least six colors), markers.
- To prepare the room, tape the paper to the wall to create a large workspace. Remove any impediments such as tables or chairs that might prevent participants from accessing the paper.

Steps

1. Before the workshop starts, verify that you have the right mix of participants from both technical and business domains. If you suspect the combination of stakeholders is not right, it's better to postpone the workshop.

2. Start the workshop by sharing the goals for the activity. You might say something like, *our goal in this workshop is to create an event map for the Hamster Production Line system.*

3. Introduce participants to the idea of domain events and describe the different kinds of events to be mapped. Assign each event type a color.

   Domain event (orange) An event relevant to domain experts that happened in the past. Domain events might be a step in a business process, scheduled, or happen as a result of another event.

   User command (blue) An action initiated by a user. Record who the user is on a yellow sticky note next to the command.

External system event (purple) Events that originate from an external system. Record the system on a yellow sticky note next to the event.

Passage of time (green) Indicate how much time has passed when time is relevant to the flow of events.

Consequences (white) An observable change in the business process that directly resulted from an event.

Questions, comments, concerns (pink) Discussion points that a participant wants to raise. Capturing issues and deliberation on a sticky note instead of talking about it encourages participants to continue moving forward, avoids analysis paralysis, and creates a visual indicator of potential trouble spots. Help participants to use this information to address issues during the workshop.

4. Set expectations for participation. Explain that all participants are expected to contribute and encourage participants to favor creating a sticky note over discussing whether or not a sticky note is required.

5. Make sure everyone has a marker in hand. Have everyone write down an event. The facilitator should place the first sticky note on the paper. Placing the first sticky note signals that it is OK to get started. Once the first event is on the wall, the activity has officially begun.

6. Participants place events in the order they occur from left to right. As the group discovers new events, move sticky notes around to make room. Add subflows underneath the initial event with more detail.

7. As the activity progresses, the facilitator should review events and look for issues. An event might take place in the future instead of the past or be abstract instead of concrete. As you find events that need help, rotate them a quarter turn so they look like a diamond on the map.

8. Encourage all participants to work at the same time to build the map. Help participants find areas where they can contribute. Point out hot spots or areas they should review. A smooth-running workshop will appear slightly chaotic to an outside observer.

9. After 15–20 minutes or if you notice participants winding down, encourage the group to review the map and revise events as necessary.

10. Once time has expired, discuss the map as a group. Are there concepts that seem awkward or still in need of refinement? Are there gaps or major questions in the map?

11. Take good pictures of the map. Move it to a different wall. Tape a new piece of paper. Build a new map but change the rules slightly so that the group explores the domain differently. For example, remove a central concept that appeared in the first map, encourage participants to be more specific, or build a new map in silence to try to expose ideas that didn't make their way to sticky notes.

12. To close the workshop, ask participants to share one or two things they learned during the workshop.

13. Post the maps in a common area if possible. Save the pictures and written notes. Use the lessons from the workshop and the created maps as inputs for other modeling activities.

Guidelines and Hints

- Include a diverse group of participants and ensure your have the right mix of participants before starting. It is better to cancel the workshop and try again with the right mix of people than attempt the workshop without knowledgeable business experts. With only developers present, you'll get a technical model. With a mix of developers and business experts, you'll create a visual flow of events, which is what you want.

- Ensure everyone has easy access to sticky notes and markers. Bring more than you think you'll need.

- Do your best to create an unlimited modeling space. Choose an appropriately sized room with a large wall. Bring plenty of extra big paper. If you're using a whiteboard, it should be big.

- Explore real, concrete business examples. The more specific, the better. This helps expose new events and edge cases.

- Post a visual legend of the sticky notes being used.

- Ask clarifying questions throughout the workshop. *What is a good example of…? What do you mean by…? What else might happen here?* The conversations that happen when asking these questions are extremely important.

- Encourage participants to post sticky notes first, then talk about ideas.

- Time-box the activity to encourage the group to move forward quickly.

Alternatives

The general organization of the workshop is similar in nature to *User Story Mapping [Pat14]*.

Event storming can be modified to include different experts and emphasize different modeling outcomes. Here are some ideas from Brandolini:

- Focus on big picture ideas and include many stakeholders when starting a new system or project.

- Dig into specifics required to implement event sourcing[4] or CQRS[5] systems by focusing more narrowly on a specific topic area.

- Include user experience experts and overlay a user's journey onto the event map.

- Use as the basis for evaluation to identify areas of the system that may need to be expanded or can be refactored.

- Run a workshop with new teammates and stakeholders to teach them about the problem domain.

Activity 17

Group Posters

Small groups work together to create a poster that conveys their design ideas for the architecture. This activity is well suited to summarizing outcomes from other workshops.

Benefits

- Produce several alternative models for comparison.
- Build pockets of consensus and spread knowledge within a larger group of stakeholders.
- Create artifacts that can be easily shared with people outside the group.
- Quickly explore and summarize architecture design ideas.

Activity Timing

20–30 minutes

Participants

Stakeholders work in groups of 2–5 people. Stakeholders who work together regularly should be in different groups.

Preparation and Materials

- Flipchart paper and markers

Steps

1. If needed, review architecture sketching basics.

2. Review the goals for the activity. All participants will produce a poster that solves the same problem.

3. Divide participants into groups or allow them to self-organize. Distribute flipchart paper and markers.

4. Groups create a common vision for the architecture within the scope of the agreed goals.

5. When time expires, each group shares their poster. Give each group 3 minutes to present their poster. Questions and comments should be held until after the presentation.

6. Allow 3–5 minutes to critique the poster after each presentation.

7. Once all posters have been shared, briefly discuss any trends or general observations about the posters together.

8. Initiate a round of dot voting. Given each participant 1 vote for best overall poster and 3 votes for interesting design ideas that appear on any poster. Discuss the outcomes of the voting.

Guidelines and Hints

- Remind participants to include a legend and think about which views of the architecture they are sketching—module, component and connector, or allocation.

- It's OK to sketch more than just structures. Sketches of domain models, sequence diagrams, or state diagrams can all be useful.

- Encourage participants to jot down open questions or risks that arise during their group discussions.

- Monitor participant progress closely and adjust time up or down to ensure groups are creating effective posters.

- During the critiques, remind participants to focus on facts and avoid "I like…" kinds of remarks.

- Record video or audio of the poster presentations for later review.

- Keep the posters and hang them in your workspace.

Example

This poster shows two architecture views and the stickers used during dot voting. Participants were asked to vote for an overall *best poster* and to highlight *unique design concepts* from individual posters they thought were relevant or interesting, even if the poster overall was not the best.

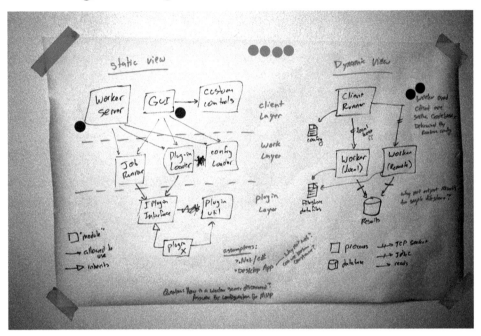

Round-Robin Design

Quickly explore a range of ideas, and then combine them to start building consensus. In a *round-robin design* workshop, participants quickly generate, share, and critique sketches of the architecture to help them see a range of possibilities. By the end of the activity, participants will have seen at least two new ideas in addition to their own.

Participants go through three rounds. In round one, participants generate a sketch. In round two, participants review someone else's sketch. In round three, participants attempt to fix the issues raised in a third person's sketch.

Use this activity as a sanity check exercise (see Activity 36, *Sanity Check*, on page 304) or to set the stage for a follow-on activity such as creating group posters, described on page 249.

Round-Robin Design Overview

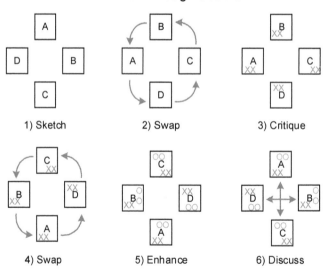

| 1) Sketch | 2) Swap | 3) Critique |
| 4) Swap | 5) Enhance | 6) Discuss |

Benefits

- Give everyone a voice and opportunity to share their design ideas.
- Foster creativity by constraining the design environment.
- Create opportunities for unintended combinations.
- Encourage group ownership of the design.
- Build consensus among possibly disparate ideas.
- Expose differences (and similarities) in thinking across the group.

Activity Timing

15–45 minutes

Participants

Since we're sketching architectural models, this activity is usually best reserved for technical stakeholders. At least 3 people are required to participate. Conversations start to break down with more than about a dozen participants.

Preparation and Materials

- Standard-sized paper
- Pens or markers of three different colors

Steps

1. Distribute pens and paper to the group.

2. Agree on the exploration goal—a specific view, quality attribute, or type of model (for example, API or domain model).

3. All participants sketch for 5 minutes. Encourage unconventional ideas.

4. Pass your sketches to the person on the left.

5. Using a different colored pen, critique the sketch for 3 minutes. Add annotations directly to the paper.

6. Again, pass your sketches to the person on the left.

7. Using a different colored pen, improve the design to overcome weaknesses identified by the critique for 5 minutes.

8. Pass the papers back to the original designer. Review the sketches as a group and briefly discuss.

Guidelines and Hints

- Do not disclose all steps at the beginning of the activity. Hold paper trading as a surprise.

- Informal views are fine during the sketches.

- Encourage participants to use any notations needed to convey an idea.

Example

This example shows the resulting sketch after three rounds of annotations:

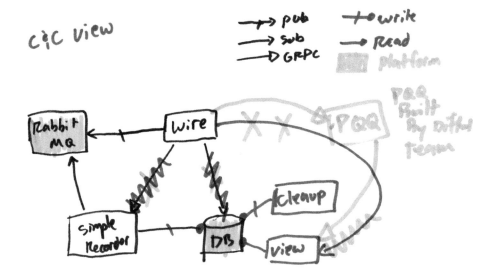

Activity 19

Whiteboard Jam

Collaboratively draw a series of diagrams that best capture the whole group's ideas. We've all done this before. Gather some teammates around a whiteboard, put a marker in everyone's hand, and start sketching. The activity described here adds a smidge of structure to something most architects do naturally. This additional structure helps the activity become more consistent and encourages better outcomes.

Benefits

- Help opinionated teams get their ideas out in the open.

- Quickly move through design alternatives by forgoing formality and immediately improving ideas based on feedback.

- Create a shared cultural experience upon which further design insights can be created.

- Include many participants in the discussion.

- Facilitate the activity as a participant.

Activity Timing

The timing is up to the group and what they want to explore.

Participants

Any technical stakeholder may participate. The number of active participants is limited by the amount of whiteboard space, though 3–5 participants seems to be a nice sweet spot. Participants will sometimes come and go throughout the session.

Preparation and Materials

- Start with a clean whiteboard and have plenty of markers of different colors.

Steps

1. Set the stage by reviewing the objectives for the whiteboard jam. Write the objectives on the whiteboard so everyone can see them.

2. Encourage someone to sketch his or her ideas on the whiteboard.

3. Take turns describing your sketches to the group. As you are describing, it's OK for others to start sketching new ideas, riffing on your work.

4. After the initial sketches are up, briefly critique the designs. Write issues that must be addressed on the whiteboard.

5. Take turns adjusting the sketches already on the whiteboard or drawing new ones.

6. Continue adjusting sketches, sharing updates together, and critiquing until time runs out, all ideas are covered, the group reaches consensus, or the group reaches an impasse.

7. Take pictures of the whiteboard and summarize the results in your team wiki along with a brief write-up of the discussion.

Guidelines and Hints

- Use during impromptu discussions to resolve confusion and capture multiple ideas under discussion.

- Write down important discussion points on the whiteboard as they are raised during the jam.

- Occasionally pause to reflect on the sketches and ask questions. Most jams follow a natural create-share-critique flow described on page 117.

- Encourage everyone to draw. It's OK to sketch while others are talking.

- The diagrams themselves are only useful as a cultural artifact for the people who participated in the jam. Pictures will jog participants' memories but won't make sense to someone who wasn't there. The discussions take place during the whiteboard jam are often more important than the sketches.

Example

This example shows one of three sketches drawn during a whiteboard jam. Notice the *responsibilities* listed on the right side. The team used these responsibilities as a checklist to evaluate their design ideas as they evolved the diagrams together.

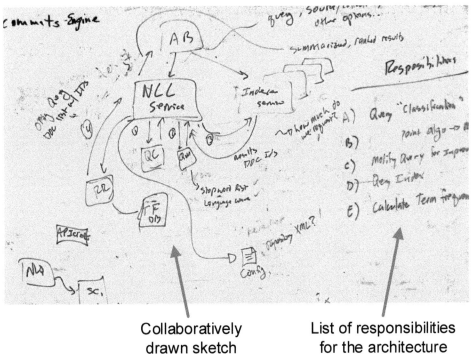

Collaboratively
drawn sketch

List of responsibilities
for the architecture

CHAPTER 16

Activities to Make the Design Tangible

Things get real when we stop talking and start making. In the make mindset, we turn abstract ideas, such as design concepts, into tangible things we can easily share with others. Tangible things facilitate communication between stakeholders. They can also be directly tested to see how well a design addresses our needs. Making something is a great way to reason about the architecture. Even making only a part of an artifact or a draft can serve as a useful thinking exercise.

Software architects make more than just box-and-line diagrams. We also have more tools in our toolbox than just diagrams. Building prototypes, writing documents, running experiments, crunching numbers, telling stories, and even play acting are all great ways to show an architecture to others instead of only telling them about it.

The artifacts in this chapter will help you make the architecture tangible. You can create most of these artifacts on your own, but sometimes it's more fun (and informative) to pair with someone or collaborate with a larger group. Most artifacts here take 30 minutes or less to create.

Since the purpose of making something is to share it, review the artifacts you make with your team and relevant stakeholders. They'll need to know about the ideas contained in the things you make. Reviews also let you check that the design concepts in the architecture align with your understanding of the problem. The activities in Chapter 17, *Activities to Evaluate Design Options*, on page 285 will show you how to facilitate reviews.

Architecture Decision Records

Capture architecture design decisions as they are made using a lightweight, text-based template. Lightweight decision records are a developer-friendly approach to a time-tested architecture practice. Documenting design decisions makes it easier to share and analyze them. Retaining a history of decisions provides context for the current architecture relative to its evolution.

Benefits

- Make recording design decisions a team responsibility.
- Keep key decisions close to the code by storing them in the code repository.
- Combine with other artifacts to create a holistic description strategy.
- Capture history to gain perspective on the evolution of the design.
- Involve the whole team in the design process.
- Train teammates in architectural thinking by providing ADR templates.
- Enable peer review of design decisions using standard development tools and an existing peer review workflow.

Description

Write down key architecture design decisions along with the context and implications of the decision. Each decision record should describe a single decision. What makes a decision architectural and not simply detailed design varies from system to system and team to team. Here are some ideas that may indicate you are dealing with an architectural decision.

- The decision directly affects another component or team.

- The decision changes how the system influences one or more quality attributes, for better or for worse.

- The decision was precipitated by a business or technical constraint.

- The decision has a far-reaching, significant impact such as a framework or technology choice.

- The decision fundamentally changes the way the team develops or ships the system.

Here is a sample ADR template:

Title Include the ADR number and a descriptive title.

Context Explain the circumstances under which the decision was made. This should be a series of simple, factual statements. Describe relevant architecture influencers such as technology, skills, previous decisions, and the business or political climate among others.

Decision Describe the decision you made.

Status Draft, Proposed, Accepted, Superseded, or Deprecated

Consequences Describe how your decision will or has changed the circumstances of the system, stakeholders, and team. Both positive and negative consequences should be included. Update this section as consequences emerge and are understood.

Guidelines and Hints

- Include only one decision per file.
- Sequentially number ADRs and keep old records. Add references to old records when a decision is superseded or changed.
- Keep ADRs short, one or two pages at most.
- Use plain language when recording decisions.
- Put architecture decisions through the same review process as code.
- Store in version control with other code artifacts.
- ADRs should not be the only architecture documentation you create. Combine with other artifacts such as views, architecture haikus, and system metaphors.

Example

Here is an example ADR for Project Lionheart, recorded in markdown syntax:

ADR 7: Public GitHub and Travis CI

Status: Proposed

We will use GitHub and Travis as our version control and continuous integration systems. All team collaboration will be conducted openly using GitHub systems.

Context

The City requires all code to be released as open source. Travis CI is free for open source. Social coding practices are expected to assist in community building. Our team is familiar with GitHub workflow and tools.

Consequences

Positive

* Everyone is able to read and edit code and documents (plain text).

Negatives

* Collaboration with City officials is decreased as they become comfortable with new tools.

* While ADRs as markdown are great, creating and storing diagrams is still a problem.

The form of decision records discussed here was proposed by Michael Nygard.[1] Examples are also widely available on the web.[2,3,4]

Many templates for recording architecture design decisions have been proposed over the years. Jeff Tyree and Art Akerman in *Architecture Decisions: Demystifying Architecture [TA05]* emphasize traceability to the issues that the decision addresses. Uwe Van Heesch, Paris Avgerioum, and Rich Hilliard in *A documentation framework for architecture decisions [VAH12]* show how decision templates can be used within the context of the IEEE 42010 standard.

---

1.   http://thinkrelevancecom/blog/2011/11/15/documenting-architecture-decisions
2.   https://github.com/
3.   Michael Keeling and Joe Runde. *Architecture Decision Records in Action.* SATURN 2017. http://resources.sei.cmu.edu/library/asset-view.cfm?assetid=497744
4.   https://www.youtube.com/watch?v=41NVge3_cYo

Activity 21

Architecture Haiku

Figure out what matters in your architecture by creating a bite-sized summary stakeholders will actually use. An architecture haiku describes a view of the architecture using only a single piece of paper. The architecture haiku was originally proposed by George Fairbanks.[5]

Benefits

- Think through and articulate the essential parts of the architecture.

- Produce an artifact that is easily consumed by readers. The end result is almost like a flier advertising the best parts of the architecture.

- Create a frame of reference for other documentation.

Description

Architecture haikus can be recorded as a slide, an image, or text. The format is less important as the focus and brevity. No matter how you record it, an architecture haiku should include *the following information [Kee15]*:

- A brief summary of the overall solution
- A list of important technical constraints
- A high-level summary of key functional requirements
- A prioritized list of quality attributes
- A brief explanation of design decisions, including rationale and trade-offs
- A list of architectural styles and patterns used
- A list of only the diagrams that add meaning beyond the information already on the page

The haiku should be only one page. In practice, nobody is counting but conciseness is the secret sauce.

Guidelines and Hints

- Do not attempt to record everything about the architecture. Focus only on what is most important.

---

5.   http://georgefairbanks.com/software-architecture/architecture-haiku/

- Establish a common vocabulary for architectural concepts so everyone speaks the same language.

- Set aside time to explore design options before starting.

- Treat the architecture haiku as a living document.

- Use the architecture haiku as an outline or executive summary for a longer architecture description.

- The architecture haiku is not a replacement for other design artifacts.

Example

Here's a partial architecture haiku for Project Lionheart. There is also a template available on my website to help get you started.[6]

Project Lionheart is a publicly available web application that will help the Springfield Office of Management and Budget manage the city's requests for proposals (RFPs) and local businesses to find RFPs of interest.

Business Goals

- Reduce procurement costs by 30%

- Improve city engagement with local businesses

- Cut the time required to publish a new RFP in half

Top Quality Attributes

Security > Availability > Performance

Architecture Patterns Used

Service-Oriented Architecture (SOA), Layered web application, REST APIs for web services

Key Decisions and Rationale

- Node.js for web app—team has experience

- MySQL database—free, open source

- Apache Solr—free, open source

- SOA with REST—decouple components, team interested in experimenting with emerging tech trends

- Java for web services—open source, low-risk, great tool support

---

6. http://neverletdown.net/2015/03/architecture-haiku.html

Context Diagram

A *context diagram* helps stakeholders understand where the software system fits in the world. Context diagrams show the people and systems that interact with the software system you are responsible for developing.

Benefits

- Provide a high-level overview of the systems and stakeholder groups the system directly interacts with or relies on.

- Make the boundary between the system you're building and the outside world obvious to stakeholders.

- Use as a natural entry point for learning about the system's architecture.

- Ensure everyone is aware of and agrees with the general system scope.

Description

In a typical context diagram, the system you are developing goes in the center. Draw the various people, software systems, and hardware your system will use or interact with around the system whose context you are describing. Arrows are used to show the relationship among these various elements to describe the overall circumstances in which the system you're designing lives.

Context diagrams can take on many forms and need not be only a box-and-line diagram. Any graphical depiction that can show where the system fits in the world can work, including drawings, storyboards, cartoon strips, and photographs. Some teams have even experimented with using video and animation to describe a system's context.

Guidelines and Hints

- It's OK to use informal notations. The most important thing is to communicate effectively.

- Show people and systems relevant to the system you are designing.

- Label arrows to tell how two things are related.

- Include a legend to describe the notations in the diagram.

Example

Here is a possible context diagram for Project Lionheart:

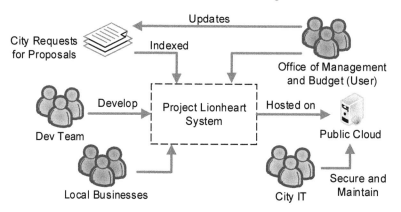

Project Lionheart Context Diagram

Greatest Hits Reading List

As a software system grows, so does the documentation that describes its architecture. A *greatest hits reading list* will help stakeholders navigate the morass of design artifacts so they can find relevant information. Creating a curated reading list provides new stakeholders with a starting point for learning about the architecture.

Benefits

- Highlight the most important design artifacts.
- Provide context for design artifacts within the scope of the whole system.
- Unify disparate, lightweight design artifacts to create a coherent, whole description.

Description

The greatest hits reading list is often a simple link page on the team's wiki. Each link should include the following information:

Title A brief, descriptive title for the artifact. Most artifacts already come with a title.

Overview Briefly explain why this artifact is important or interesting. What should the stakeholder take away from the artifact? It may also be useful to mention when and why the artifact was created.

Caveats In some cases the artifact may be incomplete or outdated. Mention any circumstances the stakeholder should know about when referring to the artifact.

Guidelines and Hints

- Organize the list around stakeholder concerns. Artifacts that address the same concern should be grouped together. Add a heading for the group.

- The same artifact can be used to address different concerns. Use the overview and caveats to help stakeholders navigate an artifact from varying perspectives.

- Take advantage of design artifacts from third-party sources. For example, if a pattern you are using is explained in a framework's documentation or a blog post on the web, use it instead of creating your own document.

- Include links to reference material that defines important concepts in the architecture as well as design artifacts.

Example

Here is an excerpt of a Greatest Hits Reading List from one team's code repository:

WIRE/FIRE/PIRE/TIRE Project: Greatest Hits Reading List

- Context Diagram - Get a feel for the lay of the land

- Inception Deck - Created in the first weeks of the project. Much of what's here has changed but it tells why we're building this system.

- Original system use cases - Largely abandoned but still useful context, skim only.

- ASR Workbook - Mostly up to date. The top quality attributes still apply.

- Checkpoint #2 Presentation - Created in March. Includes the most recent architecture diagrams that were shared with all stakeholders.

- Search and Train sequence diagrams - Shows how different components interact during specific use cases. Useful for availability analysis.

- Layers Overview - Shows how the code is organized

Inception Deck

Answer ten important questions at the start of a new project to avoid common failures and align stakeholders. The inception deck most often takes the form of a slide deck or lightweight text document and is usually created early in a project's life, during the *inception* phase. The version of the activity outlined here was described by Jonathan Rasmusson in *The Agile Samurai: How Agile Masters Deliver Great Software [Ras10]*.

Benefits

- Put important information in the open.

- Share easily with all stakeholders.

- Ensure all stakeholders have a common understanding of important system concerns.

- Discuss important information that should be covered at the start of a new project.

Description

Filling in the inception deck can take as little as 20 minutes when you have the required information handy. Finding the information needed for the deck could take days or weeks. The inception deck is highly customizable. Modify the questions presented here so that they work for your particular situation.

To create an inception deck, answer these questions and record the answers in a slide deck, markdown file, or another format that can be easily shared with stakeholders.

1. Why are we here?
   Simply and clearly describe the problem you are going to solve.

2. What's the vision?
   Concisely describe how the proposed software system will solve the problem shared by answering the first question. Rasmusson recommends creating an elevator pitch for this slide. There are many resources on this topic available on the web.

3. **What's the value?**

   List the business goals for the project. See *Discover the Business Goals*, on page 43 for ideas and hints.

4. **What's in scope?**

   List the highest-priority functional requirements that are known to currently be in scope. Usually these will be the *must haves*. Also list features that are definitely out of scope as well as functionality with potential architectural significance whose scope is still to be determined.

5. **Who are the key stakeholders?**

   List the key stakeholders and their primary concerns.

6. **What does the basic solution look like?**

   Share a sketch of the notional architecture. This can be an informal diagram such as *Let Ideas Breathe with a Cartoon*, on page 134.

7. **What are the key risks? (Why might this project fail?)**

   List the current top risks in the project. Review what makes a good risk statement in *Identify Conditions and Consequences*, on page 33.

8. **How much work? What are the costs?**

   Using what you know about the scope and notional architecture, estimate the approximate effort and costs to complete the known work. List any assumptions you make about the team size and skill sets.

9. **What are the expectations for trade-offs?**

   Have a frank discussion about key trade-offs before difficult decisions need to be made. Talk about the Big Four: scope, cost, schedule, and quality. Also discuss any interesting or high-priority quality attributes, especially if they may be in tension. Use Activity 1, *Choose One Thing*, on page 192

10. **When will it be ready?**

    Provide stakeholders with an idea for how long it takes to deliver the software. This estimate is your opportunity to start a conversation about key milestones. Create a draft time line or project schedule for the known work. The schedule is not expected to be perfect and should change as the project evolves.

Once the inception deck is completed, review it with stakeholders and make adjustments based on feedback.

Guidelines and Hints

- Use the ten questions as a checklist for kicking off a software project.

- Periodically review the inception deck as a reminder for what's important in the project.

- Slides are not required! The important thing is to answer the questions. Markdown also works well for the inception deck.

- The effort that goes into creating the Inception Deck should be commiserate with size and cost of the project. For example, don't spend a week creating an inception deck for a two-week project. At the same time, a week might not be enough time to complete an inception deck for a huge, multiteam project.

Example

Jonathan Rasmusson has shared an excellent example on his website.[7]

---

7. https://agilewarrior.wordpress.com/2010/11/06/the-agile-inception-deck/

Modular Decomposition Diagram

Show how the architecture is composed of varying abstractions that come together to create a coherent whole. A *modular decomposition diagram* is a simple tree diagram that shows how varying granularities of abstraction are related to one another. The word decomposition in this context means to break into smaller pieces, not to rot.

Modular decomposition is a general technique that can be used in many circumstances—from code package organization to organization charts to work breakdown structures used in project planning.

Benefits

- Uniquely name concepts at different granularities of abstraction.
- Map refinements in the architecture.
- Use to analyze organizational alignment with the system's composition.
- Reduce complexity without losing traceability to related elements.
- Promote system thinking within the architecture.

Description

Modular decomposition diagrams are nearly always drawn as a tree. The root node of the tree is the *system*. Each level of the tree breaks down (decomposes) a specific module to show finer-grained details. In a large system, the bottommost leaf nodes might represent a module implemented by a single team. In a smaller system, the bottommost leaf nodes might represent a specific package or class in the architecture.

Each level of the tree is an opportunity to group architectural concepts and show how they are related to ideas that are both bigger picture and also more detailed.

Guidelines and Hints

- Use the diagram to help reason about quality attributes such as agility, maintainability, time-to-market, costs, buildability, and deployability.

- Use software to make drawing a tree simpler.

- Break large diagrams into smaller ones to make them easier to understand. Be careful not to lose the context between the diagrams.

- Leaf nodes should not be connected with other leaf nodes except by way of their parent.

Example

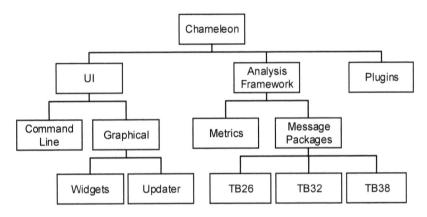

Here is the same decomposition drawn as a tree map with some additional information. In this map, size represents the amount of relative technical debt in the module.

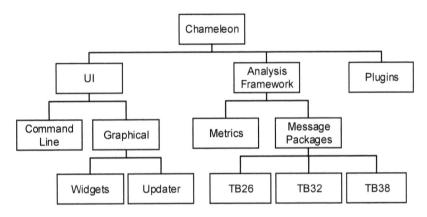

Activity 26

Paths Not Taken

Create a list of the architectural decisions you discarded with a brief note explaining why you ultimately rejected each decision. Recording the decisions you discarded, the paths not taken, provides context and rationale for a design decision.

Benefits

- Help downstream designers replay the thought process that went into the current design.

- Head off *did you consider...?* discussions with stakeholders.

- Provide an additional layer of rationale for design decisions.

Description

List design decisions you considered but rejected along with the reason for why the decision was not selected. The list can be stored in plain text or other easily accessible format.

Guidelines and Hints

- Focus on a single view or design decision. The list should not attempt to encompass all design decisions.

- Keep it brief. Include only enough detail so that stakeholders can understand the decision and why it was rejected.

- Combine with other methods to create a more complete description of the architecture. You can list the paths not taken alongside Architecture Decision Records on page 260 and architecture haikus on page 263.

Example

Here is an example of paths not taken for a hybrid cloud project in which an on-premise, shrink-wrapped software system was required to integrate with a rapidly evolving cloud platform on a continuous delivery schedule. The shrink-wrapped software was released quarterly. The scope of the decision centered on the integration between the two platforms.

Path Not Taken	Why the Path Was Rejected
Create a cloud-based "services adapter" to buffer against changes in third-party services	Heavy maintenance costs, benefits in features and quality attributes not required for MVP release, costs outweigh benefits
Release adapter as open source, have customers load it themselves	Extra steps to deployment inhibits adoption, concern that unmodified defaults could introduces security risks, concerns about training customers and consultants, does not reduce maintenance costs
Offer a client-side library	The client library will likely always be out of date (services ship continuously, shrink-wrap software ships once per quarter). Customers must learn both cloud services and how to use the client library. Documentation costs are highest. There is high risk the software will not be ready by the deadline.
No new support for web services integration in the client software	Does not improve the user experience, customers require guidance with emerging patterns and paradigms

The final decision was to release sample code for high-priority use cases in the documentation. The team was not responsible for maintaining the sample code. Customers were on their own if they chose to use or extend the sample code. Stakeholders felt this struck the right balance between costs and value. This minimally viable release allowed the product manager to collect data on the usefulness of the integration before investing further into the architecture.

Prototype to Learn or Decide

Develop or use software so you can test a hypothesis, learn information needed to make a design decision, prove a quality attribute, or gain experience. Sometimes the only way to learn what you need to know is to do it yourself. This adage is especially true of technology and frameworks.

We *prototype to learn* when we need to figure out how to do something or how something works. We *prototype to decide* when we need to gather information that will help us choose between multiple options.

Building a prototype to decide is like running an experiment. The technology or pattern under investigation is hypothesized to solve a specific design problem. The purpose of the prototype is to test the hypothesis.

Benefits

- Gather information through firsthand experience.
- Generate data to use in decision making.
- Allow stakeholders to experience a part of the system.
- Learn how something works quickly and inexpensively.

Description

The difference between a useless prototype and overdoing it is a razor-thin line. To increase your chances of success when prototyping, you need a plan. Let's look at what is involved in creating a prototyping plan.

1. Define the learning objectives and scope for the prototype. What questions will this prototype help you answer?

2. Decide on the prototype's budget and establish a delivery time line. When will you pull the plug on the prototype? How much are you willing to spend to meet the learning objectives? Limit costs and time as much as possible.

3. Decide how the outcomes will be delivered. Who is the audience for the prototype and how will you share it? For example, will you share a demo, whitepaper, presentation, or something else?

The goal is always to implement the prototype as quickly and cheaply as possible. As the prototype comes together, review the implementation relative to the plan. Once you've achieved the objectives, the prototype is complete and it's time to share the outcomes.

After the prototype is complete, perform the minimum clean-up necessary so it can be used again if required. Archive code and instructions for future reference.

Guidelines and Hints

- Look for ways to meet your learning objectives without writing software.

- Decide up front whether the prototype is evolutionary or throw-away.

- Keep tabs on the prototype implementers. Prototyping often requires that you trade quality for speed of delivery and completeness. This is a challenge for many developers who are proud of their craft.

- Time-box the prototype aggressively, but allow sufficient time to complete the work.

- Sketch out a high-level design for the prototype with the implementers before starting development.

Example

Here's an example of prototyping to learn. The team needed to understand the performance limitations of specific Apache Solr APIs. To learn this, a single developer over the course of one week developed a simple test driver using Apache JMeter,[8] ran several load tests, collected data, and wrote a two-page report summarizing the findings. Using Apache JMeter let the team quickly gather data with minimal effort.

Here's an example of prototyping to choose. The team needed to select a server-side web framework. To help them decide, the team implemented a simple blog application using the top two frameworks. The activity was time-boxed to two days. At the end of the second day, the team discussed pros and cons of each framework based on their experiences and chose a framework.

---

8. http://jmeter.apache.org/

Activity 28

Sequence Diagram

Dynamic structures are difficult to appreciate on paper. Use a *sequence diagram* to show how control or data moves through the system at runtime. Model the flow of logic, data, or control among components.

Benefits

- Simple and flexible notation
- Both graphical and text notations exist
- Useful for communication and reasoning
- Ample tool support, though tools are not required

Description

1. Choose a scenario to diagram. Use this as the title of the diagram.

2. List components involved in the scenario horizontally across the top of the page. These are the *participants* in the diagram. Draw a straight, vertical *life line* under each participant. Participants are usually listed from left to right starting with the participant that initiates the scenario.

3. Draw arrows from one participant's life line to another to indicate communication between those components. Label the line to describe the message.

4. Time goes down the y-axis in the diagram. Since the next message happens after the first, it should be further down the y-axis.

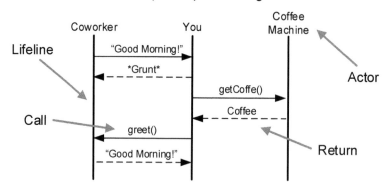

A Simple Sequence Diagram

Guidelines and Hints

- Reason about distributed systems, microservices, object communication, and other dynamic structures.

- Informal notations are fine as long as you are consistent.

- A closed arrow with a solid line indicates a *synchronous request message.*

- An open arrow with a solid line indicates an *asynchronous request message.*

- An arrow with a dotted line indicates a *response message.*

- Use a tool that renders text-based notations so you can store the diagrams with your code.

Example

Here is a sequence diagram for a set of microservices responsible for saving an item to a shopping cart, generated using js-sequence-diagrams.[9]

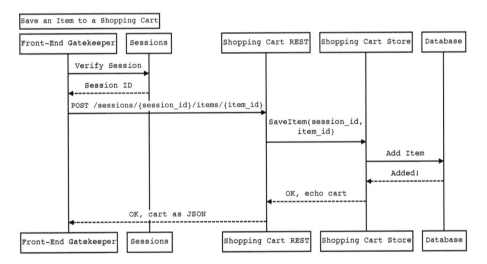

9.   https://github.com/bramp/js-sequence-diagrams

This is the text notation used to generate the diagram:

```
Title: Save an Item to a Shopping Cart

Front End Gatekeeper -> Sessions: Verify Session
Sessions --> Front End Gatekeeper: Session ID

Front End Gatekeeper -> Shopping Cart REST:
    POST /sessions/{session_id}/items/{item_id}
Shopping Cart REST -> Shopping Cart Store:
    SaveItem(session_id,\n item_id)
Shopping Cart Store -> Database: Add Item

Database --> Shopping Cart Store: Added!
Shopping Cart Store --> Shopping Cart REST: OK, echo cart
Shopping Cart REST --> Front End Gatekeeper: OK, cart as JSON
```

With the sequence diagram drawn, it's easy to see a potential flaw in the design. The first step of verifying the session creates an opportunity to validate a session that could be closed—for example, if the user checks out before the item is added. This API call by the *Gatekeeper* is redundant at best. More likely the diagram has exposed an inappropriate assumption about the state of the user's session when saving an item in the *Shopping Cart Store* service.

Activity 29

System Metaphor

Tell a simple story that demonstrates how the system influences specific quality attributes. The system metaphor was introduced by Kent Beck in *Extreme Programming Explained: Embrace Change [Bec00]* as a way to create a common vision and shared vocabulary for the architecture.

Benefits

- Lightweight description technique perfect for co-located teams to use during times of fast architectural evolution

- Can be combined with other description methods

- Cheap to create, easy to change

Description

In *Making Metaphors That Matter [KV11]*, Michail Velichansky and I summarize concrete guidance for creating useful system metaphors. Good system metaphors have the following attributes:

- Represent a single view of the system.
- Deal with only one type of structure.
- Provide clear guidance concerning design decisions.
- Shed light on system properties.
- Draw on a shared experience.
- Corollary: Even a good metaphor still requires explanation.

Every system metaphor comes with an information payload—the discussions and diagrams that went into creating the metaphor. The metaphor becomes a reference point to this other information and is meant to help team members recall these important details.

Guidelines and Hints

- Tell a memorable story and have fun.

- Be specific and focus on what makes your system unique. Every software system ever made is *like a city*.

- If a common reference point does not exist, then create a shared experience.

- Pop culture and food are common points of reference for many metaphors.

- Common architecture patterns serve the same purpose as system metaphors and can be used in the same way.

Example

In Project Lionheart we plan to build a simple data crawler, which pulls data from the city's *contracts* database, normalizes the data, and pushes it into a search index. To do this efficiently, we'll need a multithreaded crawler. But there's a catch. If the crawler is too aggressive, we might crash the database and disrupt city services. If the crawler is too slow, we might not index the data fast enough to satisfy reliability quality attributes.

To help us think through and share the design, we created the following system metaphor.

The musical *Newsies*[10] tells the story of the New York City Newsboy Strike of 1899. In the movie (and history), the newsboys (newsies) purchase newspapers from a paper distribution center every morning and then resell the newspapers to the people of New York. Our crawler threads are just like the newsies. Each thread visits a *distribution center*, requests some rows to fetch from the database, and receives a block of rows to fetch and index. Any rows not fetched are forgotten. We can always sell more *papes*—pick up missing rows— tomorrow.

Let's walk through our checklist to see if this is a good metaphor:

- Represent a single view. In this metaphor, we're considering a single view of a single component, specifically the threading model in the crawler. Check.

- Deal with only one type of structure. We're only dealing with C&C structures, so there are no mixed models in play. Check.

- Give clear guidance concerning design decisions. *Newsies* sieze the day and also fetch data to index while the *distribution center* provides a set of rows from the database. Only one *newsie* can have a database row at a time and the *newsies* are fully responsible for the rows once received from the distribution center. Leftover *papers*—database rows not crawled—are skipped. Check.

---

10. http://www.imdb.com/title/tt0104990/

- Shed light on system properties. This metaphor is trying to describe how we'll address performance. We can control our aggressiveness by controlling the number of *newsies* working at the same time. Check.

- Draw on shared experiences. The movie is a piece of 1990s cinematic gold starring a young Christian Bale. If teammates haven't seen it, create a shared experience by ordering pizzas and having a movie night, or at least watching YouTube videos. Check and team building bonus!

CHAPTER 17

Activities to Evaluate Design Options

In the evaluate mindset, we critically examine design decisions to determine how well they meet our needs. Our designs don't need to be perfect, but they do need to be good enough. Our goal is to make sure the architecture *satisfices*, that it is satisfactory and sufficient. When we've found a satisficing solution, then we say it has good fit.

During an evaluation we'll learn all the ways our architecture is not satisfactory or sufficient. We might learn we don't understand some nuance about the problem. Or perhaps a design idea that seemed good will turn out to have unacceptable trade-offs, miss an important constraint, or introduce too much risk. These things are better to know early, before it becomes difficult to change a potentially costly decision.

After an evaluation we should have enough information to decide which design mindset to embrace next. We'll always embrace the evaluate mindset during the *check* step in the do-make-check cycle, but evaluation can be the main attraction during the *do* step too.

Evaluation is a continuous activity. Waiting until the end of a design phase to do an evaluation is too late. We should evaluate our work every step of the way. Once we deem some part of the architecture to be good enough then that part of the system's design is ready to be refined further by focusing on finer-grained details. Everything in the architecture need not be *ready* before starting to build something.

The activities in this chapter help teams look deeply at different facets of the architecture and glean information needed to take action. Use them when you need to check your understanding, choose a design option, or help you figure out what to do next.

Activity 30

Architecture Briefing

This brief (no pun intended) presentation is used to bring stakeholders up to speed about some part of the architecture. By the end of the briefing, participants are prepared to provide meaningful feedback about the architecture.

Architecture briefings are a common practice used by traditional building architects to educate clients and share progress. The same general practice has been used in software development for decades. The idea of using an *architecture briefing* with software has been proposed by many, including Stuart Halloway[1] and Patrick Kua.[2]

Benefits

- Quickly bring stakeholders up to speed so they can ask questions and point out issues in a design.

- Foster a sense of shared ownership over the architecture.

- Enable more stakeholders to provide feedback, ensuring a diversity of perspectives critically evaluate the design.

- Promote accountability in architectural decision making.

- Create a platform for teaching and learning architecture design. Teammates will be exposed to other people's approaches to architecture design and have a chance to practice articulating designs concisely.

Activity Timing

Forty-five minutes to one hour. The presentation portion of the briefing should last no more than 30 minutes. Try to leave at least half of the meeting time for audience questions and feedback.

Participants

The architect presents the briefing.

---

1.   https://github.com/stuarthalloway/presentations/wiki/Architectural-Briefings
2.   Patrick Kua. *Evolutionary Architecture*. SATURN 2016. http://resources.sei.cmu.edu/library/asset-view.cfm?assetID=454345

Stakeholders and knowledgeable nonstakeholders attend the briefing. The briefing should be open to a wide audience, including people with no prior knowledge of the architecture under discussion.

Preparation and Materials

- Briefing presentation. This will usually be slides but can also be a whiteboard talk. As a rule of thumb, preparing for the briefing should require no more than about twice the briefing length. For example, preparing for a 30-minute presentation should take about an hour.

- Audience members should bring supplies to take notes.

Steps

1. Welcome the audience, introduce the architect, and share the ground rules for the briefing. Here are some sample ground rules you can use:

   > Audience's job: Question everything.
   >
   > Please hold questions and comments until the end.
   >
   > Pay attention. Take notes.
   >
   > Think about: What is missing? How does this compare to your experience? Do you agree with the decisions? Do you understand why a decision was made?
   >
   > Be respectful; remember, your briefing is next!

2. The architect presents the briefing. The presentation ends when time expires or the architect is done, whichever comes first.

3. Open the floor for comments and questions. Team members may optionally join the architect to field questions.

4. Conclude the briefing by thanking the audience and architect. The briefing ends when there are no more questions or the time has expired.

Guidelines and Hints

- Host briefings at the same time and place at a regular interval.

- Publish slides after the briefing and record it if possible.

- The team presenting the briefing should appoint a note taker during the questions portion of the briefing.

- Audience questions should be tough, but constructive.

Example

Here is one possible outline for architecture briefings. The specific outline may vary depending on the type of systems you build.

Elevator pitch: what overall business problem are you solving?

Overview and context

Top quality attributes

Relevant views

Key design decisions with rationale

Alternatives considered

Current status: quality, work remaining, next steps

Costs

Top risks and other concerns

Future plans

Halloway included an example briefing and an alternative outline in a talk available in his GitHub repository.[3]

---

3. https://github.com/stuarthalloway/presentations/wiki/Architectural-Briefings

Activity 31

Code Review

A form of peer review in which code is incrementally inspected with an eye toward architectural concerns as the code is developed. Code review is a fantastic practice that every team should do anyway. Extending code reviews to include architectural concerns makes them even more powerful.

Incrementally inspecting code as the architecture manifests helps fight architectural rot by keeping tabs on the system's evolution relative to the planned design. Reviews are also a great time to identify design inflection points that emerge during development. Such inflection points may require further analysis.

Every review presents a potential coaching opportunity. Watch out for synchronization mismatches in mental models so you can fix them before real problems arise. Coach teammates on architectural principles as well as the specific architecture you're developing together.

Benefits

- Keep architecture design at the forefront of every developer's mind.
- Allow finer-grained details to emerge without losing a connection with coarser-grained architectural concerns.
- Manage emergent details that can cause problems in the architecture.
- Influence the detailed design as required.
- Create teachable moments to grow the team's architecture design competence.

Activity Timing

Ongoing for the life of a project. An initial code review might take as little as 10 minutes with more time needed to resolve any identified issues.

Participants

The author submits an artifact, in this case code, for review. The reviewer inspects the artifact and provides feedback. Many teams encourage multiple reviewers to participate.

Preparation and Materials

- A prepared code artifact, patch, or pull request.

Steps

1. Skim the change set to get a feel for the overall scope of changes.

2. Perform the code review as you normally would, focusing on detailed design, style issues, and defects.

3. Once the first pass review is complete, reflect on potential architectural implications of the change set. See the sample checklist on page 291 to get an idea of what you might look for during this part of the review.

4. Add comments related to your architectural concerns. If there are potential gaps in understanding, reference relevant resources.

5. After sharing your review with the submitter, follow up with that person directly. Architectural issues usually require more discussion.

6. Reflect on the results of the review. Were there issues that could have been avoided with more education or documentation? Is there an implied design decisions that should be explicitly stated? Add design tasks to the backlog to address ideas you think will bear fruit, such as improving a document or hosting an information session with the team.

Depending on the tool or exact situation for your code review, these steps may need to be adapted.

Guidelines and Hints

- Use code review software that integrates with your version control and build system.

- Reviews are often small. Watch out for thematic shifts in how the code evolves over time.

- Escalate the style of peer review to resolve issues quickly. For example, shift to pair programming or host a whiteboard jam on page 255 when an issue arises due to a lack of understanding.

- It's OK for the architecture to change as the system emerges. The primary goals of code review from the architect's perspective is to increase awareness of design decisions, monitor the implementation of the architecture, and guide change over time.

- Code review is not a replacement for design evaluations. Use reviews to monitor architectural drift and learn how you can better serve your team as an architect.

Example

Code review checklists improve consistency and show teammates what to look for during a review. In addition to looking at detailed design concerns, here are some architectural ideas you should look for when reviewing code:

- Correctness—Are the changes consistent with the established patterns in the architecture? Are there pattern violations? Is there an opportunity to use an architecture pattern or refactor the code so that an intended pattern becomes more obvious?

- Consistency—Look at the naming. Do the concepts at play make sense? Do any names surprise you? Are you able to form a mental model in your head of where the changes fit? How well does this jive with your expectations of what these changes would entail?

- Testability—Are there clean unit tests included with the changes? Can the tests be run with every build? Is there an opportunity for the tests to be flaky or inconsistent? Are common patterns such as *inversion of control* used appropriately and correctly?

- Modifiability/maintainability—Are there hard-coded constants or values that should be injected via configuration? What assumptions are baked into the code under review about what will change in the system? Can the code be made more flexible? Were any new dependencies introduced? Why were they introduced? Was it right to include them?

- Reliability—Are exceptions handled consistently? Are there opportunities for errors to propagate in unexpected or unhandled ways? Does the system attempt to retry when appropriate? Does the system fail fast when no recovery action can be attempted? How is error prevention (including from human mistakes) built into the design?

- Scalability—Does the code introduce potential for rampant memory use? Are the algorithms at least nominally efficient? Are thread-safe data structures used when appropriate?

Decision Matrix

A decision matrix is a visual comparison of how various alternatives stack up against one another. Use a decision matrix to qualify design alternatives so a decision can be made. A decision matrix can also be used in documentation as a part of the design's rationale.

Benefits

- Use to compare a variety of decisions such as patterns, technologies, or frameworks.

- Visualize relative strengths and weaknesses among decisions.

- Focus attention on essential factors when comparing and contrasting alternatives.

- Facilitate open discussion about trade-offs among alternatives.

Activity Timing

Varies, depending on the number of alternatives and evaluation factors.

Participants

The architect is responsible for ensuring the matrix is filled in accurately. Stakeholders validate the evaluation factors.

Preparation and Materials

- Identify a list of architecturally significant requirements, especially quality attribute scenarios to be used as the properties for comparison.

- Before starting the analysis, identify at least two design alternatives for comparison.

Steps

1. Identify evaluation factors. Collaborate with stakeholders to agree on the factors used to compare and contrast alternatives.

2. Establish a rubric. Collaborate with stakeholders to decide how design alternatives will be scored. For guidance on defining a rubric, see *Define a Design Rubric*, on page 162.

3. Do the analysis and fill in the matrix.

4. Share the matrix with stakeholders. Verify the analysis and discuss your recommended decision.

Guidelines and Hints

- Use qualitative comparisons unless you performed quantitative analysis. For example, performance or availability can only be quantified if you ran tests.

- Consider no more than seven factors in the same matrix.

- Compare up to five design options in the same matrix. Use multiple matrices with a larger number of options.

- Take good notes when filling in the matrix. The analysis is as important as the results and can provide design rationale for decisions.

Example

Here is a sample decision matrix. Additional examples are shown in *Create a Decision Matrix*, on page 71.

Project Lionheart Decision Matrix

	3-Tier	Publish - Subscribe	Service Oriented
Availability (Database unavailable)	+	O	+
Availability (Uptime requirements)	O	O	O
Performance (5-second response time)	O	−	+
Security	O	−	O
Scalability (5% annual growth)	O	O	+
Maintainability (Team knowledge)	+	−	O
Buildability (Implementation risks)	++	−	− −

Legend

Strongly Promotes ++	Strongly Inhibits − −	Neutral O
Promotes +	Inhibits −	

Activity 33

Observe Behavior

Add instrumentation to the software system so you can see runtime behaviors firsthand. Use the observations to answer specific questions about quality attributes and other stakeholder concerns. Once instrumentation is in place, either observe the system in normal use or inject stimuli to flex specific quality attribute scenarios.

Observing behavior is a great way to analyze runtime quality attributes. The ability to observe the system assumes that *observability* is designed into the architecture. Evolve the architecture as needed to promote required observability scenarios.

Benefits

- Monitor the system over time to verify design assumptions.
- Directly test how well quality attributes are promoted.
- Produce concrete metrics that can be shared with stakeholders.

Activity Timing

Varies depending on the required analysis and how well the software system promotes observability.

Participants

One or more analysts, usually developers of the system.

Preparation and Materials

- To add instrumentation there must be a working (or partially working) software system. Adding instrumentation can sometimes be a design task unto itself. Decisions around frameworks, data storage, and analysis must be made before observations can begin.

Steps

1. Define the goals of the analysis. What question are you trying to answer? Use Activity 3, *Goal-Question-Metric (GQM) Workshop*, on page 199 to identify candidate metrics and the data required to compute those metrics.

2. Decide how to generate data and design tests to drive the system.

3. Add the required instrumentation and logging to the software system. Verify that your changes work before attempting meaningful analysis. You don't want to spend a week running tests only to learn that your logging failed!

4. Implement and execute tests, or allow the software system to be used as it normally would.

5. Once data has been collected, perform the analysis. Compute metrics and answer the questions established in step 1. If you are unable to answer questions, then make adjustments and try again.

6. Prepare and share findings with relevant stakeholders.

Guidelines and Hints

- Observability is a quality attribute and must be designed into the architecture. Instrumentation can be added late, even after the system is in the wild, as long as you've designed the ability to produce and collect system events into the architecture.

- As you answer questions about the software system, think about how the data can be used in automated analysis. Consider adding your metrics to system dashboards and alerting systems.

- In theory, any runtime property of the system can be observed, including security, performance, availability, and reliability, among others.

Example

Some patterns such as event sourcing publish-subscribe (described on page 88) have observability baked in. Observability is a must-have for all modern distributed systems, especially microservices.

Netflix has done extensive work in this area and made much of their work available as open source.[4] One example is the Hystrix Dashboard, which allows developers to observe metrics produced by the Hystrix fault tolerance library for the JVM.[5] Another example is the Simian Army, a suite of tools used to stimulate a service-oriented system in various ways.[6]

In the simplest case, you can use any logging platform to record observed information. Take a look at logging platforms such as LogStash,[7] Splunk,[8] or Graylog[9] for storing, visualizing, and analyzing system events. Keep in mind that though these tools are powerful, their effectiveness depends heavily on how you've instrumented the system.

4. https://netflix.github.io/
5. https://github.com/Netflix/Hystrix
6. https://github.com/Netflix/SimianArmy
7. https://www.elastic.co/products/logstash
8. https://www.splunk.com/
9. https://www.graylog.org

Question–Comment–Concern

This is a collaborative, visual activity that gets the whole team talking about the architecture—what they know, what they don't know, and what keeps them up at night. Use this activity to shine a light on knowledge gaps, articulate issues, and establish known facts about the architecture.

The inclusion of comments during the workshop is meant to fast-track issue resolution. Issues that result from simple gaps in understanding can be resolved immediately so the team can focus on the bigger concerns. As an architect you can even choose to add questions during the workshop as a simple sanity check (described on page 304).

Benefits

- Promote knowledge sharing by flushing questions into the open along with potential answers.

- Visualize high-risk, mysterious, or troublesome parts of the system.

- Identify areas in need of further research and exploration.

- Foster shared ownership over the architecture and the direction it takes.

Activity Timing

30–90 minutes

Participants

Whole team, about 3–7 participants

Preparation and Materials

- Views of the architecture. These can be created just-in-time or printed from appropriate sources.

- Sticky notes (three different colors), markers

- Large paper, flipcharts, or whiteboard with appropriate markers

Steps

1. Start the workshop by explaining the goals. For example, *In this workshop we will learn what we know, what we think we know, and what worries us about the architecture.*

2. Sketch relevant views. All participants should help sketch views of the architecture on whiteboards or paper.

3. Brainstorm questions, comments, and concerns. Working together, participants will write one item per sticky note and immediately place them on the relevant view.

4. Stop the exercise when time expires or as the rate of stickies slows.

5. Observe and reflect. What does the team notice about the diagram? What is interesting about where sticky notes landed? Are there areas of particularly high concern or uncertainty? Were there any areas with many questions that were quickly answered?

6. Extract themes. Read through the sticky notes and write down common themes that emerge.

7. Decide on next steps. Briefly brainstorm actions that should be taken next. Prioritize and assign responsibility for next steps.

Guidelines and Hints

- Assign a color to each type of item before brainstorming starts. Create a legend that is visible to all participants.

- Comments can be facts, new ideas, tidbits of knowledge, or answers to questions raised during the workshop. To answer a question, simply write the answer on a comment sticky note and place it directly on top of the question it answers.

- Concerns can be known problems, risks, or general worries.

- Pay attention to questions. Questions can expose gaps in understanding, mismatches in expectations, or areas in need of further exploration.

Example

In this example, the team sketched diagrams during a whiteboard jam (see on page 255), took a picture with a phone, and uploaded the image to Mural[10] to run the exercise. Notice how comments are placed in close proximity to the questions they answer.

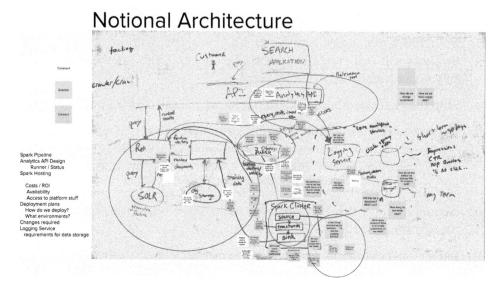

Risk Storming

A collaborative, visual technique for identifying risks in the architecture. Risk storming was proposed by Simon Brown in *Software Architecture for Developers* [Bro16].

Benefits

- Quickly identify risks in the proposed system architecture.
- Visualize the system by considering the level of risk.
- Constrain risk identification to architectural concerns.
- Provide a platform for all team members to elevate their concerns.

Activity Timing

60–90 minutes.

Participants

Small groups of 3–7 developers. Participants must be familiar with the architecture. This workshop can be self-facilitated by experienced participants.

Preparation and Materials

- Views of the architecture. These can be created just-in-time or printed from appropriate sources.

- Sticky notes (three different colors), markers

- Large paper, flipcharts, or whiteboard with appropriate markers

Steps

1. Set the expectations for the workshop by explaining the workshop goals. For example, *By the end of this workshop we will have a list of prioritized risks to help us decide on next steps.*

2. Sketch relevant views. All participants should help sketch views of the architecture on whiteboards or paper. Include a range of views.

3. Brainstorm risks. Working individually, participants will write one risk per sticky note. The color of the sticky note used to capture the risk should correspond to the risk's degree of exposure: high, medium, or low. Exposure is a relative qualification of how bad a risk is by considering probability, impact, and time frame.

4. Cluster risks on the diagrams. Participants place their risks on the diagrams where they think the risk most directly applies.

5. Prioritize and discuss the identified risks. Look at clusters of sticky notes, high-exposure risks, or other interesting patterns.

6. Develop mitigation strategies and decide on next steps.

Guidelines and Hints

- Place sticky notes directly on the diagrams.
- Stick duplicate risks directly on top of each other.
- Leave time for team discussions. This is the most important part.
- Use no more than 2–3 sketches. More than that can be overwhelming.

Example

Here is a tentative agenda for the workshop:

Introduction and goals	< 5 minutes
Sketching	15–20 minutes
Risk brainstorming	7–15 minutes
Discussion and prioritizing	15–30 minutes
Brainstorm mitigations for top risks	10–15 minutes
Wrap-up, review actions	< 5 minutes

In this example, a sticky note legend is posted on the left side. High-exposure risks are orange, medium risks are pink, and low-exposure risks are purple. It's easy to see clusters of high-exposure risks around certain elements and relations. These areas should receive more design attention. Likewise, there appear to be areas of low risk that may already be in development or could get fully underway soon.

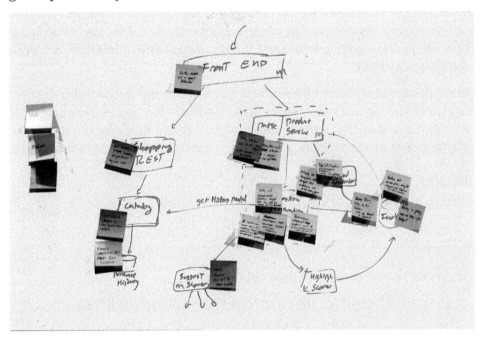

Activity 36

Sanity Check

A fast, simple exercise designed to expose issues in team communication or understanding. Sanity checks verify everyone is indeed on the same page. They can also identify opportunities for improving team operations, artifacts, and design methods.

When designing a sanity check, think back to the pop quizzes you dreaded in elementary school. Any short-burst activity that forces teammates to actively think about the architecture is a great sanity check candidate. Verbal sanity checks are an efficient way to end most collaborative design sessions.

Benefits

- Reinforce architectural responsibility across the team.
- Identify problems caused by misunderstandings and gaps in knowledge early.
- Create teaching and coaching opportunities.
- Document knowledge the team feels is essential to the design.
- Pinpoint opportunities for improving artifacts and communication.
- Uncover the unknown unknowns.

Activity Timing

5–10 minutes

Participants

Whole team, assign one team member to prepare the sanity check.

Preparation and Materials

- A prepared exercise or quiz.

Steps

1. Remind the team that sanity checks are for process improvement and helping uncover knowledge gaps before they become problems.

2. Complete the exercise.

3. Review answers to the exercise. Briefly discuss answers that differed from the key.

4. Decide whether follow-up actions are required. If so, the person who led the sanity check will lead the team in determining next steps.

Guidelines and Hints

- Keep it simple and short. A good sanity check can be completed in 5 minutes or less.

- Always remember: Sanity checks are really about improving the team's knowledge. Do not use sanity checks to punish or promote teammates.

- Share responsibility for creating sanity checks among the team.

- Host regular sanity checks—for example, at the beginning or end of a weekly status meeting or retrospective.

- Get creative and use a variety of formats. This keeps the sanity checks fresh and helps expose different kinds of understanding gaps.

Example

Sanity checks can take many forms. Some examples include true/false, fill in the blank, matching, and multiple choice. And this is just the beginning. In the following example sanity check, the team verified the rationale for specific technology choices by playing a simple matching game.

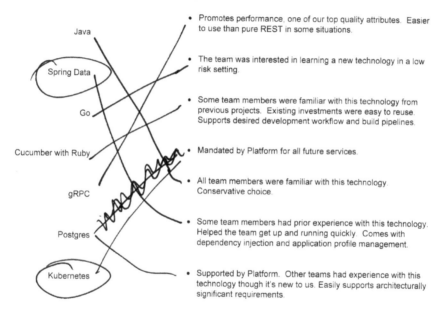

Sanity Check: Technology Choices!

Instructions: For each technology draw a line to connect it with the rationale for why we chose it. Circle any technologies that you didn't know we use.

Scenario Walkthrough

Describe step-by-step how the architecture addresses a specific quality attribute scenario. Scenario walkthroughs can be used any time but are most applicable early in the life of the software system, before the system's behavior can be observed directly.

A scenario walkthrough is like telling a story about the architecture. Pick a quality attribute scenario and describe what the system would do in response to the scenario stimulus. As you walk through the various elements in your design, show how the quality attribute is promoted (or not) by the system.

Benefits

- Assess the architecture design early, even while it's only on paper.
- Identify different concerns in the architecture.
- Reason about how the architecture will respond to different stimuli.
- Qualify the design. Walkthroughs are not strict pass or fail.
- Quickly determine the extent to which the architecture promotes or inhibits different quality attributes.

Activity Timing

Walking through the architecture for a single quality attribute scenario might take 20–30 minutes depending on the system. A scenario walkthrough meeting will typically run 1–3 hours and cover several quality attribute scenarios.

Participants

Scenarios walkthroughs require that the following roles are filled:

- The *architect* is someone knowledgeable in the architecture's design. This person describes how the system responds to stimuli.

- The *recorder* take notes during the meeting. This person will write down any issues, risks, unknowns, gaps, and other general concerns raised during the session.

- The *reader* reads scenarios to start the discussion and facilitates the walkthrough. This person is also the session moderator.

- Every walkthrough will have one or more *reviewers*. Reviewers are relevant stakeholders or knowledgeable non-stakeholders who can ask questions and poke holes in the architecture during the review. On small teams, the recorder and reader might also be reviewers.

Walkthroughs should be small, with no more than 3–7 participants.

Preparation and Materials

- Reviewers should look at the quality attribute scenarios, relevant architecture descriptions, and other background materials as homework prior to the review meeting. If such materials do not exist, prepare an introductory presentation (such as the architecture briefing described on page 286) and allow extra time to bring reviewers up to speed.

- Prioritized quality attribute scenarios must be prepared prior to the start of the meeting.

Steps

1. Distribute scenarios and architecture artifacts to the group. Set up projectors or screen sharing so the architect can easily share relevant views.

2. The reader picks a quality attribute scenario and reads it out loud. The purpose of reading the whole scenario is to ensure everyone knows the context and general scope of the scenario.

3. The reader then repeats the stimulus of the quality attribute scenario, thus kicking off the walkthrough.

4. The architect describes how the system responds to the stimulus, by *walking through* elements in the architecture.

5. Once the architect has completed the initial walkthrough, reviewers may ask questions and point out potential architectural issues.

6. The architect may briefly respond to questions. Issues, risks, and questions raised should be recorded for further analysis by the team after the review meeting.

7. After all reviewers have shared their feedback or time has expired, pick another scenario and repeat the process.

Guidelines and Hints

- Avoid turning the review into a witch hunt. The whole point is to find potential problems while they are still cheap to fix—on paper. Finding issues is a good thing.

- To keep the meeting moving, the time spent on each scenario should be time boxed.

- Avoid problem solving during the review. The purpose of this activity is to surface issues, not solve them.

- The reader and recorder roles can be combined but should be separate from the architect role.

- Rotate roles to help build teammates' skills.

- Write or project the current the quality attribute scenario so reviewers can see it during the walkthrough. If this is not practical, distribute a packet with quality attribute scenarios.

- Record new quality attribute scenarios raised during the walkthrough.

Example

Let's walk through an availability scenario from Project Lionheart. A user's searches for open RFPs and receives a list of available RFPs 99 percent of the time on average over the course of the year. To walk through an availability scenario we'll need to focus on specific conditions. Recall that Project Lionheart consists of a small handful of web services, a few databases, and a search index.

Here's a specific quality attribute scenario:

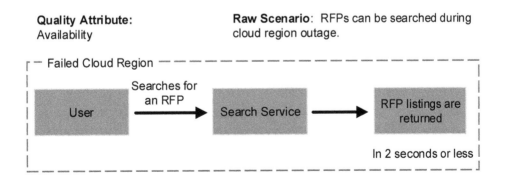

The City of Springfield's IT Department has decided to host Project Lionheart services using a popular cloud provider. Services and processes are hosted in Docker containers in two different cloud regions. This way, when one region fails another is still available.

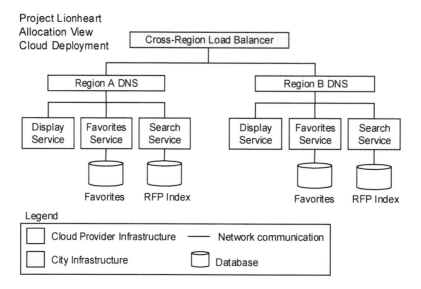

Here is one potential walkthrough for the given quality attribute scenario:

Reader: *The next scenario covers availability during a region failure. Let's start by assuming everything is up and running. OK, bam! Region A just went down.*

Architect: *Within 60 seconds, our cross-region load balancer will detect the failure and automatically route traffic to the available region. If a user was unlucky enough to be on the website at that moment, they'll get a failure. Refreshing the browser should fix the problem.*

Reviewer 1: *Where is the multiregion load balancer hosted?*

Architect: *In the closet across the hall.*

Reviewer 1: *So all site accessibility is determined by load balancers we're managing? Why bother with the cloud platform at all if our weakest link is in the building?*

Reader: *Reviewer 1, let's work to keep our conversation constructive. Can you try to phrase your concern as a risk?*

Reviewer 1: *Sorry, I was just a bit surprised. How about this: There is a single point-of-failure in our cross-region strategy; might not be able to meet required service-level agreements. (Recorder verifies the concern is captured.)*

Reviewer 2: *How is the data kept up to date in the proposed multiregion deployment...*

Sketch and Compare

Sometimes a design only seems good because there isn't a baseline for comparison. With the sketch and compare activity, we create two or more alternatives of the same design so it's easier to see the pros and cons.

Any design alternatives can be sketched and compared. This includes current and future, ideal and reality, technology A and technology B, and many others. Sketching the extremes can also be compared. To do this, pick a quality attribute or design concept and design the architecture for that one thing at the exclusion of all else. Then pick another high-priority quality attribute or interesting design concept and sketch an alternative design for comparison.

Benefits

- Expose both the positive and negative aspects of a decision by comparing it to something else.

- Create a platform for discussion and build consensus around a design decision.

- Avoid *buyer's remorse* when making a design decision by doing at least a basic comparison.

Activity Timing

20–30 minutes, up to an hour

Participants

This activity works best in small groups of 3–5 people, including the architect and other stakeholders.

Preparation and Materials

- Whiteboard or flipchart, markers
- Alternatively, prepared views (for example, in slide software), projector

Steps

1. Establish the goals of the activity by saying something like, *It seems like there are at least two alternative designs on the table. Let's put them side by side and pick one.*

2. Sketch or show the alternative designs so everyone can see them.

3. Open the discussion by pointing out an advantage or disadvantage of one design compared to the other. Invite others to share their thoughts.

4. Write down participants' ideas as they share them. If necessary, change or annotate the diagrams to clarify meaning or add new insights.

5. As the group begins to reach consensus, summarize the decisions made. Give a just-in-time sanity check (introduced on page 304) to verify that participants understand and agree with the decisions.

6. Take pictures, record the decisions in your team wiki, and use the discussion to help flesh out design rationale.

Guidelines and Hints

*   Help participants avoid argumentative confrontations and encourage constructive participation. Sometimes participants will pick sides and entrench themselves, strongly favoring one design over the other.

*   Be ready to sketch compromises as the discussion progresses. Some of these new ideas will become new design alternatives.

*   Always summarize the findings. Skipping the final summary can leave participants confused about the decisions made.

*   Follow up with skeptics to win them over and drive consensus.

Example

In this example, the team was struggling with a few ideas. Parts of the software system were undergoing major refactoring and the team had a strong desire to avoid rework if possible. Several new responsibilities needed a home and two alternatives had been proposed. A deadline was looming and a decision had to be made with imperfect information.

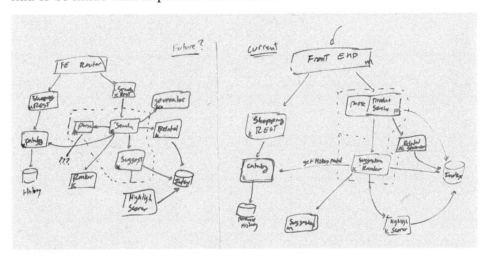

In this case, the team sketched diagrams of the *current* and *possible future* designs. Some team members were not satisfied with the current architecture. After seeing how it compared to the potential future state, they were much more willing to go along with the current design. The discussion that went with these sketches also created a shared understanding for the future direction of the system and identified areas with potential technical debt.

Community Contributor Bios

Len Bass is the coauthor of two award-winning books in software architecture: *Software Architecture in Practice [BCK12]* and *Documenting Software Architectures: Views and Beyond [BBCG10]*, as well as several other books and numerous papers in computer science and software engineering, including his latest book, *DevOps: A Software Architect's Perspective [BWZ15]*. Len has over 50 years' experience in software development, 25 of those at the Software Engineering Institute. He also worked for three years at National ICT Australia Ltd. (NICTA) and is currently an adjunct faculty at Carnegie Mellon.

Bett Bollhoefer has worked in the software space since 1999. Today, Bett is an architect at GE Digital focused on Predix Industrial Internet of Things Platform Architecture. Before joining GE, she first worked as a developer, then as a solutions architect at Verizon. Bett speaks and writes on software design and is the author of several books, including *You Can Be a Software Architect [Cor13]* and *The Zen of Software Development: A Seven Day Journey: A Handbook to Enlightened Software Development [Cor15]*. Bett cohosted the popular Software Architecture Concepts podcast for two years.[1] She is a Distinguished Toastmaster, former president of Distinguished Division Governor in Toastmasters, and winner of the Division Governor of the Year award. And for fun, Bett is a professional improv actor, and enjoys swing dancing, painting, and playing the cello.

Simon Brown is an independent consultant specializing in software architecture and the author of *Software Architecture for Developers [Bro16]*, a developer-friendly guide to software architecture, technical leadership and the balance with agility. He is also the creator of the C4 software

---

1. http://www.architecturecast.net/

architecture model and Structurizr,[2] which is a collection of tooling to help software teams visualize, document, and explore their software architecture. Follow him on Twitter @simonbrown[3] or his website, http://www.simonbrown.je.

George Fairbanks has been teaching software architecture and design since 1998, is the author of the book *Just Enough Software Architecture: A Risk-Driven Approach [Fai10]*, has a PhD in software engineering from Carnegie Mellon University, and is a software engineer at Google.

Thijmen de Gooijer brings business and software together through architecture, putting the customer and quality first. Thijmen co-authored over ten research publications on architecture, while collaborating with other architecture and user experience researchers throughout Europe, India, and the United States. He graduated cum laude in software engineering with a double MSc degree from VU University in Amsterdam, the Netherlands and Malardalen University in Västerås, Sweden.

Patrick Kua is a principal technical consultant for ThoughtWorks in London and the author of two books: *The Retrospective Handbook: A Guide for Agile Teams [Kua13]* and *Talking with Tech Leads: From Novices to Practitioners [Kua15]*. Patrick is a frequent conference speaker and blogger who is passionate about bringing a balanced focused between people, organizations. and technology. Follow him on Twitter @patkua[4] or his website, https://www.thekua.com/atwork.

Ipek Ozkaya is a senior member of the technical staff at the Carnegie Mellon University (CMU) Software Engineering Institute (SEI). Her primary interests include developing techniques for improving software development efficiency and system evolution with an emphasis on software architecture practices, software economics, and agile development. Her most recent work focuses on building the theoretical and empirical foundations of managing technical debt in large-scale, complex software-intensive systems. Ozkaya serves on the advisory and editorial boards of *IEEE Software Magazine* and as an adjunct faculty member for the Master of Software Engineering Program at CMU. She earned a PhD in computational design from CMU. Follow her on Twitter @ipekozkaya.[5]

---

2. https://structurizr.com
3. https://twitter.com/simonbrown
4. https://twitter.com/patkua
5. https://twitter.com/ipekozkaya

Bibliography

[AISJ77]   Christopher Alexander, Sara Ishikawa, Murray Silverstein, Max Jacobson, Ingrid Fiksdahl-King, and Shlomo Angel. *A Pattern Language: Towns, Buildings, Construction.* Oxford University Press, New York, NY, 1977.

[Ale64]   Christopher Alexander. *Notes on the Synthesis of Form.* Harvard University Press, Boston, MA, 1964.

[Amb04]   Scott Ambler. *The Object Primer: Agile Model-Driven Development with UML 2.0.* Cambridge University Press, Cambridge, United Kingdom, Third edition, 2004.

[App11]   Juregen Appelo. *Management 3.0: Leading Agile Developers, Developing Agile Leaders.* Addison-Wesley, Boston, MA, 2011.

[App16]   Juregen Appelo. *Managing for Happiness: Games, Tools, and Practices to Motivate Any Team.* John Wiley & Sons, New York, NY, 2016.

[BBCG10]   Felix Bachmann, Len Bass, Paul C. Clements, David Garlan, James Ivers, Reed Little, Paulo Merson, Robert Nord, and Judith A. Stafford. *Documenting Software Architectures: Views and Beyond.* Addison-Wesley, Boston, MA, Second edition, 2010.

[BC89]   Kent Beck and Ward Cunningham. A Laboratory for Teaching Object-Oriented Thinking. *ACM SIGPLAN Notices.* 24[10], 1989, October.

[BCK12]   Len Bass, Paul C. Clements, and Rick Kazman. *Software Architecture in Practice.* Addison-Wesley, Boston, MA, Third edition, 2012.

[BCR94]   Victor Basili, Gianluigi Caldiera, and H. Dieter Rombach. The Goal Question Metric (GQM) Approach. *Encyclopedia of Software Engineering 1.* 528–532, 1994.

[Bec00]   Kent Beck. *Extreme Programming Explained: Embrace Change.* Addison-Wesley Longman, Boston, MA, 2000.

[BELS03] Mario R. Barbacci, Robert J. Ellison, Anthony J. Lattanze, Judith A. Stafford, Charles B. Weinstock, and William G. Wood. Quality Attribute Workshops (QAWs), Third edition. *Software Engineering Institute Digital Library.* 2003.

[Bra17]   Alberto Brandolini. *Introducing Event Storming: An Act of Deliberate Collective Learning.* LeanPub, https://leanpub.com, 2017.

[Bro16]   Simon Brown. *Software Architecture for Developers.* LeanPub, https://leanpub.com, 2016.

[Bro86]   Frederick Brooks. No Silver Bullet—Essence and Accident in Software Engineering. *Proceedings of the IFIP Tenth World Computing Conference.* 1986.

[Bro95]   Frederick P. Brooks Jr. *The Mythical Man-Month: Essays on Software Engineering.* Addison-Wesley, Boston, MA, Anniversary, 1995.

[BT03]   Barry Boehm and Richard Turner. Using Risk to Balance Agile and Plan-Driven Methods. *IEEE Computer.* 36[6]:57–66, 2003, June.

[BWO10]   Barry Boehm, Greg Wilson (editor), and Adam Oram (editor). *Architecting: How Much and When?.* O'Reilly & Associates, Inc., Sebastopol, CA, 2010.

[BWZ15]   Len Bass, Ingo Weber, and Liming Zhu. *DevOps: A Software Architect's Perspective.* Addison-Wesley, Boston, MA, 2015.

[Car09]   Dale Carnegie. *How to Win Friends and Influence People.* Simon & Schuster, New York, NY, Third edition, 2009.

[Coh09]   Mike Cohn. *Succeeding with Agile: Software Development Using Scrum.* Addison-Wesley, Boston, MA, 2009.

[Cor13]   Bett Correa. *You Can Be a Software Architect.* CreateSpace, an Amazon Company, Seattle, WA, 2013.

[Cor15]   Bett Correa. *The Zen of Software Development: A Seven Day Journey: A Handbook to Enlightened Software Development.* CreateSpace, an Amazon Company, Seattle, WA, 2015.

[Eva03]   Eric Evans. *Domain-Driven Design: Tackling Complexity in the Heart of Software.* Addison-Wesley Longman, Boston, MA, First, 2003.

[Fai10]   George Fairbanks. *Just Enough Software Architecture: A Risk-Driven Approach.* Marshall & Brainerd, Boulder, CO, 2010.

[FHR99]   Brian Foote, Niel Harrison, and Hans Rohnert. *Pattern Languages of Program Design 4*. Addison-Wesley, Boston, MA, 1999.

[Fow03]   Martin Fowler. Who Needs an Architect?. *IEEE Software*. 20[5]:11–13, 2003, September/October.

[GAO95]   David Garlan, Robert Allen, and John Ockerbloom. Architectural Mismatch: Why Reuse Is So Hard. *IEEE Software*. 12:17–26, 1995, November.

[GHJV95]   Erich Gamma, Richard Helm, Ralph Johnson, and John Vlissides. *Design Patterns: Elements of Reusable Object-Oriented Software*. Addison-Wesley, Boston, MA, 1995.

[Glu94]   David P. Gluch. A Construct for Describing Software Development Risks. *Software Engineering Institute Digital Library*. 1994, July.

[Goo09]   Kim Goodwin. *Designing for the Digital Age: How to Create Human-Centered Products and Services*. John Wiley & Sons, New York, NY, 2009.

[Hoh16]   Gregor Hohpe. *37 Things and Architect Knows: A Chief Architect's Journey*. LeanPub, https://leanpub.com, 2016.

[HW04]   Gregor Hohpe and Bobby Woolf. *Enterprise Integration Patterns: Designing and Deploying Messaging Solutions*. Addison-Wesley, Boston, MA, 2004.

[Int11]   International Organization for Standards (ISO). ISO/IEC/IEEE 42010:2011 Systems and software engineering – Architecture description. *IEEE*. 2011, December.

[Kee15]   Michael Keeling. Architecture Haiku: A Case Study in Lean Documentation. *IEEE Software*. 32[3]:35-39, 2015, May/June.

[KKC00]   Rick Kazman, Mark H. Klein, and Paul C. Clements. ATAM: Method for Architecture Evaluation. *Software Engineering Institute Digital Library*. 2000.

[Kru95]   Phillippe Krutchen. Architectural Blueprints — The 4+1 View Model of Software Architecture. *IEEE Software*. 12[6]:42–50, 1995.

[Kua13]   Patrick Kua. *The Retrospective Handbook: A Guide for Agile Teams*. CreateSpace, an Amazon Company, Seattle, WA, 2013.

[Kua15]   Patrick Kua. *Talking with Tech Leads: From Novices to Practitioners*. CreateSpace, an Amazon Company, Seattle, WA, 2015.

[KV11]   Michael Keeling and Michail Velichansky. Making Metaphors That Matter. *Proceedings of the 2011 Agile Conference*. 256–262, 2011.

[MB02]   Ruth Malan and Dana Bredemeyer. Less is more with minimalist architecture. *IT Professional*. 4[5]:48, 46–47, 2002, September-October.

[Mey97]   Bertrand Meyer. *Object-Oriented Software Construction*. Prentice Hall, Englewood Cliffs, NJ, Second edition, 1997.

[Mug14]   Jonathan Mugan. *The Curiosity Cycle: Preparing Your Child for the Ongoing Technological Explosion*. Mugan Publishing, Buda, TX, Second edition, 2014.

[Pat14]   Jeff Patton. *User Story Mapping: Discover the Whole Story, Build the Right Product*. O'Reilly & Associates, Inc., Sebastopol, CA, 2014.

[PML10]   Hasso Plattner, Chrisoph Meinel, and Larry Leifer. *Design Thinking: Understand - Improve - Apply (Understanding Innovation)*. Springer, New York, NY, 2010.

[PP03]   Mary Poppendieck and Tom Poppendieck. *Lean Software Development: An Agile Toolkit for Software Development Managers*. Addison-Wesley, Boston, MA, 2003.

[Ras10]   Jonathan Rasmusson. *The Agile Samurai: How Agile Masters Deliver Great Software*. The Pragmatic Bookshelf, Raleigh, NC, 2010.

[RW11]   Nick Rozanski and Eoin Woods. *Software Systems Architecture: Working With Stakeholders Using Viewpoints and Perspectives*. Addison-Wesley, Boston, MA, Second edition, 2011.

[Sim96]   Herbert Simon. *The Sciences of the Artificial*. MIT Press, Cambridge, MA, Third edition, 1996.

[TA05]   Jeff Tyree and Art Akerman. Architecture Decisions: Demystifying Architecture. *IEEE Software*. 22[2]:19–27, 2005, March/April.

[VAH12]   Uwe Van Heesch, Paris Avgeriuom, and Rich Hilliard. A documentation framework for architecture decisions. *Journal of Systems and Software*. 85[4]:795–820, 2012, April, December.

[WFD16]   Jonathan Wilmot, Lorraine Fesq, and Dan Dvorak. Quality attributes for mission flight software: A reference for architects. *IEEE Aerospace Conference*. 5–12, 2016, March.

[WNA13]   Michael Waterman, James Noble, and George Allen. The effect of complexity and value on architecture planning in agile software development. *Agile Processes in Software Engineering and Extreme Programming (XP2013)*. 2013, May.

[Zwe13]   Thomas D. Zweifel. *Culture Clash 2: Managing the Global High Performance Team*. SelectBooks, New York, NY, 2013.

Index

Level Up

From daily programming to architecture and design, level up your skills starting today.

Exercises for Programmers

When you write software, you need to be at the top of your game. Great programmers practice to keep their skills sharp. Get sharp and stay sharp with more than fifty practice exercises rooted in real-world scenarios. If you're a new programmer, these challenges will help you learn what you need to break into the field, and if you're a seasoned pro, you can use these exercises to learn that hot new language for your next gig.

Brian P. Hogan
(118 pages) ISBN: 9781680501223. $24
https://pragprog.com/book/bhwb

A Common-Sense Guide to Data Structures and Algorithms

If you last saw algorithms in a university course or at a job interview, you're missing out on what they can do for your code. Learn different sorting and searching techniques, and when to use each. Find out how to use recursion effectively. Discover structures for specialized applications, such as trees and graphs. Use Big O notation to decide which algorithms are best for your production environment. Beginners will learn how to use these techniques from the start, and experienced developers will rediscover approaches they may have forgotten.

Jay Wengrow
(218 pages) ISBN: 9781680502442. $45.95
https://pragprog.com/book/jwdsal

Python for Everyone

For data science and basic science, for you and anyone else on your team.

Data Science Essentials in Python

Go from messy, unstructured artifacts stored in SQL and NoSQL databases to a neat, well-organized dataset with this quick reference for the busy data scientist. Understand text mining, machine learning, and network analysis; process numeric data with the NumPy and Pandas modules; describe and analyze data using statistical and network-theoretical methods; and see actual examples of data analysis at work. This one-stop solution covers the essential data science you need in Python.

Dmitry Zinoviev
(224 pages) ISBN: 9781680501841. $29
https://pragprog.com/book/dzpyds

Practical Programming (2nd edition)

This book is for anyone who wants to understand computer programming. You'll learn to program in a language that's used in millions of smartphones, tablets, and PCs. You'll code along with the book, writing programs to solve real-world problems as you learn the fundamentals of programming using Python 3. You'll learn about design, algorithms, testing, and debugging, and come away with all the tools you need to produce quality code. In this second edition, we've updated almost all the material, incorporating the lessons we've learned over the past five years of teaching Python to people new to programming.

Paul Gries, Jennifer Campbell, Jason Montojo
(400 pages) ISBN: 9781937785451. $38
https://pragprog.com/book/gwpy2

Explore Testing

Explore the uncharted waters of exploratory testing and delve deeper into web testing.

Explore It!

Uncover surprises, risks, and potentially serious bugs with exploratory testing. Rather than designing all tests in advance, explorers design and execute small, rapid experiments, using what they learned from the last little experiment to inform the next. Learn essential skills of a master explorer, including how to analyze software to discover key points of vulnerability, how to design experiments on the fly, how to hone your observation skills, and how to focus your efforts.

Elisabeth Hendrickson
(186 pages) ISBN: 9781937785024. $29
https://pragprog.com/book/ehxta

The Way of the Web Tester

This book is for everyone who needs to test the web. As a tester, you'll automate your tests. As a developer, you'll build more robust solutions. And as a team, you'll gain a vocabulary and a means to coordinate how to write and organize automated tests for the web. Follow the testing pyramid and level up your skills in user interface testing, integration testing, and unit testing. Your new skills will free you up to do other, more important things while letting the computer do the one thing it's really good at: quickly running thousands of repetitive tasks.

Jonathan Rasmusson
(256 pages) ISBN: 9781680501834. $29
https://pragprog.com/book/jrtest

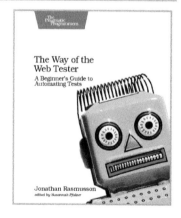

The Modern Web

Get up to speed on the latest HTML, CSS, and JavaScript techniques, and secure your Node applications.

HTML5 and CSS3 (2nd edition)

HTML5 and CSS3 are more than just buzzwords – they're the foundation for today's web applications. This book gets you up to speed on the HTML5 elements and CSS3 features you can use right now in your current projects, with backwards compatible solutions that ensure that you don't leave users of older browsers behind. This new edition covers even more new features, including CSS animations, IndexedDB, and client-side validations.

Brian P. Hogan
(314 pages) ISBN: 9781937785598. $38
https://pragprog.com/book/bhh52e

Secure Your Node.js Web Application

Cyber-criminals have your web applications in their crosshairs. They search for and exploit common security mistakes in your web application to steal user data. Learn how you can secure your Node.js applications, database and web server to avoid these security holes. Discover the primary attack vectors against web applications, and implement security best practices and effective countermeasures. Coding securely will make you a stronger web developer and analyst, and you'll protect your users.

Karl Düüna
(230 pages) ISBN: 9781680500851. $36
https://pragprog.com/book/kdnodesec

The Pragmatic Bookshelf

The Pragmatic Bookshelf features books written by developers for developers. The titles continue the well-known Pragmatic Programmer style and continue to garner awards and rave reviews. As development gets more and more difficult, the Pragmatic Programmers will be there with more titles and products to help you stay on top of your game.

Visit Us Online

This Book's Home Page
https://pragprog.com/book/mkdsa
Source code from this book, errata, and other resources. Come give us feedback, too!

Register for Updates
https://pragprog.com/updates
Be notified when updates and new books become available.

Join the Community
https://pragprog.com/community
Read our weblogs, join our online discussions, participate in our mailing list, interact with our wiki, and benefit from the experience of other Pragmatic Programmers.

New and Noteworthy
https://pragprog.com/news
Check out the latest pragmatic developments, new titles and other offerings.

Save on the eBook

Save on the eBook versions of this title. Owning the paper version of this book entitles you to purchase the electronic versions at a terrific discount.

PDFs are great for carrying around on your laptop—they are hyperlinked, have color, and are fully searchable. Most titles are also available for the iPhone and iPod touch, Amazon Kindle, and other popular e-book readers.

Buy now at *https://pragprog.com/coupon*

Contact Us

Online Orders:	*https://pragprog.com/catalog*
Customer Service:	*support@pragprog.com*
International Rights:	*translations@pragprog.com*
Academic Use:	*academic@pragprog.com*
Write for Us:	*http://write-for-us.pragprog.com*
Or Call:	+1 800-699-7764